Monographs of the
Hebrew Union College
Number 19

———

No Way Out:
The Politics of Polish Jewry
1935–1939

Monographs of the Hebrew Union College

No Way Out

The Politics of Polish Jewry
1935–1939

—

Emanuel Melzer

Hebrew Union College Press
Cincinnati

No Way Out: The Politics of Polish Jewry is a revised and updated
English translation of *Ma'avak medini be-malkodet* published in 1982
by the Diaspora Research Institute of Tel Aviv University and based
on research sponsored by the Institute

Library of Congress Cataloging-in-Publication Data

Melzer, Emanuel.
    [Ma'avak medini be-malkodet. English]
    No way out: the politics of Polish Jewry, 1935–1939 / Emanuel Melzer.

p. cm. — (Monographs of the Hebrew Union College; no. 19)

Includes bibliographical references and index.
ISBN 0-87820-418-0

1. Jews — Poland — History — 20th century. 2. Antisemitism — Poland.
3. Poland — Ethnic relations. I. Title. II. Series.

DS135.P6M4313 1997   96-30841
943.8'004924 — dc20   CIP

Design and composition by Kelby and Teresa Bowers
Printed on acid-free paper
Manufactured in the United States of America

In memory of
my parents Shachne and Gusta
and my brother David
who perished in the Holocaust

Contents

Preface

This study deals with the efforts of Polish Jews to secure their existence and advance their interests in the political arena from 1935 to 1939. These years represent the final period in the existence of a Jewish community of 3.5 million — the largest in Europe and the second largest in the world — before it perished in the Nazi Holocaust.

Although historically the beginning of the period is organically related to the years that preceded it, its course of events was abruptly aborted with the outbreak of the Second World War and the sudden end of the centuries-old community — an end imposed from the outside, not foreordained by events that occurred during the period discussed in this book. Nevertheless, it is worth exploring, even indirectly, the changes that took place in Polish attitudes toward Jews during the four years prior to the war and the extent to which they might have contributed to the manner in which the people of Poland looked upon the Nazi final solution being executed in their country. At the same time, it seems particularly pertinent to ask whether and how the manner in which Polish Jews organized themselves to fight against forces inimical to their interests during the immediate prewar period might have affected the manner in which they confronted the subsequent Nazi onslaught.

If the outbreak of the Second World War forms the *terminus ad quem* for this study, the *terminus a quo* is marked by the death of Marshal Józef Piłsudski in May 1935. Piłsudski was the personality whose influence on both the domestic and foreign policy of Poland had been most decisive during the preceding nine years, and his exit from the Polish political stage resulted in a significant deterioration in the political status of Poland's Jews. During his lifetime Piłsudski had managed to put a brake upon expressions of anti-Jewish hostility from within his Sanacja camp; following his death that brake was removed.

The weakness of the Sanacja government during the post-Piłsudski years both strengthened the antisemitic Endecja camp and contributed to a radicalization of anti-Jewish tendencies within Sanacja itself. From 1935 to 1939, Polish government leaders presented the Jewish question as one of their country's central problems. Its solution through the active intervention of the governing apparatus, they believed, would clear the way for the solution of other acute economic and social problems. At the same time, in their confrontation with Endecja, the Sanacja leaders tried to forestall the disintegration of their group by officially sanctioning anti-Jewish activity, at times expressing no more than mild disapproval of its extreme violent manifestations.

In effect, this intensification of hostility toward the Jews pervaded every sector of the organized Polish community. Even groups that strongly disapproved of it were compelled to take the spreading anti-Jewish atmosphere into account in one way or another. On the other hand, there were individuals and organizations within the Polish community – some even associated with the ruling camp – that took a firm stand against the mounting wave that endangered the Jews' position in the country. And for the Jews, the situation presented new challenges to their efforts to secure their existence, both as individuals and as a collectivity, on Polish soil. The manner in which they met those challenges is the principal theme of this book.

In pursuing this theme, the book concentrates primarily upon Jewish efforts in the political arena – an emphasis that distinguishes it from other studies of Polish Jewry during the 1930s, which have tended to emphasize Jewish activity in the social and economic spheres. During the interwar period Polish Jews developed a highly ramified institutional structure, which included organizations providing services in the areas of religion, education, culture, health, social welfare, vocational training, labor relations, and financial aid.

The operation of all these organizations, however, was closely connected to political realities, and the entire structure could not have existed without the approval, and in some cases even the assistance, of the Polish authorities. On the other hand, those authorities could, and often did, interfere with the operation of Jewish organizations and place barriers in the way of their smooth functioning. Because securing the smooth functioning of Jewish institutions was in many ways a political task, the political dimension acquired central importance in the increasingly hostile atmosphere of the late 1930s. Moreover, although the various Jewish political parties basically agreed about the seriousness of the situation, they differed considerably about what strategies to use to further the Jews' best interests. The late 1930s were thus a time of lively and often vociferous public debate among Polish Jews over questions of policy.

This study, which originated as a doctoral dissertation, was first published in Hebrew in 1982 by the Diaspora Research Institute of Tel Aviv University. The present English edition is in one sense a condensation of the earlier Hebrew version, in that certain highly detailed passages – especially those dealing with the internal workings of Jewish political life – have been deleted. The organization of the material has also been modified. However, the study has also been expanded and updated in order to take into account documentary collections to which access could not be obtained earlier. In particular, the archives of the Polish Foreign Ministry, housed in Archiwum Akt Nowych in Warsaw, have now been thoroughly combed, and materials from this source have been incorporated into the English text. So too have materials from the Hoover Institution Archives at Stanford University and from the United States National Archives in Washington, D.C. In addition, several important works pertinent to the study have appeared since 1982 and their findings taken into consideration as well.

The principal source upon which the original work was based, however, remains the same: the Polish Jewish daily and periodical press, which includes newspapers and journals of all Polish Jewish political tendencies, both in Polish and in Yiddish. These publications have been approached critically, with full awareness of their limitations as historical sources — limitations imposed especially with regard to political matters, both by the censorship to which they were subjected and by their close affiliation with specific parties or public organizations. Nevertheless, the Jewish press served both as a source of information for the Jewish public and leadership and as a formative force in the development of Jewish political consciousness. It also provided an authentic reflection of attitudes prevalent among various strata of Jewish society during the period under examination.

Additional material about the Jews of Poland has been culled from various archives — principally the Central Zionist Archives in Jerusalem, which contain, among other items, the voluminous private papers of Yitshak Gruenbaum, the files of the Zionist Federation of Eastern Galicia, and the archives of the delegate of the Jewish Agency for Palestine to the League of Nations in Geneva. The Polish Jewish historian and sociologist Jacob Lestschinski left a large collection at the Institute of Contemporary Jewry of the Hebrew University of Jerusalem, which provided some important items for this study. Other archives that made material available include the Central Archives for the History of the Jewish People and the Yad Vashem Archives in Jerusalem, the Jabotinsky Institute and the Histadrut Archives in Tel Aviv, the Archive of the Israel Labor Party at Beit Berl, and the Archive of the Board of Deputies of British Jews in London.

Because what follows is primarily a study of Jews rather than of Poles, the Polish press proved to be a less important source than the Jewish press. Nonetheless, it was necessary to analyze the changes that took place during the period in question on the Polish political scene, both in general and with regard to the Jewish question, in order to understand the Jewish response to those changes. As a result, a number of major representative Polish newspapers were consulted, as were the minutes of the Sejm and Senat for the relevant years. Another valuable source in this context were the reports of German, British, French, and U.S. diplomatic representatives in Poland, supplemented by the reports of the Polish ambassador to Great Britain, to be found at the Polish Institute (formerly the General Sikorski Historical Institute) in London.

My sincere thanks go to all those in the various archives and libraries on three continents who spared no effort to provide relevant materials and to clarify difficult problems that arose in the course of research. In addition, it is my privilege to thank several individuals without whose help and encouragement this book would not have come into being. Professor Moshe Mishkinsky supervised the original dissertation upon which it is based. Professor Shlomo Simonsohn made possible the publication of the earlier Hebrew version. Professors David Engel, Matityahu Minc, and Minna Rozen worked assiduously to bring about the production of this English version, ably translated from the Hebrew by Ronit Librozen. Financial assistance in producing the translation was provided by the Jacob and Clara Egit Foundation (under the auspices of the Histadrut Assistance Fund) and by the Yoran Schnitzer Fund for Research in the History of the Jewish People. Special thanks are due to Professor Michael A. Meyer, Publications Committee Chair at the Hebrew Union College Press, for the support he has given to the publication of this book, and particularly to Barbara Selya, its Managing Editor, for her patient and meticulous editing of the manuscript.

Finally, my greatest debt of thanks, in this as in so many other endeavors, is to my wife, Shoshana.

Tel Aviv 1996

1
Background: The Piłsudski Years

The political struggles of Polish Jewry took place in a country itself beset with political problems — in this case, those created by the renewal of Poland's independence at the conclusion of World War I. The war had brought actual fighting to more than 80 percent of the territory eventually included in the new Polish state, upsetting its economic foundations from the start. For a time it appeared that a liberal capitalist regime would enable the country to maintain the economic role it had assumed during the partition period, serving Western Europe as an agricultural resource and Eastern Europe as an industrial area. Within a short time, however, it became clear that such hopes were illusory. The economic handicaps with which the new state was beset made it impossible for most Polish products to compete with those of other countries.[1]

The reborn Polish state also faced the enormous task of uniting the country's three regions, long partitioned among Germany, Austria, and Russia into a single economic and administrative unit. Even within these regions, significant differences in economic development were noticeable — in the former Russian area between the ostensibly autonomous Congress Kingdom and the eastern provinces that had been incorporated directly into the Russian Empire; in the former German zone between Upper Silesia and the districts of Poznań and Pomorze; and in the former Austrian provinces between Western Galicia, with a large Polish majority, and Eastern Galicia, populated largely by Ukrainians. Developing a single set of economic procedures for the entire country was a slow process. Only in November 1919, a year following the new state's establishment, for example, was a uniform customs policy implemented, and not until the beginning of 1920 did the country operate under a single monetary system.[2]

The 1920s saw much fluctuation in the state of the Polish economy. From 1921 to mid-1923, the country experienced a relative upturn as it began to rebuild from the damage of the war. Following this interlude, however, it entered a period of fiscal crisis that lasted until early 1926. During that year the situation improved noticeably, as evidenced by increased industrial output, decreased unemployment, and a heightened standard of living for the work force. The same year also witnessed the coup d'état of Marshal Józef Piłsudski, which was accompanied by an increased influx of foreign investments and credit. This period of relative prosperity notwithstanding, the number of unemployed, especially in the countryside, was high — providing the impetus for permanent or seasonal migration abroad.[3]

The root of these economic and social problems, though, lay in the country's outmoded agrarian regime and in the unwillingness of the Polish leadership to initiate radical reform of it. Some 65 percent of the work force earned its living in agriculture. According to the 1921 census, 70.5 percent of this rural population was made up of farm owners and their families, 15 percent of landless peasants, and 14.5 percent of agricultural wage laborers. Moreover, 64.7 percent of all agricultural holdings consisted of less than 5 hectares — too small to support those who sought to live off the land — with another 32 percent ranging from 5–20 hectares. In contrast, although only 0.6 percent of all holdings consisted of more than 100 hectares, these large estates accounted for 44.8 percent of all agricultural lands in the country.

An agrarian reform law requiring the owners of large estates to subdivide and sell off their holdings in excess of 180 hectares (300 hectares in the eastern provinces, inhabited mainly by peasants belonging to non-Polish ethnic minorities) was passed in late 1925 but implemented in haphazard fashion. In addition, the price of the subdivided parcels was generally quite high, so that only well-to-do peasants could benefit from the reform. At the outbreak of World War II, only 15 percent of the lands affected by the law had actually been subdivided and sold.[4]

In Poland, the first signs of the Great Depression appeared as early as the end of 1928. The crisis, characterized by a contraction of foreign credit, a sharp decline in industrial output, and a drop in agricultural prices, intensified in late 1929 and reached its peak in 1932. Not only did it affect virtually all segments of society, both urban and rural, but unlike in most other countries, it did not abate in 1933.[5] In fact, it was only toward the end of 1932 that serious steps were taken to bring the deteriorating situation under control.

To revive the agricultural sector, the government attempted to impose a moratorium on peasant debt and raise farm prices. These measures, however, proved difficult to implement, owing to Poland's small internal market, itself a result of the country's flawed agrarian structure.[6] The Polish economy's dependence upon the importation of foreign capital also prolonged the crisis.[7] A poor country with limited capital resources at its disposal, Poland suffered from a rapidly growing overpopulation that available opportunities for emigration proved insufficient to relieve. Unable to cope with these problems, the government was completely overwhelmed by the early 1930s.[8]

The serious economic and social difficulties faced by independent Poland from the moment of its rebirth had deleterious consequences for the country's Jewish population, whose unusual economic structure made them easy to blame for many of the country's problems.[9] Thus trends that adversely affected the Jews' socioeconomic position were often reflected in their political standing in the new state as well.

Jews became markedly less visible in certain occupations, compared to the partition period. Whereas, for example, the 1921 census showed that they made up 62.6 percent of all merchants in Poland, their presence in commerce declined thereafter — a decline brought about not only by the factors that hurt the country's commercial life in general but also by anti-Jewish discriminatory measures imposed by the state administration.[10] The proportion of Jewish laborers in large factories decreased sharply during the early 1920s: whereas in 1914 25.6 percent of Jewish workers were employed in factories with twenty workers or more, by 1921 this figure had fallen to 16.2 percent.[11] This situation was a reflection, in part, of the government's monopolies on the salt, tobacco, alcohol, match, and lottery industries — in which many Jews had earned their livelihood — and its policy of giving priority for concessions and employment in those monopolies to discharged veterans.[12] When the government took over a factory in one of those industries, Jewish workers were dismissed.[13]

By default, the principal economic area open to Jews was artisanry, to which they gravitated not because of any government plan to improve their occupational structure but simply because poor Jews had no other options.[14] In fact, during the years of the great depression the number of Jewish artisan workshops actually grew, the result of factory closures and the dismissal of Jewish workers from other jobs.[15]

The measures taken by the government to assist the peasantry during the depression — in particular the debt moratorium legislation of 1932 — hit the Jews especially hard. The law permitted peasants to pay off their private obligations in twenty-eight semiannual payments. According to statistics gathered by the Jewish free loan and occupational retraining society CKB,[16] peasant debts to Jewish creditors during the period in question amounted to 160 million *złotych* (about 32 million dollars).[17] The moratorium thus undermined the economic position of many small Jewish shopkeepers, whose businesses were based upon the extension of short-term credit to farmers. Indeed, such shopkeepers often themselves owed monies to their wholesale suppliers, who in turn were in debt to manufacturers; yet the moratorium did not apply to commercial obligations. Thus, directly or indirectly, masses of Jews were hurt, as were, in the long run, ironically, peasants, whose possibilities for obtaining credit in the future now became quite circumscribed.[18]

A report submitted to the Committee of Jewish Delegations in Paris in 1934 determined that, in contrast to their physical security (which the Piłsudski regime at that time proved ready to protect against antisemitic violence), the economic situation of Polish Jewry was deteriorating. In addition to the debt moratorium, the report cited the disproportionate tax burden upon urban dwellers and discriminatory enforcement of tax laws against Jewish merchants and artisans. Discriminatory credit policies, the monopolization of various industries, the Sunday rest law, and the law that empowered the minister of industry and commerce to require industrialists and artisans to be organized in cartels (*cechy*) also betrayed an intent to harm Jewish interests.[19]

Thus Poland's economic crisis at the end of the first decade of its independence not only resulted in a substantial worsening of the personal situations of hundreds of thousands of Jewish petty bourgeois and proletarian breadwinners. It also led to efforts to legislate against Jewish interests, to state anti-Jewish discrimination, and to the proliferation of organized anti-Jewish economic boycotts. All of these measures contributed to the further impoverishment of the Jewish masses and gave rise to feelings of despair among them. The Jews of Poland found themselves caught in a vicious cycle: objective conditions led to a worsening of the Jewish economic position and to an intensification of antisemitic sentiments in the country, while the intensification of antisemitism contributed in turn to a further decline in the Jews' socioeconomic situation. The economic crisis made it easier to spread propaganda castigating "Jewish competition" or "Jewish exploitation," catch phrases that found credence in large segments of the Polish petty bourgeoisie and youth and contributed to a radicalization of Polish public opinion on Jewish affairs. This process of radicalization affected the manner in which both the ruling government camp led by Piłsudski and the right-wing opposition nationalist group known popularly as Endecja sought to deal with the Jewish question.

The ruling camp's attitudes toward the question had evolved steadily since it had come to power. Shortly after his coup d'état, Piłsudski had entrusted his confidant, Walery Sławek, with the task of organizing a new, broad-based political framework through which the power of the deposed parties could be broken. Sławek had responded by calling into being a Nonpartisan Bloc for Cooperation with the Regime (*Bezpartyjny Blok Współpracy z Rządem* — BBWR). This bloc, which declared that its purpose was "to heal the state"(in Polish, *sanacja państwa*, hence the regime's popular name, Sanacja), defined itself not as a party but as an alignment incorporating a wide range of interests. As a result the governing camp did not possess a clearly-defined ideological outlook; on the contrary, it had little difficulty in forging ties with differing and at times opposing ideological perspectives. Indeed, BBWR obtained support from left-wing organizations, from workers' and peasants' circles that admired Piłsudski, and from wealthy industrialists and landowners. Representatives of the ethnic minorities — Ukrainians, Belorussians, Jews, and Germans — also joined the bloc.[20]

In 1928, in the first Sejm elections after the coup, BBWR received only 122 out of 444 seats. This parliament, however, was dissolved early, and in the next elections, in 1930, the bloc emerged with an absolute majority of 247 seats. Many Jews, especially from among assimilationist circles, backed BBWR in both campaigns. Indeed, the bloc's founders had negotiated for support from the organizations of Jewish merchants and artisans and later from the Orthodox Jewish party Agudas Yisroel, and candidates from all of these groups had been included in its electoral lists.[21] In fact, in the 1928 and 1930 elections some Jewish representatives had been elected to the Sejm on the BBWR slate.[22]

Piłsudski had aimed BBWR primarily against the power of his foremost rival, the right-wing Endecja, led by Roman Dmowski. The two men had been political enemies since the beginning of the twentieth century, and many observers came to regard the history of interwar Poland as a twenty-year struggle between the opposing outlooks that they represented.[23] Among the issues dividing them was the question of how the Polish state ought to relate to the minorities residing on its territory (who made up about one third of the country's population). Piłsudski initially advanced the concept of the superiority of the state over the nation (implying a greater openness toward participation by non-Poles in the state's life), whereas Dmowski favored a clear national character in which sovereignty would be borne by the Polish people alone. The two were also divided on questions of foreign policy, with Piłsudski's orientation fundamentally anti-Russian and Dmowski's anti-German.[24] During the early 1930s, however, both camps underwent considerable ideological ferment, influenced by the economic crisis and, perhaps even more, by the rise of the Nazi party in neighboring Germany.

The changes that took place within Endecja actually had their origins in the aftermath of the Piłsudski coup.[25] Previously Endecja had been organized as a bourgeois liberal party (the National Democratic Party) supporting parliamentary democracy and participating in government coalitions. In 1926, however, Dmowski established the so-called Camp of Greater Poland (*Obóz Wielkiej Polski* – OWP), which represented the party's younger elements, who opposed its democratic orientation.[26] Following Endecja's failure in the 1928 parliamentary elections, the party changed its name to the National Party (*Stronnictwo Narodowe* – SN), and the younger elements began to gain ascendancy over the older ones. By 1934–1935, their victory was complete, no doubt in no small measure influenced by the Nazi victory in Germany.[27] The growth of OWP (which continued to exist separately from SN but operated in close cooperation with it) paralleled this development, and the camp engaged in extensive antisemitic propaganda and activity.[28] Through its front organization, the League of the Green Ribbon (*Liga Zielonej Wstążeczki*), OWP organized an economic boycott of the Jews and perpetrated frequent acts of anti-Jewish violence. Because of the camp's partisan and racist agitation as well as its organized demonstrations against the regime – which the authorities viewed as illegal, the government in March 1933 ordered that OWP be disbanded.[29]

When the Nazis came to power in Germany, Dmowski, despite his anti-German orientation, expressed great admiration for the ideological and political direction taken by the National Socialist movement. The leadership of SN looked favorably upon the non-aggression pact that was signed between Germany and Poland at the beginning of 1934, although it warned that Poland needed to remain alert to potential danger from the Germans in the future.[30] As Dmowski remarked on several occasions, "For us the German danger is unrelated to Hitlerism, whose victory we hold desirable for various reasons."[31] One of these reasons was the anti-Jewish activity of the Hitlerites – in particular the revocation of the Jews' political rights and the desire to expel them from the country – which SN saw as a rebirth of the German people and an example of the way in which other peoples might solve their Jewish problems. These two contradictory themes – fear of German expansionism on the one hand and ideological affinity on the other – account for SN's ambivalent attitude toward Nazi Germany.[32]

In 1934 two of Dmowski's pupils, Tadeusz Bielecki and Jędrzej Giertych, were coopted into the top leadership of SN. Nevertheless, on April 15 of the same year, the younger elements of the party broke away and formed their own political organization, known as the National Radical Camp (*Obóz*

Narodowo-Radykalny — ONR).The founders of this new group believed that SN had become stagnant ideologically, politically, and socially.[33] ONR was active primarily in Warsaw, where immediately upon its founding it organized shock troops called *bojówki*. Made up mainly of unemployed workers and figures from the underworld, the troops engaged in antisemitic actions in Jewish neighborhoods and attacks upon local committees of the Polish Socialist Party (*Polska Partia Socjalistyczna* — PPS).[34] Just two months after its founding (April 1934), ONR was outlawed by the government on the suspicion that its members had been involved in the assassination of Poland's interior minister, Bronisław Pieracki.[35] Its leaders were interned, most of them for three months, in the concentration camp at Bereza Kartuska, but the organization remained active illegally until the outbreak of the war.[36]

At the end of 1934, following the release of the ONR leaders from the camp, an even more extreme organization was added to the Endecja constellation — the Youth Movement (*Ruch Młodych*), led by Bolesław Piasecki. Active mainly among young people with a higher education and in areas with heavy concentrations of workers, it was influenced greatly by Nazi ideas, especially its racial doctrines. Never encompassing more than 5,000 members, the Youth Movement nevertheless distinguished itself through its organization, its internal cohesiveness, and its level of activity. In 1935 the group was dubbed *ONR-Falanga*, after the name of its newspaper. The original ONR, which represented mainly intellectual circles, was renamed (also after its newspaper) *ONR-ABC*.[37]

The great depression and the advent of the Nazis in Germany also exerted no small influence upon the ruling Sanacja camp, which began to display antisemitic attitudes similar to those espoused by its rivals on the right. The pronouncements of Bogusław Miedziński, the editor of the BBWR organ *Gazeta Polska*, for example, suggest that the bloc and Endecja did not stand far apart on the Jewish question and that BBWR's hitherto tolerant attitude toward Jews had stemmed only from "a recognition of political circumstances."[38]

Such attitudes, however, contrasted with those of Sanacja's leader, Piłudski, who, although never espousing an explicitly philosemitic position in public, still included the Jews, along with other ethnic minorities, in his vision of the Polish state and did not exclude them from the ranks of full-fledged citizens.[39] Under his authoritarian rule, widespread outbreaks of antisemitic violence did not occur, nor did the struggle against Endecja induce the state to issue formal and explicit anti-Jewish decrees. For the Jews, of course, the existence of a strong central authority that could be depended upon to protect their livelihood and security was most important. In fact, assurance of Piłsudski's opposition to antisemitism no doubt placed a brake upon the development of antisemitic feelings within the Polish community.[40] Nevertheless, antisemitism intensified within the Piłsudski camp during 1933–1934, undoubtedly because of the changing state of Polish-German relations, which powerfully influenced both the internal development of the state and the configuration of political and social forces within it.

When the Nazis first seized power, relations between the two countries became extremely tense.[41] That tension was reflected in the initial approbation shown by the Polish government for the Jewish anti-Nazi boycott[42] and in Poland's support for taking up the situation of German Jewry in the League of Nations. As early as April 26, 1933, Hans Adolf von Moltke, the German minister in Warsaw, reported to his Foreign Ministry that Poland was looking for a way to gain sympathy in the face of complaints about its treatment of its German minority.[43] He also observed that the Poles were exerting indirect pressure upon the German government not to expel some 80,000 Polish Jewish citizens who lived in Germany,[44] expressing astonishment that Poland — "the classic land of anti-Jewish pogroms" — would turn into an advocate for the Jews' defense. He concluded that the boycott being conducted by Polish Jews was but one part of the country's anti-German activities.[45]

The tension, however, was quickly dissipated. On May 2, 1933 the Polish minister in Berlin, Alfred Wysocki, acting on Piłsudski's instructions, presented Hitler with two alternatives: withdraw Germany's demands for revision of the frontier with Poland or go to war. In reply, Hitler promised to fulfill Germany's obligations under existing treaties.[46] At a conference on May 5–6, the Polish Foreign Ministry decided against issuing an official statement concerning the anti-Jewish tumult in Germany. It also decided to moderate its intervention in defense of Polish Jewish citizens living in Germany and to abandon government support for the anti-German boycott.[47] Accordingly, Polish Foreign Minister Józef Beck informed Wysocki on May 9 that "we shall not allow demonstrations against the Chancellor [Hitler] on Polish territory, although we shall not restrict the Jewish response to anti-Jewish actions in Germany — this, of course, in accordance with international custom and internal order."[48]

Wysocki, upon whom the conversation with Hitler evidently made a strong impression, disagreed with his government's position. In a letter to Deputy Foreign Minister Jan Szembek of May 19, 1933, he expressed his view that Germany had indeed been harmed by Jewish influence, adding that he knew from his own experience that the German patriots of Jewish extraction were mostly enemies of the Polish way of life. He urged the government to undertake a clear-headed, unprejudiced reevaluation of the Nazi movement.[49] That such a reevaluation was in the offing was revealed following a meeting between Poland's new minister in Germany, Józef Lipski, and Hitler on November 5, 1933 in which the German chancellor offered Poland a ten-year pact of non-aggression. Such an agreement was concluded on January 26, 1934. It was to have profound influence upon Poland's domestic policy as a whole and upon its policy toward the Jews in particular.[50]

One of the first areas in which such influence was felt was in the Polish government's treatment of the Jewish anti-Nazi boycott. During the period immediately following the signing of the non-aggression pact, Jewish organizations stepped up the pace of their boycott activity, a fact noted by German minister Moltke in his dispatches to Berlin. Moltke reported that the boycott organizers were applying "terror tactics" against Jewish merchants who did not go along with the boycott policy, threatening to damage their property and to withhold credit from them, and he complained that the Polish authorities were maintaining a neutral attitude toward such actions.[51] In response to these complaints, Polish Foreign Minister Beck promised Moltke on July 17, 1934 that the Polish Interior Ministry would take legal measures against the boycott.[52] Accordingly the Polish censorship authorities began to confiscate issues of Jewish newspapers containing pro-boycott articles.[53] The Polish Foreign Ministry also forbade Jewish organizations to conduct pro-boycott propaganda — or even to offend official visitors to Poland from Germany.[54] Finally, on June 23, 1935, the Central Committee for Economic Action against Hitler, the principal organizer of the boycott, was forced by government order to cease operations.[55]

Another effect of the Polish-German rapprochement was an intensified effort by the Polish government to rescind the obligations it had incurred under the international treaty for the protection of the rights of national minorities, signed at Versailles on June 28, 1919. Poland had long argued that such obligations ought to be placed upon all states containing national minorities, not only upon those Eastern European countries that had been forced to accept them at the Peace Conference. As early as 1922, Poland's delegates to the League of Nations had introduced a motion to that effect, but it had met with opposition from many other countries.[56] On April 10, 1934, following the signing of the non-aggression pact, Edward Raczyński, Poland's permanent delegate to the League, reintroduced the same motion; but although many states with minority populations supported it (along with neutral countries such as Holland, Sweden, and Switzerland), the great powers remained opposed, and Poland was forced to withdraw it. Instead, however, the Polish government decided to issue a unilateral declaration renouncing its obligations under the treaty; the declaration was actually issued by Beck at the League's plenary session on September 13, 1934.[57]

The response of Polish public opinion to Beck's statement was divided. BBWR organized mass demonstrations of solidarity with the foreign minister's action. A portion of the Polish press greeted the declaration as the beginning of Poland's full independence. Endecja viewed Beck's statement as overly moderate; it would have favored an absolute and unconditional renunciation of Poland's obligations under the minorities treaty, especially because the treaty included the Jewish minority under its protection. The Polish Socialist party, on the other hand, criticized the declaration as a blow to the Franco-Polish alliance and to the Versailles agreement.[58]

The reaction of the minority groups in Poland, especially of the Ukrainians and Belorussians, was weak. Even the German minority, which up to the time of the renunciation had cited the treaty in various petitions to the League of Nations, responded mildly to Beck's statement.[59] This response, however, was formulated in accordance with instructions from the German government, which approvingly viewed the Polish declaration as weakening yet another brick in the façade of the Versailles treaty.[60]

Jewish reaction to both the agreement with Germany and to Beck's declaration was mixed. There were Jews connected with BBWR who took part in the demonstrations of joy that accompanied it.[61] Following the announcement of the non-aggression pact, Ozjasz Thon, a longtime Sejm deputy and Zionist leader from Kraków, wrote that no matter how little trust was to be placed in German promises, the agreement had to be viewed as an achievement for Polish diplomacy and an indication of the weakness of German policy.[62] Typical of one segment of the Jewish press, this viewpoint was held by those who hoped the agreement would reduce tensions in Eastern Europe and permit Poland to pursue its own development tranquilly in the coming years. Obviously, its proponents did not anticipate that it would lead to the penetration of Nazi totalitarian and antisemitic thought into Poland.[63]

There were, however, other opinions. Another Jewish Sejm deputy, Fischel Rottenstreich, criticized the pact fiercely, claiming that it would only divert public attention from Germany's preparations for war, as evidenced by the sabre-rattling speeches of German leaders and the expansion of the country's military industry.[64] Zionist leader Moshe Kleinbaum observed in a letter to his mentor Yitshak Gruenbaum, the former chairman of the Jewish parliamentary caucus who had left Poland for Palestine in 1933,that prior to the conclusion of the agreement with Germany most Jews had looked upon Sanacja as their "sole salvation." Since that time, however, the ruling party had "lost all of its popularity in the Jewish street, mainly because of the pact with Hitler."[65] As the months passed, even Thon came to share this view; in November 1934, as chair of the Jewish caucus, he attacked the non-aggression pact during a session of the Sejm. Not only was it harmful to Polish Jewry, he said, but also damaging to the future security of the state.[66]

Although Beck's renunciation of the Minorities Treaty was roundly rejected in the Jewish press, Jewish newspapers refrained from placing special emphasis upon the damage done to the legal status of Polish Jewry. Rather, they commented mainly upon the dangerous precedent created when international contractual obligations under the Versailles Treaty were undermined — a precedent that would in the long run prove detrimental to Poland, whose legal existence was largely rooted in the Treaty. The newspapers further pointed to the value of the Minorities Treaty in protecting Poles abroad.[67]

This hesitancy and confusion among Polish Jews regarding the dangers facing them during the final period of Piłsudski's life was accompanied by an increase in their political, social, and economic isolation — and by internal fragmentation and divisiveness. In the absence of a unified representative organization and authoritative leadership with a mandate to speak for all — or even most — of them, it was impossible for Polish Jews to plan and expedite an independent policy that would allow them to deal with the political and economic problems they faced as a national minority. This situation in turn made Jews incapable of responding appropriately to the repeated attempts to undermine their position.

The internal fragmentation of Polish Jewry was reflected in the multiplicity of Jewish political parties that vied for their allegiance. During the early 1930s these parties were divided into three large camps: the Zionists, who constituted the largest, although they were split into general, religious, leftist, and revisionist factions; the Orthodox Jews, led by the Agudas Yisroel party; and the Socialists, led by the party known as the Bund.[68] Two other political groups had at one time exerted a measure of influence on the Jewish street, but by the early thirties their power was on the decline: the Communist Party of Poland (KPP), which maintained a Jewish bureau; and the so-called Folkist Party, which advocated the institution of a regime of national autonomy on a personal basis (as opposed to a territorial one) for Polish Jews.

In addition to the aforementioned political groups, there were also Jewish organizations that had an economic focus. The so-called assimilationists, consisting mainly of the intelligentsia and the extremely wealthy, exerted some influence in these groups. Although the assimilationists operated on the periphery of Jewish political life and urged Polish Jews to divest themselves of virtually all attributes that set them apart from Polish society, it is interesting to note that at times they would form a common front with the extreme Orthodox Jews in fighting against the Zionists.[69]

Within the Zionist camp, the General Zionists dominated until the early 1930s. They were split into three independent regional federations — one for the territories that had formerly been under Russian rule, the other two for the eastern and western halves of formerly Austrian Galicia.[70] The first of these had been further divided since 1923 into two factions known as *Al HaMishmar* and *Et Livnot*. Al HaMishmar, under the leadership of Yitshak Gruenbaum, was oriented somewhat toward the political left and actively opposed the Sanacja regime. In 1930 it gained control of the Central Committee of the Zionist Federation of [Congress] Poland. Et Livnot, in contrast, demonstrated a desire to cooperate with Sanacja while still looking out for Jewish interests. In this respect the faction's policies were similar to those of the two Galician federations as well as to those of the rightist Revisionists and the religious Zionist party, Mizrahi.[71] The Zionist left in Poland was on the ascendancy following the 1932 unification conference of Po'alei-Tsiyon Right and Hitahdut. However, unification was actually achieved only in Eastern Galicia. The Po'alei-Tsiyon Left party continued its separate existence.[72]

In the 1930 parliamentary elections, in which a Minorities Bloc did not present a list, the Galician Zionist federations received four seats (in contrast to the six that they had received during the previous elections, in 1928), and the Zionists of Congress Poland saw their representation diminished from seven seats to two.[73] These results seriously damaged Gruenbaum's standing as the leader of the Polish Zionists; shortly after the elections he left the country altogether (although he retained his seat in the Sejm until parliament was dissolved in 1935). His departure weakened the Jewish parliamentary representation, especially since, by 1933, the Jewish caucus as a whole felt driven toward the oppositional stance that Gruenbaum had long advocated.[74]

The internal divisions and factional strife that characterized the General Zionists contributed — at least in the former Congress Poland and the eastern territories — to an upsurge in the strength of the Zionist left on the one hand (especially that portion represented by the moderate socialist party

Po'alei Tsiyon Right) and of the right-wing Revisionist Party on the other.[75] This trend was apparent in the results of the elections in these regions to the eighteenth congress of the World Zionist Organization held in 1933. In these elections the parties of the Zionist left received more than 40 percent of the votes, with 30 percent for the Revisionists, 18 percent for Mizrahi, and only 12 percent for the General Zionists. In Galicia, on the other hand, the General Zionists retained their strength, garnering 40 percent of the vote, as opposed to 30 percent for the parties of the left, 18 percent for the Revisionists, and 11 percent for Mizrahi.[76]

Non-Zionist Orthodox Jews were represented mainly by Agudas Yisroel. This party was strongest in Congress Poland; its primary political goal was to take power in the local Jewish community councils. Like the assimilationists, Agudas Yisroel called for loyalty to the authorities and cooperation with Sanacja; one of its two representatives in the fourth Sejm was elected from the BBWR list. The government was well aware of the party's strength in the elections of 1930 and of the importance of its support.[77] In return for its loyalty, Agudas Yisroel received government assistance in matters of religion, welfare, and education. To be sure, during the early 1930s the party contained a small oppositional faction that opposed close cooperation with the government, but not until after Piłsudski's death did a radical change take place in its pro-government orientation.[78]

The Socialist Bund grew stronger during the early 1930s, although its electoral strength remained limited, and it never managed to return a deputy to the Sejm.[79] In 1930 the party had joined the Second International, following the victory at its 1929 national convention of the faction led by Henryk Erlich and Wiktor Alter, who advocated cooperation with PPS and with the socialist parties of the national minorities.[80] The Bund's strength lay primarily within the Jewish trade union movement headed by Alter, which was part of the overall Polish trade union movement.[81] In principle, the party was not prepared to cooperate with the Jewish bourgeois parties, and it continued to condemn notions of a common Jewish front or a unified Jewish policy.

The Polish government was aware of a leadership crisis among Polish Jewry: an official confidential report issued by the Interior Ministry for the first quarter of 1935 stated,"It must be noted that almost all of the Jewish political parties are suffering greatly from the absence of recognized authoritative leaders. Mediocrity reigns everywhere."[82] Indeed, it appears that Yitshak Gruenbaum's departure from the Polish political scene was acutely felt at a time when Polish Jewry was especially in need of a strong leader to forge a bold line of opposition in the face of mounting antisemitism in Polish ruling circles and among Polish public opinion.[83] Those who remained failed to evaluate correctly the significance and implications of the non-aggression pact with Germany and the abrogation of the Minorities Treaty, the two major and undoubtedly interconnected events for Polish Jewry in the final phase of the Piłsudski years.

2
Political Changes after Piłsudski

Two events in the first half of 1935 initiated a major political transformation in Poland, resulting in a realignment of political forces and a sharp decline in the status of the national minorities, including the Jews.

The first, on April 23, 1935, was the ratification of a new Polish constitution. Reflecting Piłsudski's conception of the state, this so-called April Constitution was to strengthen the hands of the Sanacja regime and the president of the Republic while diminishing the power of the Sejm. The constitution placed all three branches of government under the direct supervision of the president, who was entitled to select one third of the members of the new, more powerful Senat. He was also granted the authority to legislate by executive order.

Having fought for its approval by the Polish parliament ever since the convening of the third Sejm in 1930, Piłsudski evidently had intended to serve in the office of president under the new constitution. But on May 12, less than three weeks following its adoption, he passed away. His death left a political vacuum; no concrete plans had been agreed upon for such a contingency.[1] It is no wonder then that many historians view 1935 as the beginning of a new period in the history of interwar Poland.[2]

The ratification of the new constitution and the death of Piłsudski led to a worsening of the situation of Polish Jewry and to a strengthening of antisemitism in the country. To be sure, the constitution's opening article stressed that "the Polish state is the common property of all of its citizens." Moreover, articles 111 and 112 of the former constitution, which promised Jews freedom of religion and freedom from discrimination on account of their religious practices, were incorporated into the new document. However, a clause in article 7 placed a potential limitation on the protection of Jewish civil rights: "The rights of a citizen to influence public affairs will be estimated according to the value of his efforts and services for the general good."[3]

The Jewish parliamentary caucus and representatives of the other national minorities abstained from the ratification vote, mainly because the new constitution eliminated the electoral system based upon proportional representation. Some Jewish leaders, notably Ozjasz Thon, had called for an explicit vote against the constitution; but when his call was rejected under pressure from the Jewish deputies from East Galicia, Thon resigned the chairmanship of the Jewish caucus, and Zionist circles met the caucus's conciliatory position with criticism.[4] The Bund also criticized the national minorities' abstention and castigated the behavior of the Jewish Sejm deputies. According to a Bund publication, although the latter consistently maintained that the new constitution would be bad for the Jews, they did not vote against it.[5]

Jewish fears were well-founded. Endek circles viewed the new Polish constitution as supportive of anti-Jewish legislation and discrimination by government agencies. The National Party's daily newspaper explained the party's stand:

> We do not deceive ourselves that the Jewish problem can be solved by pogroms. It will be necessary to solve it through reliance upon the state, its laws, and its policies.... We hope that the Polish constitution will be the basis for a solution to the Jewish problem. In the meantime we should appreciate the fact that there have been improvements in some facets of the state's life.... The army is beginning to forge [direct] contacts with manufacturers and to pass over the Jewish middleman. This is a great step forward toward breaking the monopoly of supply that has been in the hands of the Jews.[6]

Thus Piłsudski's death in the aftermath of the vote on the constitution sent a wave of trepidation through the Jews of Poland, many of whom believed that only the Marshal was capable of maintaining public order and restraining the strong antisemitic currents flowing deep within Polish society. Nor did they believe that the Piłsudski camp would be able to retain power following his death, or that, without his leadership, it was prepared to repudiate antisemitism or to fight against it.[7] The organ of the Bund, for example, viewed the ratification of the new constitution and the death of Piłsudski as sharp turning points in the road toward fascism. It held that the purpose of the constitution was to perpetuate the existing regime and that Piłsudski's death had removed one more obstacle to an understanding between Sanacja and Endecja, which the Bund regarded as two branches of Polish fascism. The issue of antisemitism, according to the newspaper, would not impede their coalescence; the differences between the antisemitism of Sanacja and Endecja were differences of style and method about which the two sides could compromise.[8]

Indeed, Endecja did see the death of the Marshal as a propitious moment for increasing antisemitic agitation. An anti-Jewish offensive in the Endek press, bearing a style reminiscent of the Nazi press in Germany, was evident only a few days after Piłsudski's demise. On May 29, 1935 the Endek newspaper *Warszawski Dziennik Narodowy* quoted from a pamphlet on the Jewish question published by the *Westdeutscher Beobachter* in Köln, agreeing with the assertion that world Jewry regarded the Jews of Poland as its reserve force. The Polish newspaper estimated that 99 percent of all Poles were anti-semitically inclined, and two days later set forth its wish in an article head-lined "Removal of Jews from German Press Desirable also in Poland."

The first parliamentary elections to be held after the new constitution's ratification provide one early indication of how the new constitution and Piłsudski's death affected the political standing of Polish Jewry and how its leadership responded. An electoral ordinance under the new constitution was approved by the Sejm and Senat on July 8, 1935. According to its terms, 208 Sejm deputies were to be chosen from 104 electoral districts, with candidates selected by local curiae made up of representatives of municipal and regional governing councils, economic organizations, and independent trade unions. The Senat was to consist of 96 members, 64 of whom were to be chosen by regional assemblies elected according to a restricted franchise, the remaining 32 to be appointed directly by the president.[9] On July 10 the president, Ignacy Mościcki, dissolved both houses of parliament, with new elections set for September 8.

The electoral ordinance assured Sanacja of almost total domination of the process of selecting candidates; no wonder, then, that the major opposition parties of both the right and the left — Endecja, PPS, and the Peasant Party — decided to boycott the elections.[10] As a result, voter turnout at the polls was only 46.5 percent, compared to 74.8 percent in 1930 and 78.3 percent in 1928.[11] This low turnout indicated that the political framework built up under Piłsudski, centered around BBWR, was in the process of disintegration.

Indeed, in the wake of the Marshal's death, signs of a struggle for succession within the ruling camp had begun to appear. Although during his lifetime Piłsudski had named Gen. Edward Rydz-Śmigły to succeed him as commander-in-chief of the armed forces, he had not given him a role in the regime alongside the president. Thus shortly following his death the governing camp was split into three factions: the so-called *Zamek* (Castle) group, led by President Mościcki; a group of generals, coalesced around Rydz-Śmigły; and the so-called colonels, led by Prime Minister Walery Sławek.[12]

Sławek's standing suffered the greatest damage as a result of the electoral debacle. BBWR, which he had founded, was experiencing internal strife, with relations between its conservative and radical factions increasingly tense.[13] Moreover, the inability of the bloc to attract a following among the younger generation became apparent.[14] Sławek was forced to admit the failure of his leadership; on October 12 he resigned as prime minister, and on October 30 disbanded BBWR.[15]

The question of whether or not to participate in the elections divided the Jewish public. From the outset the Bund associated itself with the position of PPS; it boycotted the elections and helped organize the general strike on June 25, 1935 of workers protesting the electoral ordinance.[16] Immediately after the ordinance was published, Po'alei Tsiyon also decided to boycott.[17] Agudas Yisroel, on the other hand, resolved from the outset to participate.[18]

The greatest degree of Jewish ambivalence was noticeable among the General Zionists, who were concerned with guaranteeing a Jewish representation in the Sejm that would not be dependent upon the authorities.[19] They realized that the new electoral law would make that goal difficult to achieve and might open the door to anti-Jewish discrimination.[20] Nevertheless, at a meeting of the Zionist Federation of East Galicia on July 16, 1935, Sejm Deputy Henryk Rosmarin argued that precisely in order to obtain such an independent representation, Jews must not boycott the elections. The organization accepted Rosmarin's view.[21]

In contrast, leaders of the Zionist Federation of the former Russian partition, who belonged to the Al HaMishmar faction, made their organization's participation in the elections conditional upon being able to nominate its own candidates with no restrictions.[22] In this regard Moshe Kleinbaum defined the Zionist position as "abstention from voting" rather than an "electoral boycott" of the type called for by the Polish opposition parties. He argued that the Zionists, unlike the Polish opposition, were not a political party wishing to hold state power, but merely an ethnic minority seeking the right to choose its own candidates without Sanacja approval.[23] With this distinction between "abstention" and "boycott," the Zionists dissociated themselves from the Polish opposition and indicated a tendency to avoid direct confrontation with the ruling camp. At the same time, however, they attempted to justify abstention from voting to a Jewish public increasingly convinced that Jewish interests demanded a Jewish presence in the Sejm.

In the end, Jewish voter turnout was quite low; in Warsaw, for example, only 17 percent of registered Jewish voters went to the polls. Four Jewish deputies were elected to the Sejm — Wacław Wiślicki, a representative of the Association of Jewish Merchants in Warsaw; Leyb Mincberg, the candidate of Agudas Yisroel in Łódź; Rabbi Izaak Rubinsztein, the Mizrahi candidate from Wilno; and Emil Sommerstein, a leader of the General Zionists from Lwów.[24] No Jews were elected to the Senat, although two — the Zionist Moshe Schorr and the Agudas Yisroel representative Jakub Trockenheim — were among the 32 senators appointed directly by the president.[25]

Public Jewish debate over the Sejm elections illustrates just how divided and confused the Jewish community was and how much it lacked a clear direction vis-à-vis the changes that had been taking place in Poland after Piłsudski's death. The rival Jewish camps failed to reevaluate their domestic policies in light of these changes or to inaugurate a frank exchange of views among themselves to forge a common stance toward the dangers facing them. No matter how much Zionist leaders spoke about the need for internal unity, the fragmented Zionist camp could not even unify its three regional centers. Indeed, following Yitshak Gruenbaum's move to Palestine[26] and Ozjasz Thon's refusal to stand for election to the Sejm in 1935,[27] the camp clearly suffered from a loss of leadership.

Agudas Yisroel continued to express its readiness to collaborate with the regime and to put forth its candidate for the Sejm within the framework of BBWR. The Bund rejected calls from Jewish Communists to form a Jewish popular front similar to the Popular Front then being formed in France.[28]

The Bund's position regarding cooperation with other Jewish parties deserves further clarification. With the Bund's strength within the Jewish community on the rise in 1935, many of its leaders urged the party to seek an active role in the administration of the local Jewish communities, on the grounds that the community councils dealt not only with religious matters but also with social services essential to the welfare of the Jewish masses.[29] By participating in the community councils, they argued, the Bund could win large numbers of adherents. At the same time, they opposed any form of political cooperation with the "bourgeois Jewish exploiters."[30] In particular, the Bund claimed that the Zionists had deviated from Gruenbaum's strategy of conducting an "independent Jewish policy." And it castigated the Zionists as allies of Sanacja, which allegedly had promised them diplomatic backing. Against the Zionist argument that Polish Jewry's paramount problem was its lack of a homeland and that emigration was the only solution, the Bund contended that the difficulty was not homelessness but rightlessness.[31]

In short, after Piłsudski's death, each of the various Jewish parties became more deeply entrenched in its own position and even less willing to compromise. This tendency, blatantly obvious during the 1935 election campaign, was exploited by Endecja. It launched a new antisemitic offensive, which in turn forced Sanacja to adopt certain of its features in order to compete for the sympathy of the Polish public.

Antisemitic ferment in the country increased during the seven-month term of Marian Zyndram Kościałkowski as prime minister, from the time of Sławek's resignation in October 1935 until mid-May 1936. Kościałkowski had been regarded as a member of the so-called Young Piłsudskist group and as a man of liberal views, and at the outset of his term he enjoyed a supportive attitude from the leadership of PPS.[32] Kościałkowski also added two reputed liberals to his cabinet: Eugeniusz Kwiatkowski as deputy premier and minister of finance, and Juliusz Poniatowski as minister of agriculture. Both were close to President Mościcki, and their appointment had been opposed by Rydz-Śmigły.[33] Still, some of those close to Sławek remained in key positions, including the speaker of the Sejm, Stanisław Car, and the speaker of the Senat, Aleksander Prystor.

Sławek's resignation, together with Kościałkowski's appointment as prime minister and the dissolution of BBWR, hastened the impending crisis in the Sanacja camp, which was composed of disparate social groups that depended upon the Piłsudski legend to unite them. Once the authoritative figure of the Marshal was gone, the government found itself without widespread popular support. As a result, despite the liberal image of some of its senior ministers, it was not able to stand up to mounting antisemitism, which became radicalized precisely during Kościałkowski's term of office, when Poland seemed to be recovering somewhat from its economic woes.

Some felt that this antisemitism was only a lower class phenomenon. Indeed, in an interview granted in November 1935 to the Palestinian Jewish emissary Leib Yaffe, President Mościcki expressed his opinion that although strong antisemitic currents were present only within the lower social levels of the Polish people and not among its leaders, it was still possible that a "little Hitler" might seize power in the country.[34] More likely, this radicalization was part of a general liberation of pent-up forces that Piłsudski had managed to keep in check during his lifetime. It was also a reflection of the consolidation of the Nazi regime in Germany and of the recent improvement in German-Polish relations. These developments induced Endecja to move from a policy of simply expressing antipathy toward Jews to one of anti-Jewish violence. This shift, in turn, pulled Sanacja in its wake, forcing the governing camp to change its attitude toward Jews from one of tolerance to one of enmity.

The government expressed that enmity first by seeking the complete

Polonization of various branches of the economy. It encouraged Christian small merchants and artisans to migrate from Western Poland, where the concentration of Jews was small, into areas in the east with greater Jewish populations, where it promoted the formation of Polish producers' and consumers' cooperatives by granting them favorable credit terms.[35] This relocation of Polish urban elements proved even more dangerous to the Jews than the migration of Polish peasants from the countryside to the cities.

An economic policy deliberately injurious to the Jews was pursued with even greater vigor upon the accession of Felicjan Sławoj-Składkowski to the premiership in May 1936, together with the de facto installation, in contravention of the constitution, of Rydz-Śmigły as the country's second most powerful political figure.[36] In Składkowski's first programmatic speech to the Sejm on June 4, 1936, he succinctly stated his government's position on the Jewish question: "The government is of the opinion that in Poland no person should be harmed, for a proper host does not allow anyone residing in his house to be harmed. [If you want] an economic struggle, then by all means go ahead; but no [physical] harm."[37]

The new premier in this statement appeared to reflect a neutral stance toward all forms of an anti-Jewish economic boycott, and indeed, the expression "go ahead" (*owszem*) gave a green light to low-level administrators throughout the country to encourage attempts to remove Jews from their jobs and interfere with their livelihoods.[38] In particular, various municipalities began to take actions that seriously injured the welfare of Jewish merchants and forced many to vacate their stalls in the markets. Jewish-owned structures containing Jewish shops were frequently demolished for "aesthetic" reasons. And a law of December 10, 1936 requiring all merchants or workshop owners to display their names as written on their birth certificates on the front of their establishments proved damaging to many Jews.[39] Anyone who wished could thus interpret Składkowski's statement as meaning that the Jews were a foreign element in the country, although in dealing with them it was necessary to preserve certain standards of "fairness."[40]

Whatever Składkowski's scruples may have been, however, it appears that his words, coming in the wake of the economic measures taken by the Kościałkowski government, served not only to encourage an economic boycott but to direct it into violent channels. Indeed, groups advocating and fomenting violence had appeared on the scene even before Składkowski's speech. In May 1936, for example, a branch of the so-called Polish Union (*Związek Polski*) — founded under Sanacja auspices in Poznań two years earlier to support the Polonization of local commerce — was established in Warsaw.

Its picketers at times used physical force to discourage Christians from patronizing Jewish shops. Although picketing in labor disputes was illegal in Poland, the authorities took no action against those preventing entry into Jewish stores. Slogans such as "Market stalls for peasants" or "Marketplaces without Jews" were heard with increasing frequency.[41] At the same time, ONR and other Endecja circles stepped up their own boycott activities. Their *bojówki* formations used terror tactics against Christian merchants who maintained commercial relations with Jews.[42] Indeed, as Sanacja leaders had already recognized, Endecja and its allies sought to encourage popular violence at every turn, hoping to take advantage of public anti-Jewish attitudes and transform them into a means of seizing state power for their camp.[43]

This approach was demonstrated graphically in June 1936, when the National Party began to provoke physical attacks upon Jews Their obvious intention was to come into confrontation with the governmental administration. The first occurred in the small town of Liszki near Kraków where, following the destruction of several Jewish shops, the local police station was also attacked. Subsequently, on the night of June 22–23, National Party members, led by the party's district head for Kraków, Adam Doboszyński, not only attacked Jewish stores in the town of Myślenice but also destroyed the home of the district governor and disarmed local police.[44]

Indirect support for an anti-Jewish boycott came from the Catholic Church as well. On February 29, 1936 the primate of Poland, Cardinal August Hlond, published a pastoral letter accusing Jews of spreading atheism and revolutionary Bolshevism throughout the country and contributing to a decline in Polish morals through publication of pornographic literature. He called upon Catholics to limit their contacts with Jews in the economic realm as much as possible.[45] Similarly, before the Easter holiday in 1936, Archbishop Adam Sapieha of Kraków reportedly issued a proclamation emphasizing the importance of Catholic solidarity and instructing his flock to patronize Catholic businesses in order to insure their prosperity.[46] Other clergymen openly advised Catholics not to deal with Jewish businesses; some even urged children to pressure their parents to take part in boycott activities.[47] That same year clergymen and intellectuals took the initiative in establishing Polish free loan societies in cities and villages throughout the country, one of whose primary purposes was to bring together resources to be used in the economic fight against Jewry. The organizers of these funds made no secret of this purpose, and the Catholic Youth League (*Związek Młodzieży Katolickiej*) adopted a resolution obligating its 350,000 members to cooperate with them.[48]

Indeed, during the time in question, close connections existed in general between Endecja and the Catholic Church. In 1928, immediately following the establishment of the National Party, an official delegation requested the archbishop of Warsaw, Cardinal Aleksander Kakowski, to entrust the party with the task of defending Church interests; the archbishop responded with sympathy. In 1930 the National Party leadership established a special bureau for Catholic propaganda, led by churchmen.[49] And although Cardinal Hlond's pastoral letter of February 1936 condemned violent attacks upon Jews and stipulated that no one outside of the Church itself could claim that its program was based exclusively on Christian principles, the accusation put forth by him and repeated by other clergymen that Jews were an element that could facilitate a Communist revolution in Poland undoubtedly served to validate the activities of the Endecja camp.[50]

To be sure, there were Endecja conservatives who were not anxious to be drawn into the tide of anti-Jewish extremism. To an extent, this hesitation was rooted in considerations of foreign policy, as an interview granted by one of Endecja's more moderate leaders, Stanisław Stroński, to the Yiddish-language newspaper *Haynt* in early 1936 indicated. Stroński denied that Endecja was sympathetic to Nazi elements in Poland's ethnic German population and insisted that the relations between these two sides continued to be hostile. Even the most extreme Polish antisemite, he explained, objected to the Nazis: the Polish camp was founded upon Christian principles, while Nazism was not. In his view the problem of the Jews in Poland was unique and could not be solved according to models developed in other countries. He expressed sympathy for Zionism, not so much because of that movement's potential for reducing the number of Jews in Poland but mainly because of "one national movement's sympathy for another national movement."[51]

Other reservations about Endecja's approach to the Jewish question were expressed by certain individuals within the Polish intelligentsia, who maintained that Endecja was directing the main thrust of the anti-Jewish economic boycott against poorer Jews in the countryside and small towns while doing nothing about the wealthy Jews in the larger cities. Even a major Endek newspaper gave voice to this argument, although the same issue of the newspaper also contained a reply claiming that the war against the weaker Jews — who purportedly constituted the basis for the wealthy Jews' existence — in fact severely weakened the latter.[52]

Nevertheless, in spite of these indications of less than complete accord in the Endek camp, an official proclamation of the Central Committee of the

National Party issued on May 10, 1936 declared Jews a serious threat to the security of the Polish state. According to this proclamation, Communism was on the march in Poland, aided by certain socialist organizations participating in the so-called popular front. That front, however, according to the National Party's Central Committee, was in reality a Jewish one, because the Jews possessed decisive power within the Communist Party of Poland, and they were the ones preventing the country from transforming itself into a great independent power. Only a united National Party, the party's leaders warned, could succeed in the struggle against the threatened Jewish-Communist takeover.[53]

The proclamation proved to have a powerful influence upon the Polish political scene. Within Endecja, the radicals' strength steadily increased, drawing along most of the party veterans and even pulling the rival Sanacja camp behind them. As early as January 1936 a dissident Sanacja group led by former Polish ambassador to the United States Tytus Filipowicz formed a new Polish Radical Party (*Polska Partia Radykalna*). Although in general this party espoused liberal principles, it believed that Poland should be a Christian state; on the Jewish question it demanded that ethnic Poles be given preference in all areas of the country's life and that Jews emigrate from Poland en masse.[54]

On the other hand, significant voices were also raised against the rising tide of antisemitism by those who perceived its dangers. In early 1936 the League for the Protection of the Rights of Man and the Citizen held a public meeting devoted to heightening public awareness of the manner in which antisemitic agitation was, according to the meeting's organizers, being used to divert the public's attention from the fundamental problems facing the country.[55] In Łódź a Polish group was formed expressly to combat anti-semitism. Comprised of students, workers, and even several clergymen, it proclaimed that anti-Jewish activities represented a departure from true Christian principles; it even published a weekly newsletter, *Wolny Człowiek* [The Free Man], that endeavored to counter antisemitic propaganda.[56]

Opposition to the antisemitic agitation of Endecja came from organized political parties as well. During 1935–1936 PPS distributed flyers against Endecja, broke up Endek meetings, and physically confronted Endek pickets and fighting squads.[57] PPS took a more moderate stance in opposition to Sanacja, fearing that should the Sanacja regime fall, Endecja would take over the government. On the other hand, some PPS members voiced negative opinions about Jews during this time. For example, in commenting upon the joint May Day demonstrations held by Polish and Jewish workers in 1936, the editor of the party organ *Robotnik*, Mieczysław Niedziałkowski, noted that "only in Warsaw, for reasons having nothing to do with us, ... were we unable to march together with the Jewish workers, [because] 'various elements' felt a certain panic on account of the threats of the 'national camp.'" This fear of Endecja, however, was also evidently accompanied by some indigenous hostility toward Jews, for Niedziałkowski went on to write: "In terms of the economy we are imprisoned by a foreign element in our own home. Commerce and finance are ninety percent in Jewish hands, and in industry the share of foreign capital reaches sixty percent. No wonder that in this situation, given current economic policy, our army lacks the equipment currently needed for our nation's armed forces."[58]

Still, as anti-Jewish violence increased, Niedziałkowski was moved to take a bold and forthright stand against it. In July 1936, following the outbreak of riots against Jews in Mińsk Mazowiecki, he enunciated three principles according to which PPS must conduct itself: the notion of collective responsibility — such as when a Jewish community was attacked in retaliation for the actions of an individual Jew, was unacceptable; attempts to create situations of interethnic warfare in Poland were to be opposed vigorously; and the recent wave of anti-Jewish riots was not only an attack on Jews, but a transparent attempt to divert the attention of Polish society from its true difficulties.[59]

The Communist Party of Poland (KPP) also opposed antisemitism. In November 1935 it called upon all antifascist forces in Poland to join together in combating "the pogrom atmosphere in the country" as part of a "broad popular front."[60] In July 1936 it proposed that all Polish and minority workers' parties respond jointly to anti-Jewish violence by forming defense units within the trade unions and even summoning an international conference to discuss the problem.[61]

During the same period many Jews placed great hopes in the powerful Peasant Party, which had cooperated with PPS in numerous areas. However, following the adoption of its platform on national minorities at the third party congress in late 1935, Jewish leaders were disappointed.[62] The platform divided Poland's national minorities into three categories — the Slavic minorities, the Germans, and the Jews. With regard to the latter, the document stated that despite attempts at assimilation, the Jews remained a foreign element in Poland. And because historical circumstances had prevented the Poles from developing their own middle class, Jews had taken over the country's commercial and financial functions. Now, the party platform decreed, the time had come for these functions to pass into Polish hands. Hoping that this goal could be achieved without violence, the party called for the creation of ethnic Polish producers' and consumers' cooperatives and official support for the "Polish element" in all aspects of economic life. Jews should not be stripped of their civil rights, the platform declared, but they should be encouraged to leave the country.[63] The Bund leader Wiktor Alter stated that this platform reflected the victory of right-wing circles possessing antisemitic tendencies within the Peasant Party.[64] In the spirit of the party platform of December 1935, its leader Stanisław Thugutt stated that although he opposed anti-Jewish violence and supported equal rights for Jews, he favored encouraging Jewish emigration and supported "the aspirations of the peasants to take the national economy into their own hands."[65]

As we have seen, following Piłsudski's death the weakness of the Sanacja camp, lacking a firm ideological base and open to clashes between various competing interest groups, was exposed. The camp was certain that the new parliamentary electoral ordinance would permit it to remain in power, but the low voter turnout in the 1935 parliamentary elections and their boycott by the right and left opposition parties demonstrated that it did not represent the majority of the Polish public at all. In response to the strengthening of the so-called Endek National Camp and to a radicalization of antisemitism within it, various efforts were made to bring the divided Sanacja camp together. Led by the competing Zamek and Generals factions against the Colonels faction led by Sławek, these efforts brought about the establishment of an effective diumvirate of Mościcki and Rydz-Śmigły. A government was formed representing a compromise between these two factions, in the hope that such a solution would allow the Piłsudski camp to continue to rule in the future.

It appears, moreover, that the pervasive antisemitic atmosphere engendered following Piłsudski's death also began to infect members of the left and left-leaning opposition parties. Like Sanacja, these parties could no longer ignore the anti-Jewish public passions that Endecja had succeeded in arousing. Still, for the Jews of Poland, the response of Sanacja to the intensification of hostility was of greater consequence than that of the opposition parties of the left. In early 1937 that response took an ominous turn.

The event that signalled the inauguration of a new stage in the decline of the Jews' political position in Poland was the founding of a new pro-government bloc to replace BBWR, which had been disbanded sixteen months earlier. Known as the Camp of National Unity (*Obóz Zjednoczenia Narodowego* –

OZON), this new bloc was established in February 1937 under the leadership of Adam Koc. Koc was known within Sanacja for his conservative views, and in founding OZON he enjoyed the support of Rydz-Śmigły. Hoping to avoid the mistakes that had beset BBWR, he sought to take a lesson from the illegal and radically antisemitic organization belonging to the Endek camp, ONR-Falanga, led by Bolesław Piasecki.[66] After visiting a secret Falanga youth training course, Koc managed to persuade many of its young members that by joining his camp they would be able to conduct their activities legally within the framework of OZON's new Young Poland Union (*Związek Młodej Polski* — ZMP), which was to be led by Piasecki's former lieutenant, Jerzy Rutkowski. To further weaken the Endek National Party, he also courted other dissident elements within Endecja, coming to terms with them on such issues as the constitution, foreign policy, and the Jewish question.[67]

The desire to imitate Endecja, albeit in a somewhat more moderate guise, was evident in OZON's platform, published on February 21, 1937. It was based upon three principles: totalitarianism, which implied close connections with the army and unreserved obedience to Rydz-Śmigły; nationalism, which referred to the necessity for the Polish state, made up of many national groups, to promote primarily the interests of the ethnic Polish nation; and Catholicism, which recognized the Church's special standing in the Polish state and special relationship to the Polish people.[68] Nevertheless, unlike Endecja's, OZON's platform did not encourage physical violence. In its plank concerning the Jewish question, it stressed that OZON opposed all manner of violent attack upon Jews, even though the camp "looked with understanding upon the feeling of cultural self-defense and upon the natural desire of the Polish people for economic independence."[69]

Still, when compared with previous statements on the Jewish question from the Sanacja leadership, Koc's OZON platform represented a new departure. In all official declarations since the coup of 1926, Sanacja had upheld the principle of the equality of all citizens of the state. By allowing that the Jews were a foreign element who represented a danger to Poland's cultural and economic development, Koc's declaration broke with that tradition.[70] In effect, it indicated that it was now prepared to mobilize the most radical antisemitic forces, undoubtedly in order to steal some of Endecja's thunder and to guarantee that the reins of power would remain in Sanacja hands.[71]

On April 20, 1937, two months after Koc's declaration about the establishment of OZON, a press conference was held in Warsaw at which OZON's chief of staff, Colonel Jan Kowalewski, announced details about the camp's policy on the Jewish question. Asked if Jews would be admitted into OZON, he replied that they should be viewed as members of a separate national group. And just as Poles would not be accepted into a Zionist party, so too would Jews not be accepted into OZON.[72] The next day he declared that the Jewish question would be solved only by the emigration of the Jews from the country. But even before the Jews left, he stated, authorities should do everything possible to permit Poles to find employment in industry, commerce, and artisanry. In his words, "The desire of the Poles to achieve economic independence and their struggle for cultural self-defense is understandable."[73] In excluding Jews altogether, OZON departed fundamentally from the approach taken by BBWR in its platform.

Following the formation of OZON, the summer months of 1937 were marked by variegated antisemitic activity carried out by the youth of ZMP. Together with extreme elements of Falanga, these young people distributed antisemitic literature and manned picket lines in front of Jewish-owned stores. With the beginning of the academic year, students affiliated with ZMP were able to force Jewish students in several institutions of higher learning to occupy segregated benches in the lecture halls. The youth organization issued a public statement proclaiming the necessity of fighting the "Jewish-Communist Conspiracy (*Żydokomuna*)" by all means possible[74] and even invited Belorussian youth to join them in antisemitic actions.[75]

Acting in accordance with a policy seemingly set at the top levels of the government, local authorities generally ignored antisemitic outbursts. In Warsaw, police reportedly received special orders to intervene only in the event that public order was seriously disturbed.[76] Rydz-Śmigły at one time sought to replace Składkowski as prime minister with Justice Minister Witold Grabowski, who had announced that after taking control of the government he would shut down the leftist newspapers, disband PPS, liquidate the Jewish-Communist conspiracy, and introduce anti-Jewish legislation.[77] Although Składkowski's government managed to remain in power, Rydz-Śmigły and Koc continued to plot against their opponents within Sanacja[78] in a fashion that often included anti-Jewish motifs. According to some opposition sources, the two actually planned to carry out a coup d'état on the night of October 25–26, 1937. The plan, which reportedly was to have included attacks upon Jews, was said to have carried the code name "Night of the Long Noses (*Noc długich nosów*) — a clear hint as to its character.[79]

Rydz-Śmigły and Koc, however, were not strong enough to carry out the coup. In fact, under pressure from more left-leaning circles within Sanacja, Koc was dismissed as head of OZON in January 1938, to be replaced by

Gen. Stanisław Skwarczyński, military commander of Wilno. This move was taken as indicating a fundamental change in OZON's political direction, and indeed led to the severing of ties between the camp and Falanga.[80] In accordance with instruction from Falanga leader Piasecki, one of the heads of ZMP, Rutkowski, announced on April 20, 1938 that his organization was withdrawing from OZON. In response, Skwarczyński removed Rutkowski and all other Falanga members from ZMP, temporarily turning over the leadership of that organization to Edmund Galinat.

All of this might also have been taken as pointing to an alteration of the camp's policy toward Jews. However, it appears that the new leadership of OZON took pains to avoid giving such an impression. When the new head, Skwarczyński, spoke at ceremonies marking the first anniversary of OZON's founding, he declared that the organization would adopt an attitude of conciliation toward the political opposition and toward all of the national minorities — except the Jews.[81] A short while later he remarked during a visit to Poznań — unusual among Polish cities for its lack of a large Jewish community — that "the city of Poznań, which is free of Jews, ought to serve as an example for the cities of Poland" and that Polish merchants and artisans from the western provinces, with their relatively small Jewish populations, were obligated to take part in the struggle against the Jewish element throughout the country.[82] Similarly, Deputy Prime Minister and Minister of finance Eugeniusz Kwiatkowski, who represented OZON's left wing, told a meeting at Katowice on April 24, 1938 that even though Poland's constitution was based upon egalitarian principles, some reservations must be applied with regard to the Jews. Repeating OZON's claim that Jews represented a foreign element in the country, he called for their emigration. He also called for half of all ethnic Poles to take up residence in cities so as to guarantee the cities' Polish character.[83]

The British ambassador in Warsaw, Sir Howard Kennard, who observed the organizational and personnel changes that took place in OZON at the beginning of 1938, was pessimistic about the camp's future. He considered neither Koc nor his successor Skwarczyński capable of attracting the support of the masses. Nor did he believe that the change in OZON leadership signalled an alteration in the camp's Jewish policy, although he remarked that "a tendency toward the left and toward understanding with the Peasant Party is noticeable in OZON."[84]

On May 19–21, 1938, OZON's Supreme Council, meeting in Warsaw, adopted thirteen theses on the Jewish question. Their essence was as follows:

1. The primary purpose of OZON is to guarantee Poland's strength and greatness. This goal guides the camp with respect to the Jewish question. The starting point for evaluating the role of the Jews in Poland as a political factor is the fact that they belong to a pan-Jewish group that extends beyond the bounds of the state and has separate national goals.

2. The Jews weaken the development of the power of the Polish nation and state and represent a barrier to the "social evolution" going on in Poland.

3. Those who support the Polish state must work toward a solution of the Jewish question. Actions of an anarchic or demagogic character impair a solution and threaten peace and public order.

4. The solution to the problem will come mainly through a large-scale reduction in the number of Jews in Poland. The state must support the existing emigrationist tendencies in the Jewish population.

5. Palestine must be regarded as the principal destination for Jewish emigration.

6. Because of restrictions upon immigration to Palestine, other sites for emigration must be secured through international action.

7. It is desirable to reach a state of economic independence in the towns and in the countryside. Thus the large role played by Jews in the country's economic life must be reduced.

8. The Jews' high involvement in certain professions must be reduced through legislation that will permit selection in accordance with the interests of the state. Opportunities for all elements of the Polish population to study in vocational schools and institutions of higher learning must be augmented.

9. The independence of Polish social and cultural life from Jewish influence — which stems from the Jews' concentration in the cities and their penetration of the press, literature, the theatre, music, the cinema, and the radio — must be strictly maintained.

10. With regard to education, the authorities must adopt a uniform policy toward the Jews and not permit the young people to interfere.

11. The goal is not the assimilation of the Jews, although Jews who have demonstrated their value through service to Poland will be recognized as belonging to the "Polish national partnership."

12. OZON condemns violence against Jews, but at the same time demands that Jews be loyal to the needs of the state. The Jews' international connections do not accord with this principle.

13. The young generation of Poles is called upon to play a positive role in

solving the Jewish question. Such a solution depends upon this generation's ability gradually to take over basic positions in Poland's social, economic, and cultural life.[85]

The thirteen theses detailed for the first time the basic principles of OZON's policy toward Jews — heretofore embodied in no more than a few general sentences contained in the speeches of OZON leaders and never having been adopted formally by the camp's official apparatus. The theses not only formulated concrete assumptions concerning the status of the Jews in the country; they also pointed to definite operational goals that were to be embodied in action concerning the Jews.

The Jews' loyalty was called into question and their foreignness affirmed; they were not to be integrated into Polish society (unlike the other national minorities in OZON's scheme) but were rather to leave the country. Legislation restricting their access to certain branches of the economy and to higher education was to be enacted. The departure of OZON's thirteen theses from the egalitarian principles of Piłsudski's April constitution was clear.

Shortly following the adoption of the theses, Rydz-Śmigły and President Mościcki decided to dissolve both houses of parliament and to hold new elections in November — marking the first time that OZON acted as a political party. The camp must have been pleased with the results: in the Sejm it returned 161 out of 208 deputies. Its greatest success, however, lay in the fact that in contrast to the 1935 elections, in which only 46 percent of eligible voters had taken part, voter turnout in the current elections had reached 67 percent — for which OZON took the credit. The election marked a turning point for the government's totalitarian element, which attempted to weaken the standing of the moderate Zamek group, represented in the government by Kwiatkowski.[86]

When the new Sejm convened on December 3, 1938, OZON head Skwarczyński called for limitations to be imposed upon the percentage of Jews in commerce and in the free professions.[87] In the same spirit he challenged the government, on behalf of 117 OZON deputies, to state what steps it had taken in order to radically reduce the number of Jews in Poland and obtain international assistance for financing mass Jewish emigration.[88] OZON also planned the introduction of legislation that would divide the citizens of Poland into three categories — those of Polish nationality, who would enjoy full rights; members of the Slavic and German minorities, who would be asked in a plebiscite to affirm their loyalty to Poland and whose rights would be adjusted according to their vote; and the Jews, who would have no

civil rights and would be entitled to remain in Poland on a temporary basis
only. It is unclear whether this plan encompassed all Jews or only those who
had obtained Polish citizenship after 1918.[89] Two Sejm deputies, one a former OZON member, Franciszek Stoch, the other an active member, Bene-
dykt Kieńć, even sought to introduce bills stripping Jews of most of their
rights immediately.[90]

In spite of the rhetoric, none of the proposed legislation reached the Sejm
floor. Poland's general political situation was growing more difficult day by
day.[91] As its relations with Germany worsened, Poland needed the good will
of Western public opinion, which the government feared would be withdrawn if they enacted anti-Jewish legislation at this time. Nevertheless, the
proposals were evidently intended to prepare the Polish public for drastic
changes in the legal status of the Jews — as well as to frighten the Jews themselves and weaken their capacity to resist.

The Jewish community in Poland followed events in the Sanacja camp's re-
organization in OZON with consternation. Shortly after Koc's initial ideological declaration in February 1937, with its paragraph denying Jews equal
rights, a secret meeting of Zionist leaders active in the World Jewish Congress was held in Vienna to discuss the future of Polish Jewry in the wake of
OZON's establishment. Among those in attendance were Yitshak Gruenbaum (already a resident of Palestine), Moshe Kleinbaum, Yitshak Schwarzbart, Henryk Rosmarin, Anshel Reiss, and Baruch Cukierman. All were
highly pessimistic about the situation and considered Rydz-Śmigły to be
the force behind Koc's declaration and the real initiator and proponent of
the policy of economic boycott. Further, they feared that should the opposition manage to retain its strength in spite of OZON's propaganda efforts,
OZON's leaders of the organization would dissolve all political parties and
proclaim an open dictatorship.[92]

The participants at the Zionist meeting knew that many former Sanacja
adherents — even large bodies such as the Union of Trade Unions (*Związek
Związków Zawodowych*) and the Polish Teachers Union — had thus far refused to become affiliated with OZON. They were also aware of opposition
to Rydz-Śmigły and Koc within the regime itself, to the extent that some senior government figures were even reportedly interested in receiving aid
from Jewish funds for the conduct of anti-OZON propaganda.[93] They believed this opposition group was connected with military circles seeking to
replace Rydz-Śmigły with Gen. Kazimierz Sosnkowski, who had worked
closely with Piłsudski and who, although generally identified with the right

wing, reputedly felt the authorities should show greater concern for the preservation of law and order in the country.

Despite these possibilities, however, some of the assembled Zionist leaders expressed the belief that the Jews in Poland were even more vulnerable than the Jews in Germany. The Polish population, they felt, was "undisciplined and uncivilized," and unlike in Germany, had always been even more aggressively inclined toward the Jews than the line taken by the government in its anti-Jewish propaganda. In consequence, they resolved to convene an international conference on Polish Jewry; to endeavor to induce the British and French embassies in Warsaw to intervene on the Jews' behalf; to step up the economic and political struggle for Polish Jews in conjunction with international Jewish organizations; to establish a special fund to support opposition elements within Sanacja;[94] to hold a Jewish congress in Poland under the auspices and with the material support of the World Jewish Congress; and to seek reform in the deliberations of the Congress of National Minorities.[95]

The Jewish Sejm deputies and senators did not take part in this meeting, whose primary importance was in the renewal of the internal Jewish debate over the conduct of a long-range independent Jewish policy seeking practical measures extending beyond defense against expropriation. Indeed, in retrospect the major weakness of the program adopted at the meeting was that most of the recommended steps involved obtaining the assistance of Jewish and non-Jewish elements outside of Poland. It seems the participants did not consider Polish Jewry capable of exerting any meaningful political influence on its own; and in the end, none of the measures called for came to fruition.

For their part, the Jewish parliamentary deputies spoke out against the so-called "Jewish paragraph" in OZON's founding declaration. In the debate over the government budget held in March 1937, Senator Moshe Schorr announced that the Jewish caucus would, as an expression of no confidence, vote against the government's budgetary proposal. In Schorr's view, Koc's declaration indicated that OZON intended to pursue an antisemitic policy and lead Poland toward totalitarianism.[96]

The emphasis placed by OZON on the need to bring about the disassimilation of Polish Jewry was particularly troubling to the Jewish assimilationists, such as the Polish Jewish Veterans Organization. At their meeting on December 5, 1937, Zdzisław Żmigryder Konopka, the principal speaker, commented that OZON's slogans regarding Jewish emigration sounded like calls to expel the Jews from the country. Although the members of his organization felt they belonged to the Polish nation and had sought to dissuade Jews from adopting extreme positions, OZON was now frustrating their efforts and feelings.[97]

Another group that became increasingly estranged from the Sanacja camp was Agudas Yisroel. Although it had strongly identified itself for a long time with Sanacja, the process of estrangement had begun in 1936, even before OZON's founding, when a law was passed restricting the slaughtering of kosher meat.[98] With the adoption of OZON's thirteen theses, a virtually unbridgeable rift was created. The party's newspaper, *Dos Yudishe Togblat,* viewed the theses as a policy of official antisemitism that would most likely lead to further anti-Jewish legislation. As a result, speeches and articles would no longer suffice for combating antisemitism. Instead, practical measures would have to be taken to help Jews hold onto their sources of livelihood despite the efforts being made to wrest them from them.[99] Moreover, at a meeting of the party's central committee in late May 1938, Sejm deputy Leyb Mincberg stated that Agudas Yisroel would now coordinate its defense activities with the other members of the Jewish parliamentary faction. At stake were not only religious matters — which were also not receiving favorable treatment at the hands of the Polish authorities — but the preservation of the rights guaranteed Jews in the April constitution. Further, the party's central committee called upon the enlightened elements of Polish society not to become swept up in the wave of hatred toward Jews, a hatred that was, he believed, foreign to Poland.[100]

At the opposite end of the Jewish political spectrum, the Bund expressed the opinion that the thirteen theses indicated that OZON had adopted Endecja's approach to the Jewish question and had turned its back upon the constitution that its own people had drafted. The Bund's central committee declared that the theses made Jews the victims of the bitterness that had been building up within the Polish population, both in the cities and in the countryside. This strategy, the committee warned, however, was fraught with danger not only for Jews but for Poles as well, for it would result in the strengthening of the reactionary forces in the country. Moreover, the party's newspaper observed, the theses would not bring any political benefit to OZON, for Poland's antisemites had already found their leader in Endecja.[101]

In addition to the political parties, a major vehicle for the formation of Jewish opinions and actions regarding what was going on in Poland was the Jewish press. The primary organizer of a press campaign to inform the Jewish public about OZON's plans regarding the Jewish question was Moshe Kleinbaum. In a speech to a Zionist convention in March 1937, Kleinbaum argued that Koc's February declaration had given official sanction to anti-semitism and was in full accord with Poland's foreign policy, in particular with its friendly relations with the Third Reich. He saw the regime — which, to his mind, lacked a strong base of public support — using OZON as a vehicle for building bridges to the Dmowski camp in order to ensure its survival in power. The Jews of Poland, however, would not abandon their demand for recognition of their rights as a national minority. The best way for them to realize this goal was, he maintained, to align themselves politically with the democratic elements in Polish society, represented mainly by PPS and to an extent by the Peasant Party.[102]

After the change in OZON's leadership, Kleinbaum modified his emphasis somewhat. Noting that some OZON elements were seeking a rapprochement with the Peasant Party and a cooling of relations with PPS, he warned that OZON's left wing was no less inclined toward a policy of economic antisemitism than was the camp's right wing. Jews, he argued, should have no illusions: they were now being subjected to a policy of "secret extermination." Since their only hope lay in internal Jewish unity, he called upon his readers to rally around the idea of a Jewish congress in Poland, an event that could, he believed, serve as a catalyst for the formation of a unified Polish Jewish leadership that would speak for all the country's Jews.[103] That leadership would need to mobilize the potential political power of the three million Jewish citizens of Poland "and to set it upon the balance of political decisions" through the conduct of an independent Jewish policy aimed against the Sanacja regime.[104]

Still, Kleinbaum realized that a policy of opposition to the regime could be carried out only by encouraging the democratic elements in Polish politics, chiefly PPS and the Peasant Party.[105] The continuation of these groups' support for the Jewish struggle in the wake of the formation of OZON, however, could not be depended upon. To be sure, the platform adopted at the twenty-fourth congress of PPS, which concluded on February 2, 1937, contained a strong demand for Jewish civil equality and for the waging of a struggle against antisemitism.[106] Nevertheless, as we have noted above, the antisemitic sentiments permeating Polish society appear at times to have influenced even this party.[107] When, for example, the authorities moved in several instances to prohibit common demonstrations by Jewish and Christian workers under joint PPS-Bund sponsorship, the provincial governor of Łódź noted that the PPS leadership did not object to such prohibition, as it could not ignore the spread of antisemitism among the Polish middle class, working class, and intelligentsia. Indeed, several regional PPS branches, notably the one in the Kielce province, refused to hold joint demonstrations with the Bund because the Peasant Party had refused to demonstrate together with Jews.[108] On May Day 1938 there were no demonstrations held in common by PPS and Jewish socialist groups, both because of opposition within PPS and because of prohibitions by local authorities.[109]

Nonetheless, in 1937 there were instances of active collaboration between PPS and the Bund, most notably in demonstrations following the pogrom in Brześć and in protests against the institution of the so-called ghetto benches in Polish universities.[110] In these anti-antisemitic activities, however, PPS focused its energies mainly against Endecja. At the same time, it constantly attempted to reach an understanding with the more moderate elements in Sanacja, such as those loyal to President Mościcki and Deputy Prime Minister and Minister of finance Kwiatkowski.[111] This strategy drew the fire of the Communist Party of Poland (KPP), which charged that the Sanacja regime was no less responsible than Endecja for the recent antisemitic upsurge.[112] A May 1937 KPP proclamation equated the war against antisemitism with the struggle for democracy and called upon all antifascist parties to join forces against antisemitic violence.[113] However, KPP was an extremely small group,[114] and shortly after this declaration its overall level of activity diminished sharply, one of the signs that the party was on the verge of dissolution.[115]

Similarly, the Peasant Party's attitude toward the Jewish question at the time of the formation of OZON does not appear to have been clearly defined. In contrast to earlier congresses, the special party congress that met in Warsaw in January 1937 did not mention the Jewish problem at all. Instead, it concentrated upon the demand for the complete democratization of the Polish state.[116] Nevertheless, the party did give thought to Jewish matters, as indicated by a statement appearing in the official party weekly the following October:

We are not proponents of solving the Jewish problem with whips, knives, and stones, for we believe that such means are neither effective nor moral.... [Still] the Jewish problem exists for us, and we are presently trying to solve it in a partial fashion by establishing numerous cooperatives throughout the countryside. We do not hide our opinion that if someone ought to emigrate to Madagascar, we prefer that Jews do so rather than Polish peasants.[117]

Another indication of the Peasant Party's attitude during this period came at the party congress in Kraków in February 1938. In the political resolutions adopted at this congress, the Jewish issue was mentioned only in passing, in a statement asserting that several groups calling themselves national had attached themselves to the service of dictatorship and taking part in a struggle against the peasantry under the false slogan of fighting the Jewish and Communist danger in Poland.[118]

It appears, then, that the party was not swept along in the tide of radicalization of antisemitism in Poland from 1937 onward. One explanation for this cautious and moderate stance was undoubtedly the party's realization that the problems of millions of landless peasants would not be solved by taking over 40,000 Jewish peddler stalls. Indeed, working toward such a takeover was viewed as a trap designed to distract the attention of the peasants from their primary difficulties. Like the Socialists, the Peasant Party did not wish to see the center of gravity of the public debate moved from the realm of social to that of interethnic problems.

Nevertheless, it does not appear that the various elements within the democratic camp in Poland, including those of the national minorities, were prepared to work together to change the antisemitic face of the regime. Even had they been so willing, the antidemocratic forces that controlled the country, and whose antisemitism was gaining them growing public support, were still most likely strong enough to rebuff any challenge from the left. Thus the Jewish leadership possessed few viable options with regard to the direction that their political activity should take. Some groups, most notably Agudas Yisroel, even appeared to despair of the efficacy of political activity at all. In an article published in January 1937 in the Aguda party newspaper, for example, Hillel Zeidmann contended that Jews ought to concentrate their energies upon strengthening their economic position, mainly by developing an independent Jewish cooperative movement. By increasing their economic strength in this fashion, he argued, Jews would augment their political strength as well. Jews should not identify themselves with the principles of either democracy or antidemocracy; instead, they ought to adjust themselves to the given political situation and involve themselves in economic activities that might positively influence their position in the country.[119]

A similar though by no means identical position was adopted by the Revisionist Party, which had been disappointed with the positions taken by PPS on specific issues, particularly in the Łódź city council, where the PPS party controlled the largest faction. The Revisionist newspaper thus proposed an "orientation toward ourselves," meaning that Jews ought to be prepared to accept assistance from any Polish group without being overly particular as to its general political stance. Jews should, the newspaper urged, distance themselves from the internal debates being waged by the Polish parties.[120]

This attitude, of course, was shared by neither the Bund nor the mainstream Zionists, both of which called for a left-leaning Jewish political orientation.[121] That commonality notwithstanding, these two groups continued to battle one another and showed no inclination to join forces. Moshe Kleinbaum explained that whereas the Bund sought to become part of a unified proletarian camp in Poland, the Zionists wished to remain an independent force allied with that camp.[122] For its part, the Bund argued that the Zionists actually helped to strengthen "Polish Hitlerism" by accepting the notion that Palestine rather than Poland was the true homeland of Polish Jewry and that the Polish state was made up of a "landlord people" and a "tenant people."[123]

Thus even the mounting pressures against them during the two and a half years between the formation of OZON and the outbreak of the second world war — years during which anti-Jewish sentiments in Poland continued to undergo a process of steady expansion and radicalization — proved insufficient to forge Polish Jewry into a politically unified body pursuing a coherent strategy aimed at securing its position in its country of citizenship.

3
The Economic Campaign Against the Jews

For all of its internal divisiveness and inability to coalesce about a single strategy for self-defense, Polish Jewry did make serious stands against many of the specific manifestations of the country's increasingly hostile attitude toward it. The Jewish political leadership, however, was not always at the forefront of such resistance. Such was the case, for example, in the campaign to overcome the effects of the anti-Jewish economic offensive waged by several elements of the Polish community — an offensive that became far more intense from 1936 to 1939, just when Poland's economic situation had improved noticeably following the depression of the early 1930s.

The secondary role played by the Jewish political leadership in this campaign is surprising, for, as we have seen, the economic campaign was sanctioned and organized with the far-ranging powers granted to the executive branch by the Sejm and Senat in the post-Piłsudski governments. The regime initially wished to use these powers, among other things, to extend the debt moratorium — hitherto applied only to peasants — to urban clerical workers as well. This moratorium, initially adopted in 1932, had especially deleterious effects upon Polish Jewry, and its proposed extension was likely to do Jews even further economic damage.[1]

To be sure, Jewish parliamentary deputies did raise their voices against this proposal,[2] as well as against what they took to be deliberate government encouragement of other measures to eliminate Jews from participation in the economic life of the state. The Zionist representative Emil Sommerstein spoke out loudly before the Sejm plenum in February 1936, during the course of a debate on the government budget, against what he called the government's economic antisemitism, which, to his mind, went hand in hand with "the antisemitism of pogroms." He charged that terror tactics were being applied to dissuade Poles from any economic cooperation with Jews and that anti-Jewish agitation in Polish newspapers (and not only those of Endecja) was never condemned by the government. On the contrary, the Kościałkowski government itself was erecting barriers against Jewish participation in many branches of the Polish economy. Consequently he demanded that the government affirm that its slogan, "Work and Bread for All," applied to the Jewish population as well as to ethnic Poles.[3] He also called for greater government supervision of its lower-echelon administrators to prevent them from supporting the anti-Jewish boycott and its accompanying terror. Each of these administrators, he charged, conducted his own independent Jewish policy.[4]

On a later occasion, in June 1936, Sommerstein warned that those who supported the economic campaign against the Jews and sought to deny them means of subsistence would in the end merely drive them closer to Communism. "People try to excuse pogroms and economic antisemitism as opposition to Communism," he declared, but in fact these manifestations of antisemitism were the most powerful and effective means of spreading Communism among the Jewish masses. In his view, sanction of the "go ahead (*owszem*)" policy announced by Prime Minister Sławoj-Składkowski[5] necessarily involved doing injustice to Jews and led to violence against them.[6]

Sommerstein also expressed strong opposition to the government's refusal to employ Jews in the civil service. In his speech to the Sejm on October 29, 1935 he complained that the Jews of Poland were being denied "the right to work," and that the younger Jewish generation faced a hopeless future with public employment closed to it.[7] Similarly, in a June 1936 Senat debate, Senator Trockenheim argued that the anti-Jewish economic boycott was more dangerous to the Jews than violence, for it represented a systematic way to deprive Jews of their livelihoods. He also responded to charges that the occupational structure of Polish Jewry was out of balance, arguing that were they allowed to do so, Jews would want to work — and indeed would be able to — in agriculture, large industry, public transportation and utilities, and government service. As proof, he cited the fact that many Jews of Polish origin living in Palestine were employed in those very fields.[8]

Such efforts to counter the economic offensive through political channels appear to have had some effect. For example, following Sommerstein's protest to the Interior Ministry,[9] the government placed a ban upon a "Polish Commerce Week" scheduled to be held in Częstochowa in March 1936. By this time, however, it appears that most Jewish leaders realized it would be necessary to carry the economic battle into other arenas. Thus deputy Leyb Mincberg of Agudas Yisroel told the Sejm shortly after Sommerstein's earlier speech that the economic boycott was actually "a double-edged sword." Some Jews, he said, had begun to consider whether they ought to refrain from consuming the products of Polish fisheries owned by boycott supporters.[10] Similarly, the Polish Jewish newspaper *Nasz Przegląd*, noting the peasantry's increasing pressure on the Jews' economic positions, proposed that Jews attempt to exert economic counterpressure in the countryside.[11]

In June 1936, a few days after Sławoj-Składkowski's announcement of the *owszem* policy, former Sejm deputy Henryk Rosmarin called a general meeting of the Jewish Economic Committee (*Żydowski Komitet Gospodarczy*) established in 1934. The purpose of the meeting was to convene a Jewish Economic Congress to extricate the Jewish community from its growing feeling of helplessness and desperation.[12] It was hoped that the Committee and the Congress would coordinate the activities of Jewish economic organizations, provide assistance to unemployed Jews, create new jobs for them, and develop possibilities for vocational retraining – as well as maintain contact with the Jewish parliamentary representation. In short, by mid-1936 the mounting sense among Polish Jews was that the economic offensive against them could best be fought by an economic counterattack combined with self-help activities.

In retrospect, the notion of economic counterattack was not realistic in the political climate of post-Piłsudski Poland. The notion of self-help, on the other hand, proved to be increasingly important in the Jews' struggle to maintain sources of livelihood and locate new ones. A leader in this area was the Jewish free loan and occupational retraining society CKB (Cekabe),[13] which supported Jews as they underwent retraining and researched possibilities for moving them into other occupations.[14] In 1935 it also announced the establishment of a self-help fund of 3 million *zł.* for assisting Jewish economic rehabilitation.[15] In addition, in 1935 it maintained 722 free loan funds throughout the country, with a total capital of some 10 million *zł.*[16] The number of such funds increased in the next few years, and according to the director of the office of the American Jewish Joint Distribution Committee (JDC) in Warsaw, Yitshak Giterman, they represented one of the most effective ways to combat economic antisemitism.[17]

The JDC was also active in the establishment of Jewish producers' cooperatives and credit unions. Together with the Jewish Colonization Association, it established a common fund, known as the American Joint Reconstruction Foundation. In an attempt to do for Jews what the Polish authorities and government banks did for non-Jewish cooperatives, the fund offered financial support to Jewish cooperative associations. In particular, the credit unions, which in 1935 made up some fifty percent of all Jewish cooperative enterprises, played an increasingly important part in helping Jews protect their economic positions.[18] During the first half of 1936, 336 separate unions granted 55,000 loans worth a total of 16 million dollars.[19] Their assets came from two principal sources: private capital and members' deposits; and low-interest loans from the Joint Reconstruction Foundation, which dealt only with credit unions and not with individuals.[20] In many instances the credit they extended offered the only possibility for Jewish small artisans, shopkeepers, and peddlers to maintain a livelihood.[21] In July 1935 a meeting was held in Warsaw to create a central financial support system which, according to Sejm deputy Wacław Wiślicki of the Jewish Merchants' Association, would coordinate the entire Jewish economic struggle. At this meeting it was decided to establish a Credit Center (*Centrala Kredytowa*) to unite the various branches of the Jewish cooperative movement throughout Poland.[22]

Despite such efforts, however, the Jewish political leadership failed to realize the importance of the cooperatives in the battle against economic antisemitism and did not exert much energy in promoting them. As a result, the number of such cooperatives began to decline. The Jewish press criticized the management of the Joint Reconstruction Foundation for not allocating more funds for this endeavor precisely at the time of great economic crisis and growing hostility from the Polish sector.[23] Indeed, in 1935 the Foundation called in loans to cooperatives totalling 634,000 zł. and issued only 229,000 zł. in new ones.[24] Other voices criticized what seemed to them excessive concentration of the cooperative movement upon credit unions and insufficient attention to the essential problem of vocational retraining.[25]

Another aspect of the Jewish economic struggle involved efforts to counteract the tendency of public and government agencies not to offer employment to Jews. The Bund played a leading role in this regard, opening a special office called Right to Work (*Rekht oif Arbet*). In April 1936 its representatives met with officials in Warsaw, demanding that unemployed Jews be included in a government-sponsored project to provide public works jobs to 150,000 jobless citizens.[26] At the same time, demands concerning the right to work continued to be voiced by Jewish deputies in the Sejm and Senat. Sommerstein castigated antisemitic propaganda related to economic matters, which, he claimed, masqueraded under the guise of patriotism. Once again he complained that Jewish youth had no chance to secure their future in Poland as long as jobs in public enterprises were closed to them and the etatist economy shut Jews out of chances for employment.[27] However, such demands lacked force, especially since at the same time even many Jewish factory owners refused to hire Jewish workers. The labor branch of Agudas Yisroel attacked this practice in a special proclamation, reminding Jewish factory owners that their Jewish customers were liable to cease patronizing them in light of such behavior.[28]

Finally, Jews and Jewish organizations in other countries occasionally inveighed against the economic policies of the Polish government. Immediately following Sławoj-Składkowski's *owszem* speech in June 1936, the Board of Deputies of British Jews addressed a protest to the Polish ambassador in London, Edward Raczyński. In response, the ambassador was instructed by the Foreign Ministry in Warsaw to explain that the prime minister's speech had specifically expressed opposition to violent acts and illegal anti-Jewish actions and had taken a neutral stance, based upon its inability to intervene in the economic struggle between Poles and Jews.[29]

Chaim Weizmann, president of the World Zionist Organization, also tried to encourage British Jewish leaders to apply pressure of behalf of their Polish co-religionists. In October 1936 he wrote to the Sir Simon Marks, enclosing a letter that Zionist official Berl Locker had written in the wake of his recent visit to Poland, that painted a highly pessimistic picture of the Jewish future in that country in light of the economic boycott and government policy.[30] Weizmann urged Marks to meet with Foreign Minister Beck on his upcoming visit to London and to inform him that Jewish organizations throughout the world would soon be coordinating all of their activities in extending aid to Polish Jewry.

That same year, at a meeting of the World Jewish Congress in August, the head of the central office of the Association of Jewish Merchants in Warsaw spoke about Polish Jewry's economic difficulties. He suggested that the Congress establish a special committee on economic affairs, which would seek to increase the number of Jewish merchants and artisans in Poland capable of producing merchandise for export. The committee would also assist in the export of their products organizationally and financially. The Association of Merchants also proposed to found a Central Jewish Cooperative Bank, through which all funds sent to Polish Jews by relatives abroad (a sum that amounted to some 120 million *zł.* annually) would be channeled.[31]

Unfortunately, most plans for international Jewish cooperation in this area remained on paper and never actualized any really effective or coordinated counteractions to persuade the Polish government to repudiate economic antisemitism or anti-Jewish violence. This lack of effective Jewish pressure was reflected in an intensification of anti-Jewish activity from 1937 to 1939, both on the part of political circles in the ruling party and on the part of the opposition Endecja camp. Moreover, during this period such activity became systematic and institutionalized. Its advantages over sporadic violence, which antagonized world public opinion, came to be widely recognized; Jews could be discriminated against within the framework of existing laws. The founding declaration of OZON of February 1937 included a paragraph concerning the "natural desire of the Polish nation for economic independence"; the use of the word "nation (*naród*)" rather that "state (*państwo*)" made it clear that the practical meaning of this phrase was a call to weaken the Jews' economic standing through government-initiated action, rather than through the neutrality of which Składkowski had spoken only a few months earlier.

This semantic shift, indicating that the government actually took a positive attitude toward the attack upon the Jews' economic position and viewed itself as an active agent in it, was revealed during a session of the Budget Committee of the Sejm on January 25, 1938. There, regarding the Jewish question, Składkowski reiterated his government's opposition to violent action, but he added that the Jews felt discomfort with the social and economic changes that had led to a rise in the peasants' standard of living and to the migration of some of them to the cities. "The Polish government must support this process," he declared, "and therefore the Jews must understand that the economic struggle against them does not represent any injury to their rights, nor does it constitute an attack against them as citizens of the state. There are also several undesirable instances in which Jews abroad interfere with our economic and social difficulties."[32]

This statement incorporated an attitude frequently expressed by government spokesmen — that the economic offensive against Jewry did not contradict the clauses of the 1935 constitution guaranteeing Jews equal rights. The principle of the Polonization of the country's economic life, which in practice meant the separation of the Jews from their sources of livelihood, was a principal feature of government economic policy. And while such a principle resulted in discrimination against Jews, it was not meant to interfere with the Jews' enjoyment of their rights. At the same time, government spokesmen do not appear to have made any positive statements concerning the government's obligation to preserve the civic equality of its Jewish citizens.

The attitude of the authorities was further revealed in their approach to the boycott. During the two years preceeding the outbreak of war, boycott activities reflected government plans for achieving far-reaching political goals. The formation of picket lines around Jewish stores became a daily occurrence, and in some locations Jewish stalls in the marketplace were forcibly concentrated into a sort of ghetto, separated from the stalls of non-Jews. In the provinces of Poznań and Pomorze, Jewish merchants were not allowed to participate in fairs. The authorities dismantled and demolished many stores and other structures owned by Jews, ostensibly in accordance with municipal ordinances.[33] A 1921 law had empowered municipal authorities to demolish any structure that interfered with the esthetic appearance of the surroundings, without compensation to the owners. However, this law came to be widely applied throughout the country only beginning in 1938, and then only against Jews, evidently as a result of instructions from higher authorities.[34]

To be sure, some Polish circles had doubts as to the effectiveness of the boycott, maintaining that only through government initiative and with the means at the government's disposal would it be possible to strike at the true source of Jewish economic power — the Jewish bankers and wholesalers — and thereby to facilitate the movement of peasants into the cities. Small-scale actions against scattered Jewish stores, they argued, might impress with their high visibility, but actually brought meager results.[35]

On the other hand, one of the younger leaders of the National Party, Jędrzej Giertych, disagreed. He held that after Polish shopkeepers, through the anti-Jewish boycott, managed to destroy Jewish petty commerce, wealthy Jews would also suffer damage. Pointing with pride to the boycott's accomplishments thus far, he noted that although it had begun in isolated villages, it subsequently spread to the largest urban centers. In particular he cited the small town of Odrzywół, where anti-Jewish incidents had taken place as early as 1935. All of the Jewish market stalls had been liquidated within three years and replaced by two hundred Polish stalls.[36]

Indeed, anti-Jewish boycott activities intensified beginning in the second half of 1937 — primarily instigated by the group called *Związek Polski*, in which representatives of the Polish Merchants Union, the Organization of Small Businessmen, and a host of professional associations of the Polish intelligentsia participated. Connected to OZON, with some active members of ONR in it as well, the organization's raison d'être was to bring about the removal of the Jews from Polish economic life, so that they would be forced to leave the country. To accomplish this goal, it planned to organize and fund picket lines outside Jewish businesses; expose the Jewish ownership of stock in various corporations; conduct research into the extent of Jewish involvement in the various branches of trade and industry; open Polish wholesale supply houses, through which Polish factory owners would offer their products to Christian merchants at special discounts; take action against Christian merchants who maintained business contacts with Jews; and help merchants and artisans in the Western provinces relocate to other parts of the country. At its first national convention, held behind closed doors in Poznań in March 1938, a resolution was adopted demanding the liquidation of Cekabe, on the grounds that with the support that it received from American

Jewry it severely impeded the Union's work in Central and Eastern Poland.[37]

Even before this convention, however, boycott activities gathered momentum. An "Anti-Jewish Week" was organized by ONR in Poznań from September 12–19, 1937, and according to a report sent by the German Consulate-General in that city to the German Foreign Ministry in Berlin, the week was termed "a success." It was preceded by much preparatory work, including intensive propaganda in the local mass media and public meetings by Polish economic organizations calling upon authorities to institute a ghetto for the Jews.[38] On November 12, 1937, an All-Polish Congress of Christian Merchants met in Warsaw under government sponsorship. The opening session, attended by the president of the republic and by senior government ministers, was addressed by the minister of industry and trade and by the mayor of the Polish capital.

Much of the Congress's deliberations dealt with the Polonization of commerce, which was deemed essential both for economic and security reasons. As its resolutions emphasized, the Jews were not only a source of social ferment. They played a decisive role in Poland's foreign and domestic trade and posed a danger to the state. Thus the Congress called upon state and municipal authorities to assist Polish merchants by establishing special credit and licensing terms for them, by ordering supplies from them, and by granting them tax breaks.[39] Jews, on the other hand, should be denied the right to trade freely in the country because they cheated on their taxes, did not keep honest accounts, maintained stores that did not meet the requirements of the Ministry of Health, and thus had a lower cost of doing business than did Polish merchants.[40]

This Congress represented a turning point in the anti-Jewish boycott in that it involved the central and local authorities directly in its activities. On January 28, 1938 the minister of industry and trade, Antoni Roman, announced that the government supported the activities of the Association of Polish Christian Merchants, which, he said, was working for the Polonization of commerce. He added that the government would assist in promoting the natural migration of peasants to the cities.[41]

At around the same time, the government established an interministerial committee, consisting of senior officials from the Ministries of Industry and Trade, Treasury, and Agriculture, for the purpose of assisting in carrying out the decisions of the Congress. In a February 1938 debate over the budget of the Ministry of Industry and Trade, the rapporteur of the Sejm's budget committee, Brunon Sikorski, warned the Jewish public against an intemperate reaction to the Congress's resolutions concerning the Polonization of the country's commercial life.[42] And in May 1938 Treasury Minister Eugeniusz Kwiatkowski gave an important programmatic speech in Katowice in which he spoke about the need to remove non-Polish elements from the country's economic life.[43] In addition, central and local governmental agencies and the Polish army refrained from purchasing merchandise from Jewish suppliers.[44]

The government's support for the boycott was also revealed in an exchange between Składkowski and the Jewish Senator Jakub Trockenheim in February 1938. Trockenheim complained to the Senat Budget Committee that the placing of picket lines outside Jewish-owned stores — an important element of the anti-Jewish economic struggle — violated the principle of free and fair competition. He demanded that the prime minister take a clear stand on this matter. Skladkowski claimed to be uncertain about the legal status of the picket lines. But if it turned out that they were in fact illegal, he said, it would then be necessary to arrest two hundred people in every small town and village. The prime minister added that the Jews had started the picket lines themselves when they demonstrated against Polish peasants to prevent them from selling their produce on the free market.[45]

Meanwhile, the picket lines continued to grow. By April 1938 pickets organized by Związek Polski were even demanding job security and a monthly salary in return for their services.[46] The pickets often behaved violently; in Upper Silesia they reportedly prevented Jews from entering marketplaces and threatened peasants who patronized Jewish merchants.[47] In various locations they pressed for market days to be set for Saturdays so that many Jewish merchants would not be able to participate.[48] In April 1938 pickets were reported to be standing outside almost every Jewish shop in Łódź.[49]

To be sure, the Endek camp also contributed its share to the offensive, establishing a special boycott department headed by Stanisław Trzeciak and supported by such National Party leaders as Tadeusz Bielecki, Roman Rybarski, and Father Godlewski.[50] So active were Endek circles in this regard that at many gatherings of Christian merchants, it was decided to contribute a fixed percentage of monthly receipts to the National Party.[51] ONR-Falanga set up a similar boycott department, which sought to frighten Christian enterprises that did business with Jewish factories or wholesalers.[52]

Jewish parliamentary representatives continued their efforts to counter the accusation that Jews dominated the Polish economy. Jakub Trockenheim told the Senat that, according to official government figures from 1933, Jews constituted 52.5 percent of those engaged in commerce and trade. He claimed that had municipally- and publically-owned industries been willing to hire Jews, this percentage would have been considerably lower. Even the small number of Jewish land-owners were targets for official attack: 68 percent of the lands slated for redistribution in the provinces of Lwów and Tarnopol were owned by Jews.[53] Similarly, Emil Sommerstein advised the Sejm that for all of the talk about the need for newly-urbanized peasants to acquire economic positions held by Jews, in fact Polish urban dwellers were increasingly taking over failed Jewish businesses. To his mind, government involvement in the entire anti-Jewish economic struggle was only an attempt by those in the Sanacja camp to win public opinion to their side.[54]

Indeed, by late 1937 the boycott appeared to be taking an unmistakable toll upon Jewish economic life. A report prepared by a committee of the Jewish community organization in Białystok in October 1937, for example, indicated that in many small towns in the area the majority of Jews were living on relief funds provided by the community. In the town of Sokoły, fifteen Jewish families had recently been forced to close their businesses and move elsewhere, and similar occurrences were reported in the Łomża area and in Wysokie Mazowieckie.[55]

Although the Jewish public was well aware of the dangers of the intensification of the boycott — particularly the activities of the All-Polish Congress of Christian Merchants and the authorities' complicity in its activities — it was not properly organized to fight back effectively. To be sure, the Jewish Economic Committee stepped up the pace of its activities during the summer of 1937, but it could not provide sufficient counterweight to the conduct of the anti-Jewish economic policy. At first the committee limited its activities to Warsaw, where it attempted to exert pressure on over five hundred government and municipal enterprises to employ Jewish workers.[56] Later it expanded its scope, but in protesting the exclusion of Jewish workers from public enterprises, it was hampered by a similar exclusion being practiced in many Jewish-owned factories.[57]

In November 1937 it organized a conference in Warsaw, chaired by Henryk Rosmarin. In his opening address Rosmarin offered what purported to be the first United Jewish response to the All-Polish Congress; he called for Jews to coordinate and unify the activities of all of the organizations working among them in the economic and social spheres, including the Joint, the Jewish Colonization Association, ORT, and Cekabe. He also pledged to continue the fight for the right to employment in government enterprises, and he announced the formation of a special committee for the encouragement of Jewish organizations abroad to acquire products made by Polish Jewish artisans or in Jewish-owned factories.[58] This committee eventually set up a program to increase the export of Jewish-made products. Slated to begin in 1939–40, it was predicated upon a contribution by the Joint of 10 million *zł.* for the purpose of increasing production. Of course, subsequent events prevented the program from being realized.[59]

At the same time that authorities encouraged Polish merchants to move from the Western provinces to the central and eastern regions (Jews referred to such transplants as "owszem merchants"), some Jewish merchants migrated in the opposite direction, to areas where the Jewish population was sparse. When the anti-Jewish boycott made it difficult for these Jews to make a living, the JDC office in Warsaw or local Jewish community funds assisted them. In 1936 a sizeable number settled in Katowice in Upper Silesia. Many Jews also came to Poznań at this time, including numerous artisans who had acquired machines and tools with JDC assistance. These Jews also benefited from the activities of free loan societies established by the JDC and from a special help fund organized by British Jewry.[60]

In the meantime, the Joint and Cekabe continued to function. At Cekabe's annual meeting on December 19, 1937 attention was focused upon the problems of rural Jews who had been forced to flee to the cities as a result of terror directed against them. Special funds were set up to help them reestablish themselves, an act that helped to calm a mounting sense of panic among many village Jews.[61] Altogether the Joint budgeted $945,000 for assistance to Polish Jewry during 1937, with Cekabe functioning as the primary distributor of those funds.[62]

Whether or not such monies were sufficient to make any major difference in the economic condition of Polish Jewry, the activities of the Joint and Cekabe proved to be a major irritant both to Endecja circles and to the government.[63] On April 16, 1937 Foreign Minister Beck sent a coded telegram to Poland's ambassadors in London, Paris, and Washington, informing them that the government would soon be forced to take vigorous action against Cekabe, "for the protection of state interests." The telegram was obviously sent so that the ambassadors in the west could prepare the groundwork for explaining the steps that were about to be taken against the Polish Jews. Polish security authorities, it said, had determined that Cekabe and its various branches throughout the country were serving as fronts for the Comintern and were engaged in espionage and other subversive activities. For evidence, the authorities were said to possess "numerous monographs" written by Cekabe employees that described various sections of Poland's eastern

territories in great detail. In addition, treasury officials were said to have un-
covered evidence of Cekabe involvement in illegal financial maneuvers. Although Beck indicated that he had no intention of interfering with the Joint,
"whose work the government regards with thanks," the infiltration of Communist agents into Cekabe obliged the government to take steps against that
organization in the near future.[64]

The plans for the liquidation of Cekabe were evidently kept strictly secret, for no hint of them appeared in either the Jewish or the Polish press at
the time. Nor do Cekabe documents themselves indicate an awareness of
such a threat. In any case, Beck's charges against the organization should not
be believed. The government knew that the free loan associations operated
by Cekabe were the Jews' most important defense against the economic boycott and the government's own policy of discrimination. Beck's trumped-up
charges were most likely intended to justify the liquidation of the Jewish
organization in the eyes of Western – especially Western Jewish – public
opinion.

In the end, however, no action against Cekabe was taken – probably because at the time the government was involved in serious negotiations with
representatives of the United States, including important Jewish financiers
such as Felix Warburg and Bernard Baruch. The discussions centered
around the possibility of creating a special fund for Jewish emigration from
Poland under Polish government auspices. In the course of these conversations, held mainly in Paris during the summer of 1937 between Baruch and
the Polish ambassador to France, Juliusz Łukasiewicz, and in November of
that year in Poland between representatives of the Polish government and
President Roosevelt's special envoy, William Bullitt, the possibility was
raised that the United States would grant Poland fifty million dollars in
credits toward the rehabilitation of Polish Jewry. The Poles demanded that
these credits be given unconditionally and not be earmarked only for the
immediate needs of the Jews.[65] The negotiations eventually foundered, but
while they were going on the Poles appear to have been reticent about taking any steps that might appear to strike a blow at the Joint or other international Jewish charitable agencies.

Thus Cekabe continued to expand its activities. In 1938 it opened 45 new
free loan societies throughout Poland, bringing the total number of such
societies to 915. Cekabe funds created new jobs, extended significant aid in
vulnerable areas, and represented virtually the only source of credit for Jewish shopkeepers and artisans.[66] At the same time, new actions were under-

taken to counteract attempts to drive Jews out of the economy. For example, when both houses of parliament passed a law requiring special new licenses for selling tobacco (as a result of which some 30,000 Jewish tobacco merchants whose earlier licenses were not renewed were injured directly), Jews organized a partial boycott of tobacco products. This boycott hurt the government tobacco monopoly and led to a slight mitigation of the so-called tobacco decree.[67] For another example, *Nasz Przegląd* took on the Endek press, which charged that the Jews were not permitting Christians to work in Jewish-owned restaurants. The Jewish action, of course, was in protest over a petition submitted by Christian restaurant owners to refuse to allow Jewish restauranteurs to sell alcoholic beverages or to maintain restaurants in central Warsaw. As the Jewish newspaper pointed out, a boycott was always potentially a two-way street; those who preached boycott had to be prepared to see similar tactics adopted against themselves.[68]

Thus even in the difficult conditions of the time, Polish Jews possessed means of resisting the economic boycott. *Haynt*, for example, gave prominence to the dignified efforts of Jewish merchants and factory owners in Łódź, who refused to bow to pressures from some commercial houses in Gdańsk to dismiss their Jewish agents as a condition for the continuation of their business contacts.[69] Yet despite such resistance activities, the Jewish public criticized its agencies for not doing enough in the field of economic self-help. Even Jewish organizations abroad were criticized in the Jewish press for not providing sufficient aid. To be sure, the Jewish public did appreciate the work of the Jewish cooperative credit unions, but these were few in number, with limited resources. Unfortunately, the cooperative concept did not widely catch on. Leading merchants did not put significant energies behind it; nor did it attract the support of the younger generation.[70]

By the end of 1938 the Joint expressed interest in transferring all of its activities in the economic and social realms to local Jewish organizations, while it would concentrate on helping to make those organizations independent.[71] As a result, on February 23, 1939, the Joint and Cekabe agreed that the latter would assume responsibility for maintaining the free loan societies in Poland and for distributing funds received from the Joint. In addition, Cekabe pledged to raise funds on its own to cover a portion of its administrative costs, with the Joint reserving the right to supervise the management of accounts and to participate in all of the directorate's deliberations.[72] This arrangement, however, proved difficult to implement, and in the end no central Jewish body was able to coordinate an economic counterattack effectively.

Meanwhile government economic pressure on the Jews increased. In December 1938 Treasury Minister Kwiatkowski revealed a Fifteen-Year Plan for economic development, which included a plank calling for the Polonization of the cities.[73] In January 1939 Trade Minister Roman reported to the Sejm budget committee that progress was being made in this area. Specifically, he mentioned a program to train young people from Poznań "to take up positions in other parts of Poland, especially in Wołyń and Eastern Galicia" — areas where the Jewish concentration in the towns was especially high.[74]

The sanction of anti-Jewish economic action by responsible government leaders, including the former liberals in the Sanacja camp like Kwiatkowski, was interpreted by local officials as a green light for them to proceed with the boycott, accompanied at times by anti-Jewish violence. The Jewish struggle became increasingly difficult from day to day. Yet although the institutionalization of the anti-Jewish economic campaign under government auspices was apparent at least from the time of the founding of OZON in 1937, no nationwide, coordinated, planned Jewish counteraction in the political realm was noticeable. There is no evidence that Jewish political parties devoted any great energy to parrying the concentrated attack against Jews in the economic field. Instead this matter was left to organizations of a purely economic or social character. Nor was the potential force of Western Jewry exploited; it was only partially mobilized for rehabilitation and relief work but not at all for a direct attack upon the official policy of boycott and exclusion.[75]

Although the Polish government was quite sensitive to the reactions of Western Jewry to its policies,[76] the Polish Jewish political parties, mired in their own internal squabbles, do not appear to have realized the depth of this sensitivity. Jewish political leaders might also have pointed out that the drive to transfer Polish merchants from the western parts of the country to its eastern regions effectively resulted in handing over many commercial positions in the former to the German minority. Had Polish Jewry taken advantage of such missed opportunities, the government might have been convinced not to go beyond its benevolent neutrality toward the boycott expressed in Składkowski's *owszem* speech. Instead, the government's open support for the anti-Jewish economic struggle ultimately led to its sanction of violence.

4

Anti-Jewish Violence: Riots, Pogroms, Recriminations and Responses

The daily agitation and Jew-baiting in the press and parliament that accompanied the organized economic boycott and its terror tactics created a pogrom atmosphere in many localities all over the country. This readiness to condone anti-Jewish violence was at times even more dangerous than the violence itself. The various factions within Endecja worked openly to promote such an atmosphere, and they benefited from a sympathetically neutral attitude toward their activities on the part of the authorities in the capital and in the provinces. Indeed, the Sanacja camp, divided no less than Endecja, did not establish a clear and uniform strategy from the outset for preventing its rivals from using the Jewish issue to strengthen their position. The weakness of the Sławek and Kościałkowski governments following Piłsudski's death was manifested by their failure to confront anti-Jewish violence, despite frequent verbal condemnations of the phenomenon by their spokesmen. This avoidance of the issue helped to intensify the climate of terror – toward Jews and recalcitrant Poles alike – that accompanied the boycott. The result was a wave of anti-Jewish riots that reached its height in 1936–37 and engendered a spirit of pessimism among many Polish Jews regarding their continued existence in the country.

Although there is no dispute that economic conditions contributed to the outbreak of the pogroms, it must also be recalled that during the second half of 1935 the economic crisis afflicting the country was noticeably mitigated.[1] In fact, the motives that led certain parties to engage in antisemitic agitation were varied. Endecja used it to undermine support for Sanacja in hopes of eventually seizing state power. Polish conservatives, including large estate owners, saw it as a way to divert the attention of the masses from internal Polish social and economic problems. Both groups were thus more interested in sustaining the tension generated by the Jewish problem than in solving it.

The pogroms of the late 1930s[2] occurred sporadically, breaking out whenever local conditions were conducive to anti-Jewish agitation. Frequently a pogrom would take place following the killing of a Pole by a Jew, whether the latter was committing a crime or acting in self-defense. Endecja put forth the notion that all Jews were collectively responsible for the deeds of each individual – providing the basis for the pogroms in Grodno in 1935 and in Przytyk and Mińsk-Mazowiecki in 1936.[3]

The Grodno pogrom, for example, took place on June 7, 1935, following the death of a Pole who had been wounded in a spontaneous scuffle with two Jews. During his funeral some of the many mourners left the procession and began attacking local Jews and their property. All the while, authorities kept police away from the scene,[4] and two Jews died as a result. During the same month, antisemitic riots occurred in Suwałki and in Raciąż,[5] and in November in Odrzywół. In the latter case the pogrom was preceded by incidents in the marketplace, by intensified boycotting of Jewish stores, and by the promulgation of a lie among the peasants that Jews had kidnapped a bishop who happened to be in the area at the time.[6]

The Jewish representatives in the Sejm protested loudly against the complete lack of response by the Polish community to the agitation and to the injuries the violence did to Jews.[7] It was the pogrom of March 9, 1936 in Przytyk, near Radom, however, that captured the attention of Jews throughout the world and dramatized the plight of Polish Jewry, for it displayed elements that had not been evident in earlier outbreaks of anti-Jewish violence. Jews constituted 87 percent of the 2,500 inhabitants of Przytyk; most of them made their livings in petty trade, operating stalls in the local marketplace. Antisemitic agitation in the town intensified in late 1935, when local peasants were reportedly terrorized into renouncing commercial contacts with Jews, mainly because of what had happened in nearby Odrzywół.[8] Also responding to the lessons of Odrzywół, twenty young Jews from Przytyk, some armed with handguns, organized a Jewish self-defense unit. Their presence appears to have prevented a violent attack by peasants at the end of 1935.[9] Nevertheless, agitation by the local Endek boycott pickets continued and Jewish requests for protection from the Radom district authorities ignored. By the end of January 1936, the Union of Petty Merchants in Warsaw was extending aid to the town's six hundred Jewish families,[10] whose anxiety mounted from day to day. A correspondent from the Yiddish newspaper *Naye Folkstsaytung* who visited Przytyk on the eve of the pogrom described the atmosphere at that time:

Today I arrived in Przytyk [and went] straight to the marketplace, for today was market day.... The large number of bands roaming about the marketplace is immediately apparent. Each band numbers some

6–8 strapping youths carrying clubs and moving through the market-place like conquerors. At one end [of the marketplace stands] a police-man armed with a rifle. Jewish sellers are not to be found. . . . Here the boycott means not buying from Jews and not selling to them. . . . The peasants have been forced to sell their produce at Radom (18 km. from Przytyk); the Przytyk merchants buy from them there.

Many additional details about the situation in early March were revealed in the testimonies presented at the June 1936 trial of those involved. For exam-ple, on March 4, 1936 a Jewish delegation from Przytyk warned the district governor at Radom that according to information in its possession anti-Jewish riots were planned for March 9.[11] And a Pole testified that several weeks before, a local Jew had told him that the Jews had five hundred hand-guns at their disposal and were preparing for an eventual showdown.[12]

The violence began, according to the indictment prepared for the trial, on the 9th, a market day, when a policeman detained one of the boycott picketers for preventing peasants from purchasing baked goods from a Jew-ish vendor. Protesting the detention, part of the crowd attacked Jewish stalls, destroying many of them. Many peasants fled after being set upon by a number of Jews, who, according to several testimonies, were armed with handguns. Several peasants were wounded, one seriously. The peasants then armed themselves with clubs and returned to town. At the same time a number of shots were fired from a house, killing a peasant named Stanisław Wieśniak. Charged with the shooting, a Jew named Sholom Yehiel Lesko later confessed to the investigating magistrate that he had fired three shots from the window of his home to frighten the crowd away. Fearful of possible riots, he said, he had purchased the gun in Radom.

Additional witnesses testified that they saw other Jews firing into the crowd of peasants, further inciting the peasants to vandalize Jewish prop-erty and attack Jews in cruel fashion.[13] According to one newspaper report, it appears that following the beginning of these attacks, some Jews remained behind in the town square and fought off the rioters. Other Jews arrived later to assist them. The vandals fled, with the Jews chasing after them.[14]

During the first days after March 9, newspapers were forbidden to pub-lish photographs or detailed reports about the riots and authorities would not allow the daytime burial of one of the Jewish victims, Pesah Minkow-ski.[15] On March 10 the district governor of Radom visited Przytyk and de-clared that an objective investigation revealed that the riots were the result of Jewish provocation.[16]

In a speech delivered from the floor of the Senat on March 12, Jewish Senator Moshe Schorr was the first to reveal details about what had occurred at Przytyk. According to him, there had been a mass attack by peasants, armed with clubs, upon Jewish residences and shops. The police had intervened late, with the result that 3 Jews were killed and 22 injured.[17] On the grounds that "no one had been killed yet," neither the police nor the district governor had taken Jewish warnings of impending violence seriously. Similarly, Jewish entreaties to the provincial governor at Kielce had been to no avail.

Interestingly, Schorr did not mention the Przytyk Jews' armed resistance at all, even though it was much easier to reveal such information from the floor of the Senat than to put it in print, where it could be censored. Indeed, at first Jewish leaders seemed uncertain as to whether they ought to emphasize the fact that local Jews had prepared for the pogroms and had been ready to meet their attackers with weapons in hand. Jewish response to violence against them was a new phenomenon and resistance in Przytyk had been organized locally, independent of a countrywide organization or direction from any political body. Jewish public opinion responded quickly to this self-defense activity. Ozjasz Thon, for example, devoted two articles in *Haynt* to it, claiming that "a few more [incidents like the one at] Przytyk would put an end to the pogroms and to the shame associated with them." He argued that "the shame of the pogroms is usually worse than the grief that they bring; Przytyk did not bring shame upon us, [even though] it caused us great sorrow."[18] Therein, he believed, lay the importance of the Jewish defense during the Przytyk pogrom; it would undoubtedly help to calm the situation in the future.[19]

Less than three weeks later, in a memorandum presented to the members of the Jewish Agency Executive on March 27, Fischel Rottenstreich announced that Jewish self-defense cells, encompassing all political orientations from Agudas Yisroel to the Bund, had been established in various cities and towns, but that the effectiveness of these groups would depend upon the extent to which the Polish police remained neutral during outbreaks of anti-Jewish violence. In his opinion the local administration of provincial towns was in the hands of a group of colonels unfavorably disposed toward the central government, who sought to use the pogroms to point up the central authorities' inability to control the unrest. These groups, together with the Endeks, according to Rottenstreich, wanted to force the government to come to the Jews' defense and thereby weaken its standing in public opinion. In other words, the various opposition parties, even those that opposed anti-Jewish violence, preferred to maintain a state of disarray in the country in order to demonstrate the ineffectiveness of the existing government.[20]

It appears that Rottenstreich's evaluation was not entirely accurate. There is, for example, virtually no corroboration for his statement that many Jewish self-defense organizations, encompassing young people from all streams of Jewish public life, already existed in Poland at the time of the Przytyk pogrom.[21] Nonetheless, after it many Jews were open to the establishment of such organizations. To this end, during his visit to Poland in September 1936, Eliyahu Dobkin, a member of the Jewish Agency Executive, met with the director of the Minorities Department of the Polish Interior Ministry to request special permission for Zionist youth groups to give "instruction in sports." Ostensibly such instruction was to prepare Jews to serve as policemen in Palestine, and on that basis he encountered no difficulties from the Polish official.[22]

That same month, Yehuda Tennenbaum (Arazi), a special representative of the Haganah Palestinian Jewish military organization, visited Poland on an arms-purchasing mission coordinated with the Polish government. Arguing that these young people would be using Polish-made arms once they arrived in Palestine, where conditions made training them to use their weapons properly much more difficult, he suggested to his contacts in the Polish military and Foreign Ministry that Polish instructors give weapons training to Jewish young people preparing to emigrate there. Tennenbaum's suggestion was eventually accepted, and in June 1937 a training course was conducted at Zielonka outside of Warsaw. It was Tennenbaum's intention, however, that some of those who participated in the course, as well as Haganah instructors who had been dispatched from Palestine to supervise, would remain in Poland to help organize self-defense among local Jews.[23]

At the same time the Revisionists took similar action. In mid-1936 Jabotinsky requested permission and assistance from Polish authorities in the founding of a Jewish military organization in Poland. At that time, however, the proposal was rejected. As Foreign Minister Beck explained it, several of the opposition parties, interested in establishing their own paramilitary formations under the guise of sports clubs, would view the granting of Jabotinsky's request as a precedent.[24]

Reactions to the fact that Jews had taken arms in their own defense in Przytyk were also published in Endek circles. The Endek newspaper *Warszawski Dziennik Narodowy* noted that their response to the violence marked the first time that Jews had taken to the streets to demonstrate their strength.[25] The indictment handed down in the Przytyk trial, however, made it clear that the Jewish press and propaganda had promoted the idea that the Polish side had been the aggressor. Actually, the newspaper claimed, the Poles had merely been responding to the Jewish shots that killed a Polish peasant. The Jews had been seeking in this fashion to break the economic boycott against them; it was only after their attack and additional Jewish provocations that Jews had been killed.[26] Indeed, the shooting of the Polish peasant Wieśniak was regarded by Polish witnesses as justifiable grounds for violent attacks upon Jews as well as for their censure in the Endek press.

On March 13, four days after the pogrom, the police searched a large number of Jewish houses in Przytyk for arms[27] – escalating the mounting panic among Jews throughout the country. Indeed, there was a tendency for Jews in smaller towns where riots had taken place or were feared to abandon their homes; following the Przytyk pogrom, for example, over thirty Jewish families fled that town for Radom. That same week, the Agudas Yisroel news-paper, *Dos Yudishe Togblat*, reported that Przytyk was typical of many towns taken over by the boycott and anti-Jewish agitation. Thus the Jewish press called upon Jews not to quit their places of residence.[28] In addition an appeal was voiced for aid in rebuilding the stricken community.[29] A Central Com-mittee for Assisting Przytyk Jews was organized, headed by Senator Schorr. The Łódź branch of this committee was especially active, dispatching a number of instructors to the town to organize vocational training courses.[30] Jewish newspapers also initiated a short-lived fundraising drive on behalf of the Jews of Przytyk; it was banned by the authorities on March 23, 1936.[31]

Another reaction to the events at Przytyk was demonstrated by the Bund, whose central committee met on March 12 and decided to call a general half-day strike for March 17.[32] In a circular sent to all party cells on March 13, the strike was presented as a protest against the antisemitism of Endecja and Sanacja and against "the constant agitation and physical extermination (*fizi-sher oysrotung*)" to which the Jews were being subjected. The circular also spoke of the need to protest "the reactionary Jewish nationalist and clerical-ist forces," the boycott against Jewish labor, plans to drive Jews out of their positions in the economy, and efforts to impose a "ghetto" for Jews in insti-tutions of higher learning. The goal was to demonstrate the Jews' commit-ment to "honorable self-defense . . . against attempts to make pogroms." Lo-cal Bund units were called upon to approach Polish workers' organizations and invite them to take part in the protest – or at least express solidarity with it.[33]

The wording of the circular indicates that the Bund did not intend for the strike to take on an all-Jewish character but rather a general working class one. However, it did not succeed. As Bund leader Wiktor Alter explained, it was necessary for his party to initiate a separate Jewish protest action by Jewish workers because the leadership of PPS had refused to issue a joint call for a protest strike. According to a PPS spokesman, the refusal was rooted in the fear that some workers, influenced by the antisemitic wave, might view a joint PPS-Bund protest as provocative.[34]

Among Jews, however, there was widespread support for the strike, thanks largely to the Bund's thorough and organized preparations throughout the country. The Labor Zionist party Po'alei-Tsiyon, in both its left-and right-wing factions, as well as the Communists, also participated, although the Bund did not permit the latter to assume an organizing role.[35] Support spread even to non-working class Jewish elements; and although non-Bundist Jewish newspapers generally mentioned preparations for the strike only briefly, on the day it took place they expressed their unqualified support.[36] Even the newspaper of Agudas Yisroel declared, quite surprisingly, that the Bund's action in calling the strike should not be regarded as a partisan political maneuver but as an expression of the bitterness felt by all Jews. The newspaper viewed the Przytyk pogrom as a manifestation of the hatred directed at Polish Jews, a hatred that made it impossible for the party to continue its previous strategy of seeking the good graces of those in power.[37] Equally surprising, even the newspaper of the Zionist Revisionists praised the Bund's initiative.[38]

The March 17 strike was widely viewed as a success in Jewish circles. The following morning *Nasz Przegląd* wrote that the protest had taken on a spontaneous character, both in Warsaw and in the provinces,[39] while the organ of Agudas Yisroel claimed that the Jewish community had not mounted such a demonstration since it protested the infamous ritual murder trial of Mendel Beilis in Kiev in 1912.[40] Although the 1936 action appears to have greatly enhanced the Bund's prestige in the eyes of the general Jewish public, the Bund did not attempt to engage non-working class Jews in cooperative responses to the pogroms. Instead, in April 1936 it began preparations for a convention of Polish Jewish workers to further a specifically proletarian struggle against antisemitism.[41] In an ideological declaration issued in advance of the proposed convention, Wiktor Alter pointed out that antisemitic agitation was being exploited by both Endecja and Sanacja camps. Thus those Jewish organizations that, in his words, served the country's rulers — his reference was undoubtedly to the Zionists and Agudas Yisroel — were also promoting rampant antisemitism.[42]

The Bund's attempts to organize a Jewish workers' convention met with a mixed reception among the other proletarian parties. The left-wing faction of Po'alei-Tsiyon joined in organizational work for the convention.[43] The right wing, on the other hand, objected to what they regarded as the Bund-inspired anti-Zionist tone of the proposed manifesto and decided to organize its own congress of Jewish workers to fight antisemitism.[44] For quite different reasons the Communist party also opposed the Bund's proposal; it was interested in convening a general workers' and peasants' congress in cooperation with all social strata "who are suffering from antisemitism and fascism in Poland." For the Communists, the notion of a "broad popular front" was paramount, whereas the Bund objected to the inclusion of non-proletarian elements. Indeed, the Bund perceived the Communists as being willing to collaborate with the "reactionary elements" within Polish Jewry in a "pan-Judaic" spirit.[45]

The election campaign for the Bund's proposed congress actually took place between May 23 and June 6.[46] However, government authorities in Warsaw prevented the assembly, which was scheduled for June 13, from taking place. Henryk Erlich and Wiktor Alter appealed to the Interior Ministry to have the prohibition cancelled, but to no avail. The authorities also forbade the convening of the rival congress organized by the right wing of Po'alei-Tsiyon.[47]

Meanwhile, the wave of antisemitic riots continued virtually uninterrupted throughout 1936. On June 1, on the eve of the opening of the Przytyk trial, violence broke out in Mińsk-Mazowiecki. It was prompted by the assassination of a Polish sergeant named Bujak by a discharged Jewish soldier named Yehuda Leib Chaskielewicz, who, after the incident, turned himself in to local police and stated that the shooting had been the result of a personal quarrel.[48] Immediately thereafter, a band of Endek rioters ran rampant in the town, beating Jews and destroying Jewish property. The riots lasted for five days and were especially severe during Bujak's funeral.[49] Again, the principle of collective responsibility was employed; all Jews in the region were subject to revenge for the actions of one individual.[50]

The police were late in intervening and arrested only a few of the perpetrators.[51] In fact, even before the actual rioting, there was anti-Jewish agitation in the town, the result of an incident that occurred during preparations for observance of May Day, when local Endeks had clashed with Jews and a member of Po'alei-Tsiyon had been killed. Two Endek rioters were wounded as a result of a Jewish counterattack.[52]

Upon the outbreak of the June riots, a Jewish delegation from Mińsk-Mazowiecki, accompanied by Senator Trockenheim, was received by the provincial governor in Warsaw. The delegation was told that the authorities had taken "appropriate measures" and that police reinforcements had been sent to Mińsk. Prime Minister Składkowski also heard the protests of Senators Trockenheim and Schorr and of Sejm Deputy Mincberg.[53] His personal visit to Mińsk on June 16 helped to calm the atmosphere somewhat.[54]

In Warsaw a public Jewish committee to aid the victims of the riots was formed; it dispatched delegates to Mińsk on June 4 to investigate conditions and distribute food to local Jews, many of whom were still afraid to leave their homes.[55] In contrast to Przytyk, many Jews from Mińsk-Mazowiecki immediately left town because of the violence, with hundreds reportedly fleeing to nearby Warsaw.[56] The Yiddish-language newspaper *Haynt* compared the responses of the two communities: in Przytyk, far from the major Jewish centers, the Jews had responded honorably, whereas in Mińsk, only 37 km. from Warsaw, an atmosphere of panic and "flight from death" had prevailed.[57]

That same month another incident occurred, this time in the small town of Myślenice, near Kraków. On the night of June 22–23, Adam Doboszyński, Kraków district chairman of the National Party, led a band of 150 armed men in an assault on the local police station. The band confiscated police weapons, destroyed the local residence of the district governor, broke into Jewish stores and took merchandise, and burned the booty in the town square. The assailants attempted to set fire to the local synagogue and later hid in the nearby woods.[58] Only after several days did the police succeed in apprehending some of them, including their leader. The Jewish press viewed the so-called March on Myślenice as a logical extension of the Przytyk and Mińsk riots; *Chwila*, for example, stated that all these actions were expressions of Endecja's intent to undermine the authority of the government, expose its weakness, and include anti-Jewish violence in its campaign.[59]

At the same time, the trial stemming from the events at Przytyk came to an end. The proceedings, which had commenced on June 2 at the district courthouse in Radom, involved 43 Polish and 14 Jewish defendants — the latter charged with aggressive behavior against Polish peasants. Throughout, the Endek press alleged that Jewish provocation had brought about the Polish counterattack.[60] Indeed, several peasants testified that the Jews of Przytyk had launched a pogrom against the Poles, using sticks, axes, and even pistols.[61] Attorneys for the Jewish defendants countered that whatever violent actions their clients had taken were only in self defense.[62]

On June 26, the court announced its verdict: eleven of the Jews were sentenced to prison terms of from six months to eight years, while thirty-nine of the Poles received sentences of from six months to one year. Three Jews and four Poles were acquitted. The court claimed no proof had been brought to identify the killers of the Jewish Minkowski family. On the other hand, it accused the Jewish young people in the town of having an aggressive attitude even before the violence, with many arming themselves illegally with live ammunition. The court thus rejected the Jews' claim of self-defense[63] and held them responsible for inciting the riots by attacking peasants on their way home from market.

The verdict created a storm in the Jewish community, and the Jewish parliamentary caucus appealed to Polish Jewry to close ranks and not spread fear and defeatism because of it.[64] Fear was difficult to avoid, however, for the Przytyk trial appeared to inaugurate a wave of court proceedings in which Jews were charged with the crime of insulting the honor of the Polish nation and sentenced severely.[65] In response, the Zionist parties adopted the protest tactic employed by the Bund after the Przytyk pogrom, calling for a two-hour work stoppage on June 30.[66] Other parties, however, did not respond to the call. Agudas Yisroel did not request its members to participate.[67] Nor did the Central Association of Jewish Merchants.[68] The Bund, whose thunder had now been stolen, as it were, by the Zionists, at first criticized the manner in which the strike was being organized — especially the idea to hold it at noontime, when traffic in stores was light and the pace of work slow in any case. Nevertheless, the Bund did not wish to have it said that the strike had failed because of them, so in the end it urged its members to take part.[69]

This lukewarm response notwithstanding, the strike turned out to be widely observed throughout Poland, even extending beyond the Jewish population. PPS and Polish trade unions issued instructions that in factories in which Polish and Jewish employees worked side by side, Polish workers would join the strike as an expression of solidarity with their comrades.[70] In the final analysis, though, the strike demonstrated once again how internally divided the Jewish community was — its leadership still unable to mount an organized, coordinated response to the antisemitism that increasingly threatened all segments of the Jewish public. Even in the wake of the strike, the continuous invective in the Jewish press indicated that the most powerful and best organized Jewish groups — the Zionists, the Bund, and Agudas Yisroel — were primarily concerned with settling internal political accounts[71] instead of rising above their partisan differences in order to fight their common enemy.

Needless to say, this lack of unity lessened the effectiveness of the Jewish response in the eyes of the authorities, who on occasion retaliated against those who participated in the strikes of March 17 and June 30. In August 1936, for example, the authorities refused to validate the rehiring of thirty teachers in Jewish schools in Białystok, not for any pedagogical reason but because, as the district superintendent of education reported, they had interrupted their teaching for several hours on March 17 in protest over what had happened at Przytyk.[72] During the same month, a court in Baranowice sentenced twenty Jews to prison terms of three months to one year because they had closed their stores in connection with the June 30 strike and thereby insulted the state's judicial institutions.[73]

Furthermore, the state showed no inclination at this time to control or condemn the radical Endek anti-Jewish propaganda that continued to be distributed. Newspapers began to agitate explicitly for Jewish blood to be spilled. At a meeting of the Sejm in December, Deputy Mincberg read into the record a passage from the Łódź newspaper *Republika* that had appeared the previous October 10:

> Blood has been spilled and will continue to be spilled in the future. Much blood will be spilled, for this is the only plank on which the debate over justice can be conducted.... Today there is no way to confront the Jew, who wishes to take over Poland, other than to strike him with sword or bullet. These are correct and useful arguments. There can be no verbal arguments or attempts to persuade; we are at war, and we must wage a war that is continuous and all-encompassing. He who seeks to dissuade us from this war is a traitor.[74]

In such a volatile atmosphere, it is not surprising that pogroms continued during 1937–38. But the goals of anti-Jewish violence now were not only to cause Jews physical harm, but also to damage Jewish businesses and place obstacles in the way of their rebuilding.

The two most vicious attacks during 1937 were in Brześć on May 13 and in Częstochowa on June 19. The incendiary events leading to both pogroms were similar to those that led to the earlier ones in Grodno, Przytyk, and Mińsk-Mazowiecki. In Brześć a Polish police inspector, Stefan Kędziora, was stabbed to death by an eighteen-year-old Jewish butcher named Wolf Szczerbowski after the constable had confiscated "contraband" kosher meat, whereas in Częstochowa a Polish porter, was killed in a personal quarrel with a Jew, Josef Pendrak.[75]

The Brześć riots began about two hours after the killing of the police inspector; Jewish market stalls were attacked, and several Jews were wounded.[76] As the attacks were beginning, the provincial governor received a delegation of leading Jewish citizens of the town. He warned the Jews to remain quiet, since the riots were due to their own provocation. Although the delegation protested that it was unfair to blame all Jews for the actions of one individual, the police did not intervene until the rioters had done their damage and dozens of Jews had been wounded.[77]

The pogrom began in mixed Polish-Jewish neighborhoods, where rioters singled out Jewish-owned shops, apartments, and warehouses. They continued their destruction the next day in the town's suburbs. Belorussian peasants from surrounding villages who worked in the railroad workshops in the town joined in the violence. But they were opposed by some Polish workers and fled from places where they encountered such resistance.

Whenever possible, the Bund endeavored to foster cooperative Polish-Jewish resistance activities. Fearing a renewal of rioting during the funeral of the Polish police inspector, the Bund Central Committee sent two of the heads of the party's so-called militia, Leyzer Lewin and Bernard Goldstein, to Brześć. Their mission was to organize Jews for self-defense, with the cooperation of Polish workers.[78] Accompanied by Jan Dąbrowski, a PPS member and editor of *Robotnik*, the party newspaper, Lewin and Goldstein quickly managed to form one Jewish defense unit. Three groups of PPS youth pledged to assist in their defense effort, and the Jewish-Polish front effectively blocked attempts to renew violence during the funeral.

Jews throughout Poland viewed the Brześć pogrom as a dangerous turning point in their deteriorating situation. Emil Sommerstein, in an analysis in *Chwila*, argued that the riots had been planned and organized well in advance at ONR headquarters in Biała Podlaska and that the rioters had merely waited for an appropriate moment to launch them.[79] Their purpose, he declared, was to ruin the livelihood of the town's Jews, especially those of the middle class, by destroying their shops, looting their merchandise, and tearing up the notes of indebtedness that they held. He also found not only the Endek but also the Sanacja press guilty of what he believed to be encouragement of the riots, the former by harping upon the alleged Jewish provocation, the latter by giving detailed attention to the extent of the pogrom.

Indeed, it appears that the OZON organ *Kurier Poranny* crossed a threshold when it responded to the Brześć incident by affirming the principle of

Jewish collective responsibility[80] and accusing the Jewish press of constant provocation against Poland. Endek publications went even farther, with *Warszawski Dziennik Narodowy* claiming that "Przytyk, Mińsk-Mazowiecki, and Brześć are the path to a better future."[81] It reported with satisfaction that in Brześć, whose population of 65,000 was half Jewish, shops and homes belonging to Christians had been appropriately marked within days following the pogrom, and Christians had stopped buying from Jewish-owned businesses. It also called upon Polish merchants from the Western provinces to open businesses in areas that Jews had previously controlled.[82] Only the press of PPS denounced the principle of collective responsibility, which had turned a criminal matter into an antisemitic one.[83]

Yet even though Jewish leaders may have regarded the Brześć pogrom as having broken new ground, their long-range response did not differ significantly from the actions they had taken in the wake of previous outbreaks of violence. The Zionists, together with Agudas Yisroel and the Folkspartay, again called for a two-hour strike, to begin at noon on May 24.[84] The Bund again scoffed at the potential effectiveness of such an abbreviated strike, contrasting it with their own walkout of March 17, 1936, which had lasted from the early morning until 2:00 p.m.[85] Its Central Committee called instead for the organization of Jewish self-defense units on a mass scale.[86]

More Jewish activity concentrated upon providing relief for the pogrom victims.[87] On May 22 a delegation of the Sejm caucus met with Prime Minister Składkowski and received permission to begin a countrywide fundraising drive on their behalf.[88] Immediately thereafter a Central Committee to Assist Brześć Jews, chaired by Senator Schorr, was established in Warsaw, and within a month 210 local committees were set up under its auspices. Within a short time approximately 550 of the estimated 1100 families who had suffered direct damage in the pogrom received assistance from the funds collected.[89] By the time the Committee disbanded a year later, the number of families assisted had risen to over 3,000, including those who had been injured by the riots only indirectly.[90] The Joint Distribution Committee also took an active role in the relief effort, contributing $50,000 within a few days of the pogrom. On a short visit to Poland, two representatives of the Joint, Bernard Kahn and David Schweitzer, visited Brześć immediately after the riots.[91]

The Brześć pogrom, occurring as it did on a large scale in a provincial capital without any intervention from the Polish security forces until it had been underway for thirty hours, shattered whatever illusions Jews still harbored that the government would defend them against violent Endek antisemitism. The prevalent feeling among broad strata of the Jewish public was one of powerlessness, of being trapped in a blind alley.[92] This feeling was reinforced by the death sentences handed down by Polish courts in June 1937 against Yehuda Leib Chaskielewicz, whose assassination of the police officer Bujak had touched off the Mińsk-Mazowiecki riots a year earlier, and Wolf Szczerbowski, whose similar deed had precipitated the pogrom at Brześć. The sentences themselves were less disturbing than the justifications issued by the courts for them: Chaskielewicz was said to have belonged to a Jewish youth group that was under the influence of the Communist Party and therefore hostile to Poland (in fact he was a member of the Bundist youth group *Tsukunft*). The court further speculated that his hostile attitude was directly influenced by the Jewish press and a portion of the Jewish people at large, which routinely expressed enmity of the state authorities and the army.[93] These suggestions infuriated Jewish public opinion. The Association of Jewish Journalists registered a strong protest against basing a sentence upon such reasoning, and Sommerstein and Schorr remonstrated vigorously with the authorities over the collective accusations that had been hurled against the Jews during the trial.[94] In both cases, appellate courts later commuted the death sentences to life imprisonment.[95]

Slightly more than a month after the Brześć pogrom, on Saturday, June 19, 1937, three days of anti-Jewish rioting broke out in Częstochowa. As stated above, these riots, too, were touched off by a personal quarrel, in which a Jewish butcher named Josef Pendrak shot and killed a Christian porter. Following this incident, a crowd gathered outside the local headquarters of the National Party; according to the indictment prepared for the subsequent trial, its numbers continued to grow until it reached 15,000.[96] Jewish self-defense groups, led by graduates of the Zionist-organized and government sanctioned paramilitary training course at Zielonka, countered the rioters. According to a contemporary description, self-defense formations bearing arms were mustered at a Zionist training farm located about 3–4 km. from town.[97] These groups stood against rioters who tried to move against the farm, but the police, instead of arresting those who were on the attack, forced the self-defense groups to disperse. Only on the third day of rioting were some of the offenders taken into police custody – not until some 250 Jewish stores and a number of synagogues had been damaged.[98]

The pace of anti-Jewish violence quickened following the pogroms in Brześć and Częstochowa, although most subsequent riots were of a smaller scale. August 1937 was a particularly difficult month for Jews, with 350 violent attacks reported against them in 80 different localities.[99] But the attacks were not without resistance. In some places, notably in Kielce and in Łomża, Jewish and Polish workers together confronted Endek bands and prevented riots from breaking out.[100] Zionist groups also stepped up their own self-defense activities; they took advantage of the fact that in June 1937 a group of Haganah military instructors from Palestine arrived in Poland to coordinate training courses among groups preparing to immigrate to that country.[101]

It is difficult to accurately assess the damage caused by these attacks. Because censorship became more severe during the second half of 1937, the Jewish press was not able to report fully and in a timely fashion about the pogroms.[102] The British Embassy in Warsaw reported frequently about the increasingly violent attacks upon Jews, but regarded the Jewish evaluation of those attacks as exaggerated and "bordering on hysteria."[103] The Joint Distribution Committee noted that in eighteen areas of anti-Jewish violence in 1937 alone, 238 Jewish businesses had been destroyed, to be replaced by 405 non-Jewish enterprises.[104]

Jewish organizations abroad attempted from time to time to marshal public opinion in their countries against the violence directed at Polish Jews, although their actions in this regard were not constant and there was little coordination among the various agencies. On June 10, 1937, for example, the American Jewish Congress called an emergency meeting in New York, which was attended by 2,462 delegates; it decided to send a 200-person delegation to Washington to submit a protest memorandum to Secretary of State Cordell Hull.[105] The British Section of the World Jewish Congress also approached the Foreign Office with a request for intervention on behalf of their Polish brethren.[106] Norman Bentwich, one of the leaders of the Joint Foreign Committee of the Board of Deputies of British Jews and the Anglo-Jewish Association, suggested, following a 1937 visit to Poland, that British and American Jewish organizations appoint a permanent representative to the Polish government and to the foreign embassies in Warsaw.[107] Bernard Kahn, a senior official of the Joint Distribution Committee, made a similar recommendation.[108] However, the principal organizations involved, including the Joint, the World Jewish Congress, and the Paris-based Alliance Israelite Universelle, could not agree on a plan of action.[109] The Joint, for example, objected to organizing mass protest demonstrations in the United States against Polish antisemitism, preferring to influence the Polish government through quiet diplomacy.[110]

It may be that the Joint's preference was influenced by the mission of Henryk Szoszkies to the United States in the summer of 1937. Director of the Jewish Cooperative Bank of Poland (*Bank Spółdzielni Żydowskiej*), Szoszkies had ostensibly been sent by the Polish office of the Joint and the Polish-American Commercial House (*Izba Handlowa Polsko-Amerykańska*), but in fact the cost of his visit was paid by the Polish Foreign Ministry, which expected him to calm the fears of American Jewish organizations and put a damper upon anti-Polish propaganda.[111] Szoszkies indeed conducted many talks with key figures in American Jewry and reported on them in detail to the Polish authorities.[112] The Polish consul-general in New York, Sylwester Gruszka, similarly requested the Joint in October 1937 to "quiet down" the propaganda activities of the American Federation of Polish Jews with regard to Polish antisemitism.[113]

Actually, there were some meetings and demonstrations held by Jews in front of the Polish Embassy in Washington and the Polish Consulate-General in New York to protest the riots in Brześć and Częstochowa, and the Polish government received reports about them.[114] However, on the whole it appears that international Jewish organizations, wishing to continue assisting Polish Jewry economically and increasingly concerned with the problems of the Jews of Germany under Nazi rule, did not want to arouse the anger of the Polish government excessively.[115] If so, then it can be surmised that they did not properly understand the Polish government's sensitivity to Western public opinion.

The U.S. ambassador in Warsaw, Anthony Drexel-Biddle, reported on this sensitivity to his government in October 1937, noting that in his discussions with key Polish officials it had become clear that the Polish government was extremely worried about the reactions of the British and American public to the anti-Jewish violence.[116] He pointed out that at a recent cabinet meeting, Treasury Minister Kwiatkowski had noted that many influential commercial circles in Britain and the United States had lately been refusing to do business in Poland. Kwiatkowski had also indicated that the latest anti-Jewish riots had caused a notable decline in tax revenues from heavily Jewish areas, especially those that had been hit by violence. Since the pogrom in Brześć, for example, tax revenues there had fallen 70 percent.[117]

International Jewish organizations were not the only ones that proved timid in challenging the Polish government. The Zionist pioneer youth group *HeHaluts*, which had earlier entered into an agreement with the Polish authorities by which its members would receive military training from Polish instructors for eventual application in Palestine, decided in January 1938 that those who received such training would not participate in Jewish self-defense activities unless their own training farms were attacked.[118]

Anti-Jewish violence continued during 1938. On March 17 the Polish government delivered an ultimatum to Lithuania, threatening that country with military action if it did not establish diplomatic relations with Poland.[119] The tense situation in the days that followed brought about a run on the banks of Warsaw, during which members of Falanga forcibly pulled Jews out of withdrawal lines and beat them. This action soon mushroomed into a series of riots against the Jews of the capital, and the violence was especially severe on Saturday, March 19,[120] when fifty Jews were injured, including three members of Po'alei-Tsiyon who fought the Falanga attackers.[121]

Once again the Jewish parliamentary representatives protested to the authorities and demanded swift action by the police.[122] Instead of condemning the attacks, however, Polish officials attempted to justify them as patriotic acts. Foreign Minister Beck, for example, explained in a cable to Raczyński in London that "the Lithuanian conflict brought about an organized siege by the Jewish population on the banks," and therefore "there were also a few attacks upon Jews."[123] Actually, there were fewer Jews in the bank lines than non-Jews,[124] and the Jewish press condemned the exploitation of a diplomatic episode for the spreading of a blatant antisemitic lie.[125] Indeed, the director-general of the Polish state bank PKO wrote in his memoirs that Treasury Minister Kwiatkowski told him on March 19 that he had known in advance of a Falanga plan to attack Jews and had given the plan his quiet support, "in order to teach the Jews a lesson that they should not arouse panic."[126]

During the next month attacks continued on the Jews of Warsaw, as well as in other cities and towns throughout Poland. In Dąbrowa, near Białystok, a pogrom broke out against the background of a medieval blood accusation.[127] In the town of Żarki, on the other hand, self-defense action by Jews on July 19 prevented an organized riot, although a Polish court later put twenty-one Jews on trial for beating up a group of Endek students.[128] Nevertheless, during the second half of 1938 the pace of anti-Jewish violence appears to have slowed significantly.[129] The authorities also began to exert more disciplinary action against Endek rioters, sending many of them to the detention camp at Bereza-Kartuska.[130]

The decline in anti-Jewish violence may well have been a conscious government decision — one that reflected its awareness that the pogroms had encouraged Jews to organize for their own physical defense and for the rehabilitation of those who had been injured in the rioting. Since 1936 the government had actively guided the campaign to Polonize the country's economic life. It moved from the hostile neutrality implied in Składkowski's *owszem* speech of June 1936 to practical identification with the intent of the Thirteen Theses of OZON to liquidate Jewish economic positions and to abolish the Jews' equality before the law. Now, two years later, rather than continue to permit sporadic outbreaks of pogroms, which served merely to solidify Jewish ranks, it evidently preferred to channel mounting popular anti-Jewish hostility into a systematic policy of discrimination carefully supervised from above. Moreover, by 1938 the government could not ignore the changes in the international political situation and did not wish to arouse Western public opinion against it — something it feared might happen as a result of pogroms. At the same time, however, it needed to lead the anti-Jewish economic boycott aggressively, in order to prevent the Endek opposition from weakening its authority by appearing to hold the initiative in anti-Jewish action.

If the government succeeded in controlling street violence against Jews beginning in the second half of 1938, though, it was not able to control violent Endek activities in another arena — the universities.

5

"Ghetto Benches," Agitation, and Violence in the Universities

Even in the final period of Piłsudski's rule, a deterioration in the status of Jewish students in Poland's institutions of higher learning was noticeable. In fact, ever since the attainment of independence, the universities in Poland had been strongholds of Endecja supporters and centers for antisemitic agitation. University authorities throughout Poland had adopted various means, often camouflaged, of limiting the number of Jews enrolled, ostensibly to reduce the future influence of Jews in the country's economic and social life.[1] The agitation against Jewish students intensified during the depression and early 1930s and continued later, when unemployment hit the intellectual classes.[2] Those interested in promoting such agitation benefited from the universities' status as autonomous corporations, as university rectors tended not to invite police to campus to protect Jews from violence.[3]

Such violence broke out in November 1931 in several universities, accompanied by demands to reduce the number of Jewish students. At the University of Wilno, Jewish students organized a self-defense action in which a Polish student, Stanisław Wacławski, was killed.[4] The demands for limiting Jewish admissions were evidently met, for the proportion of Jewish students declined steadily from the beginning of the 1930s. During the 1921–22 academic year Jewish students had comprised 24.6 percent of the entire Polish university student population, and in 1931–32, 18 percent. In 1935–36, in contrast, the number was reduced to 13.2 percent, in 1936–37 to 11.8 percent, and in 1937–38 only 10 percent.[5] The decline was reflected in absolute figures as well — from 9,694 in 1932–33 to 6,207 in 1935–36, 5,682 in 1936–37, and 4,790 in 1937–38.[6]

Discrimination was evident in other university areas as well. Even during the 1920s, Jews had been removed from student societies in a number of institutions and, beginning in 1933, had founded their own parallel societies.[7] Jewish professors and lecturers were a rarity; in 1936 only 36 out of 1,672 professors in Polish universities (2.2 percent) were Jews, and most of these had obtained their positions under Austrian rule in Galicia before the First World War.[8] Jewish students only rarely obtained tuition reductions or even postponements in payment, which made it difficult for many to attend university, especially during the depression years.[9]

The decline in the number of Jewish students was accompanied by an increase in campus anti-Jewish violence. The beginning of the 1935–36 academic year witnessed riots against Jewish students at the University of Warsaw and the Warsaw Polytechnikum; from there they spread to the streets of Warsaw.[10] Violence broke out subsequently at other universities.[11] At the same time students associated with ONR, influenced by the Nazi Nürnberg Laws, demanded that Jews be compelled to sit in separate sections in the lecture halls.[12] This demand was voiced with particular vigor at the Universities of Warsaw, Lwów, Wilno, and Kraków; there were even incidents in which Polish students attempted to move Jews to "ghetto benches" by physical force.[13]

In November 1935 constant anti-Jewish violence eventually forced the temporary closure of all of Warsaw's institutions of higher learning.[14] The Endek newspaper argued that the Warsaw University attacks were the Jewish students' own fault for refusing to adhere to the special seating arrangement set by Polish students.[15] At the University of Poznań there were also numerous attacks upon Jewish students. When a delegation of them complained to the rector, he responded that the violence was of a political character and did not warrant suspension of classes. He advised the Jewish students to stay out of classes for several days until the atmosphere became calmer.[16]

In December 1935 ghetto benches received official sanction for the first time. Following several violent attacks upon Jewish students at the Polytechnikum of Lwów, school officials instructed them to take up seats in separate sections for the time being. Afraid this sanction would be a dangerous precedent and result in the creation of "ghettos" in other areas of life, the Jews of Lwów were roused to concerted resistance.[17] They found an ally in Professor Zygmunt Szymanowski of Warsaw University, who in a newspaper article branded the benches a relic of the Middle Ages[18] and attacked the Lwów professors for their unprecedented action in giving in to violent agitators. In January 1936 Education Minister Świętosławski received a delegation of Jewish community representatives from Lwów and promised to discuss the matter with the Polytechnikum administration.[19]

Even earlier, however, the rector of the institution had tried to mitigate the seriousness of the action. On December 20, 1935 he announced to a professors' assembly that it had been decided to forcefully condemn all acts of violence against Jewish students. With regard to separate seating in the lecture halls, he declared that no permanent decisions had been made; in the meantime only temporary instructions had been issued, and only when it was felt they were necessary to allow the institution to continue its regular routine.[20] Actually, however, the ghetto benches remained in force following this announcement, bringing about violent clashes between Jewish students who refused to sit in them and non-Jews who attempted to force them to.[21] The Polytechnikum authorities imposed various penalties upon those who stayed away from classes to protest segregated seating,[22] but finally, in February 1936, the Academic Senate of the school officially cancelled the ghetto bench order.[23]

That same month Jewish representatives in the Sejm and Senat spoke out strongly against both the ghetto benches and the violence against Jewish students. Sommerstein focused on "the November unrest" — attacks upon Jews at the beginning of the academic year — that had already become an annual occurrence.[24] Izaak Rubinsztein wondered about the demand by Polish students to institute separate seating, noting that Jews had traditionally been the ones accused of separatist tendencies.[25] On the other hand, at least one prominent Jewish political leader viewed the matter in a different light. Ozjasz Thon believed that Polish students who refused to sit next to Jews were disgracing only themselves; he therefore called upon Jewish students to acquiesce to the ghetto benches, seeing in such behavior not submission but preservation of Jewish self-respect.[26] In the event of violence, he maintained, Jews should respond with force of their own, but should not call upon non-Jews to fight their battles for them.[27]

The beginning of the 1936–37 academic year brought an intensification of university antisemitism. In Warsaw, Lwów, and Wilno, Jewish students were injured almost daily in violent attacks,[28] which both Prime Minister Składkowski and Education Minister Świętosławski vigorously condemned.[29] The Congress of Rectors of Polish Universities, which took place on December 2–3, 1936, also issued a statement against violence and antisemitic agitation on campus, although it also expressed "understanding" for the right of youth to search for ways "to correct injustices in our national life."[30] These pronouncements notwithstanding, no steps were taken against those who committed violent acts. Earlier the academic senates at the Universities of Warsaw, Wilno, and Lwów ordered a temporary suspension of classes, whereupon Endek students in Wilno seized control of one of the university buildings and began to use it as a base for distributing antisemitic literature.[31] The anti-Jewish fervor subsequently spilled over into the streets, to the extent that even police reputedly took part in attacking Jews.[32] In this instance agitation for ghetto benches led to broader violence — but no non-Jewish Sejm deputy explicitly condemned what had happened in Wilno from the house floor.

Once again, however, solid opposition from within the Polish community came from PPS and Socialist youth organizations. The PPS newspaper, *Robotnik*, forcefully condemned both the idea of ghetto benches and the violence against Jewish students. It viewed what was happening in the universities as a danger to the country's very independence, in that it signified a desire to impose upon Poland the laws and customs of the Third Reich.[33] In January 1936 the organ of Polish socialist youth called upon students to put an end to the riots in the universities themselves; in their view, university authorities should not have to summon police to the campus.[34] And at the start of the 1936–37 school year, there were numerous instances in which members of youth organizations affiliated with PPS took part in confrontations with Endek students and distributed pamphlets condemning antisemitic activity in the universities.[35]

Among Jewish organizations in 1936, the Bund was most active in the struggle against the anti-Jewish tendencies in the universities. *Folkstsaytung* maintained that although the problem of the ghetto benches affected only a small segment of the Jewish population, it was in fact of paramount importance in the struggle over the Jewish question in Poland.[36] According to the Bund newspaper, those who called for ghetto benches wished to destroy the morale of Polish Jewry and create an atmosphere conducive to the enactment of a Polish version of the Nürnberg Laws.[37] It therefore urged that the Jewish working masses take up the students' cause and endeavor to win over the Polish proletariat as well. In this connection the Bund and the Jewish trade unions called a protest strike for November 26, 1936, in which some Jewish merchants and artisans, as well as many Polish workers, also participated.[38] One month later representatives of Jewish students from throughout Poland came together and resolved to use all available means to fight against the terror directed against them on the campuses.[39]

Still, the attacks upon Jews in the universities intensified. In January 1937 the most extreme among the agitators began to call for a total ban upon the admission of new Jewish students to institutions of higher learning. The demand to segregate seating was heard even more loudly, voiced especially by the OZON-led Young Poland League (*Związek Młodej Polski*), in which Falanga elements were prominent. And as anti-Jewish violence on campus continued, even the little resistance university officials had offered before to the ghetto bench idea became weaker.

On January 11, 1937 several Jewish students at the University of Warsaw were wounded when Endek students blocked the main entrance to the campus. An order to segregate Jews was evidently given, for four days later Polish socialist students joined a "stand-up strike" protesting the institution of ghetto benches.[40] One Endek newspaper suggested that quiet could be restored if a separate university for Jewish students, staffed by Jews, would be opened.[41] The Jewish press deplored the situation in Warsaw, especially the tendency of university authorities to give in to the Endek students' demands.[42]

The seriousness of the campus situation was not lost on the government. On January 22, Education Minister Świętosławski declared in the Sejm that the pressure to institute separate seating for Jews was liable to bring Poland to a state of anarchy; he announced that he would not capitulate to this pressure and threatened to close the universities if unrest in them continued.[43] The semi-official newspaper of the regime, *Kurier Poranny*, subsequently published a statement by Tadeusz Kotarbiński, a professor of philosophy at the University of Warsaw, that all Polish university students had a duty to disarm those engaged in violence and to defend students being attacked.[44] The University of Wilno was actually closed by order of the authorities between January 12 to January 27.[45]

Nevertheless, the situation worsened. In Wilno, violence by Endek *bojówki* (shock troops) on February 9, 1937 led to Jewish students' being denied entry to the university grounds. A delegation of Jewish students protested to the rector, but to no avail. As a result, five hundred fifty of them staged a twenty-four hour hunger strike.[46] Their action was met only by a counteraction from the university leadership: on February 15, individual faculty members were empowered to decide whether to segregate Jews in their classrooms, and any failure to comply with faculty directions would result in the students' expulsion from the university.[47] Jewish students challenged this action by boycotting all lecture halls and laboratories in which they were forced to take separate seats, and indeed, on March 13, 1937, fifty-four of them were expelled. They were, however, reinstated the next day as part of a compromise, according to which not only Jews but Belorussians, Lithuanians, and "Polish democrats" would be seated separately.[48]

Shortly thereafter, the government dropped all opposition to ghetto benches, probably as a result of the rapprochement between OZON and the Falanga youth and the establishment of *Związek Młodej Polski*. At a conference of university rectors on September 24, 1937, Świętosławski announced that he was giving university officials complete autonomy to regulate seating of Polish and Jewish students in lecture halls.[49] And on October 5 the rector of the Warsaw Polytechnikum became the first to issue an administrative order regarding assigned seating, which in practical terms meant ghetto benches for Jews.[50] Within a few days similar orders were given at all other institutions of higher learning in Warsaw, as well as at the Universities of Wilno, Kraków, and Poznań.[51] In Lwów a bitter fight over the issue broke out, with the final decision being to create three separate seating sections — one for Endek students, one for Jews, and one for all others.[52] In the wake of this decision the rector of the university, Prof. Stanisław Kulczyński, resigned his position, explaining in an open letter that an order to establish ghetto benches would "force the university authorities to put into practice the outlook of a political party that seeks to discriminate against Jews." Nevertheless, the next morning the vice-rector issued an instruction to set aside special "mandatory seats" for all Jewish students.[53]

The Jewish parliamentary representatives protested the government's new position to Świętosławski. The education minister justified it by claiming that the orders given by the various rectors were intended to prevent acts of violence on campus.[54] Świętosławski took a similar position in a report to the Senat on March 12, 1938, claiming that the imposition of "special seats" was an act undertaken at the initiative of the rectors rather than the government and that its purpose was not to discriminate but to preserve order.[55]

In the meantime Jewish students continued to protest. On October 8, 1937 representatives of Jewish student organizations throughout Poland met in Warsaw and resolved to resist the ghetto benches by all means at their disposal, and a student strike was called for October 14–15.[56] As stated before, the struggle over the ghetto benches had implications far beyond institutions of higher learning: the Jewish public understood that the battle being fought in the universities would serve as a proving ground for possible future attempts at segregation and ghettoization.[57] The newspaper of the Bund, for example, noted this danger in an editorial and decried the lack of Jewish action in the face of attacks with "sticks, pistols, and bombs" by "Polish Streichers" against Jewish university students.[58] It called upon "all of the active forces in the Jewish and Polish communities" to join the students in their fight.

To demonstrate their solidarity with the students, several Jewish groups, including various Zionist parties, the Folkists, the Bund, and the Organization of Jewish Artisans, decided to stage a mass demonstration on October 19, 1937 against ghetto benches and to strike the same day between 8:00–12:00 a.m.[59] Similarly, the Jewish parliamentary representation, condemning the benches as unconstitutional, proclaimed the week of October 20–27 as "Jewish Student Week," during which funds would be collected specifically for Jewish student organizations.[60] Unfortunately, in issuing their proclamation, the parliamentary representation failed to mention the strike, which, in Eastern Galicia was called for 12:00–2:00 p.m. instead of the morning hours.[61] Thus even though the entire spectrum of Jewish political parties, from the Bund to Agudas Yisroel, eventually participated, the effect of the strike was diminished by lack of coordination and once again reflected Jewish disunity and the absence of effective leadership.[62]

Nonetheless, the Jewish students were greatly encouraged by the support shown them. A conference of student representatives in December 1937 noted with gratitude the strike and special fundraising efforts, as well as actions by Polish democratic youth, progressive professors, and workers and various circles abroad on their behalf.[63] The students resolved to continue their fight without compromise and never to submit to segregated seating in lecture halls.

Incidents of violence in Warsaw institutions of higher learning increased in December 1937. On December 17 antisemites drove the few Jewish students at the Warsaw Polytechnikum from the lecture halls. At the same time a group calling itself "OZON Youth" distributed fliers calling upon all Polytechnikum students to join the boycott lines in front of Jewish shops. In response to the increasingly violent atmosphere in the institution, government officials closed it until January 8, 1938.[64] And at the Warsaw Commercial School, formations of student *bojówki* attacked and injured several Jewish students, and for several days prevented Jewish students from entering the campus.[65]

During the same period the climate of agitation began to spread into the high schools. Endek groups founded a National Organization of High School Students, whose members took up places on the boycott lines and distributed Endek literature. Members of OZON-led *Związek Młodej Polski* also distributed antisemitic publications in high schools.[66]

As the Jews had feared, after the authorities appeared to acquiesce to the idea of segregated seating, the campaign to institute ghetto benches in universities widened to other areas of Jewish life. As early as the second half of 1937, the National Party conducted widespread propaganda in favor of establishing "residential ghettos" throughout the country.[67] In the first half of 1938 various trade unions and professional associations demanded separation between Jews and non-Jews in their fields. For example, the annual convention of the Polish Bar Association adopted a resolution calling for separate chambers to be installed for Jewish and non-Jewish attorneys in Polish courtrooms.[68] Similarly, the Association of Christian Small Merchants approached the Ministry of Industry and Commerce with a request to impose a Jewish "ghetto" in all marketplaces, explaining that it was necessary to increase the Polish element in commerce until it reached the percentage of Poles in the total population.[69]

Violence in the universities escalated again at the beginning of the 1938–39 academic year, after Jewish students in all major Polish centers of higher learning resolved not to accept assignment to segregated seats.[70] In response, Endek strike formations took up positions in several universities and attempted to enforce separate seating physically. In some instances even female Jewish students were attacked. At the University of Warsaw students declared a "week without Jews," and Jews were driven by force from the campus; in the wake of these events the authorities ordered the temporary closure of the university.[71] At the University of Lwów, Jewish students in the Faculty of Pharmacology were attacked with knives, and two of them – Karl Zellermeier and Samuel Prowaller – later died of their wounds.[72] When a police investigation revealed that an Endek student group maintained a clandestine weapons store, several students were arrested.[73]

In the aftermath of these events anger mounted even further. The funeral of Karl Zellermeier in Lwów turned into a protest demonstration by local Jews and by many Poles who objected to anti-Jewish violence – including the rector of the university, representatives of the faculty, delegates from the Polish Democratic Club, independent Socialist youth, members of the Peasant Party youth organization WICI, and a delegation of Polish and Ukrainian construction workers.[74]

Nevertheless, anti-Jewish riots at the university continued. Now antisemitic students demanded that Jews be thrown out of the institution altogether.[75] The Warsaw Dental Academy officially informed Jewish students that their classes would be conducted in special lecture halls and be taught by a special teacher.[76] Similarly, the Warsaw Bar Association decided that Jews, and even people of "Jewish extraction," would have to complete their legal training in separate "ghetto seminars."[77] Jewish students at the Wawelberg School in Warsaw who did not sit in their assigned segregated seats were not permitted to take their final examinations, and forty-five of them were expelled.[78]

Sommerstein issued an interpellation in the Sejm in which he bitterly decried the refusal of state authorities to intervene and put a stop to campus violence – a refusal that they justified with the contention that the universities were autonomous institutions with complete jurisdiction over their internal affairs.[79] The reality, however, was that authorities could intervene whenever it was in their best interests to do so. This was demonstrated in February 1939, after Endek agitation against Jewish students in Lwów had come to include attacks upon the government as well. In this case the police conducted thorough searches in all dormitories.[80] In similar fashion searches were conducted at the Lwów Polytechnikum on March 10–11, 1939, in the presence of the rector. In the course of these searches an arms cache was discovered. The police encountered forced opposition; one officer was seriously wounded and 86 students arrested.[81]

Jewish organizations continued their resistance to the ghetto bench movement. The Bund proclaimed two weeks of intensive effort, from February 10–25, 1939, aimed at arousing the Jewish and Polish working classes to stand together for what it called "the right to learn."[82] Likewise the Zionists, who in October 1937 had founded a Committee to Defend the Rights of Jewish Students, announced on February 10 that they were calling upon democratic opinion in Poland to extend practical aid to those struggling against segregated seating.[83] It appears, moreover, that these calls met with a notable response. The college and university section of the Polish Teachers Association presented a memorandum to the minister of education demanding that the rights of Jews who refused to obey segregated seating orders be protected and that immediate steps be taken to correct the situation in the institutions of higher learning.[84] Former prime minister Kazimierz Bartel, now a professor at the Lwów Polytechnikum, spoke out in the academic senate against government passivity toward the campus violence, reporting that in the corridors of the institution one could see "beaten Jewish students lying surrounded by pools of blood, while Aryan students pass by with smiles on their faces."[85] He called for a public discussion of the Jewish question "without knives, without violence, and according to civilized means."

Bartel's speech, however, had little practical effect, at least at his own institution. On May 24 Polytechnikum student Marcus Landsberg became the third Jew in six months to be killed on a Lwów campus.[86] In none of the three cases was the murderer apprehended. In protest, sixteen professors from Lwów institutions of higher learning addressed a memorandum to the prime minister condemning the murders and demanding that authorities take steps against the destructive elements on campus.[87] Similarly, the academic senate at the Polytechnikum demanded that all student organizations condemn the Landsberg murder. Eighteen refused and were promptly disbanded by order of the minister of education.[88] Clearly the government began to have second thoughts about the advisability of allowing the universities to maintain autonomy.[89]

It is noteworthy that anti-Jewish violence in the universities increased in 1938–39, a period in which, as we have seen, physical attacks upon Jews in general declined — most likely due to changes in Poland's international situation. Hatred of Jews was evidently so strong in a portion of Polish university youth that many chose to perpetuate the terror in their institutions of higher learning rather than worry about their country's security and prepare for a possible war. It is remarkable, too, that the state authorities took no serious action against these students, as might have been expected in a time of impending national emergency.

As for the Jewish students, their efforts to defend themselves were impeded by the steady reduction in their numbers, a reduction that was particularly noticeable during the two years prior to the outbreak of war.[90] An increasing number sought to further their education abroad. And those that remained knew that even sympathetic Polish comrades could not effectively counteract the violent behavior of the Endek students.[91]

Nonetheless, the Jewish students that persevered in Polish universities demonstrated remarkable unity and tenacity in their struggle — more, in fact, than was demonstrated by the Jewish community at large in its battles against the different aspects of the mounting attack against it. Jewish students were never prepared to acquiesce to any instructions from university officials to take up seats on ghetto benches and were willing to take the penalties attached to their refusal. The various means by which they fought, including sit-ins and hunger strikes, were not always effective, but they did demonstrate to the Polish community that the young Jews of Poland would not give in to pressure or sacrifice their honor. And to the Jewish community they showed that it was possible to withstand antisemitic pressures, even when accompanied by violence, under the most adverse conditions.

6

The Kosher Slaughtering Ban
and Other Anti-Jewish Legislation

Attempts to enact legislation hostile to Jewish interests and sensibilities – in particular the proposal to ban the kosher slaughtering of meat (*shehita*) – can serve as a gauge of the strength of antisemitic forces in Poland at various times. The changing positions of the Polish political parties, government circles, and other elements of Polish society over the *shehita* issue reflected a continually mounting discontent with the political and economic status of Jews in the country. Advocates of a ban tended to stress economic considerations, claiming that kosher slaughtering led to monopolistic practices and allowed Jewish meat wholesalers to drive up the price of beef. They argued that the Polish Christian community was actually financing kosher slaughtering and thus contributing indirectly to the budgets of the Jewish communities.[1] Jewish publications tried to prove the opposite, noting that Jews paid higher prices for meat cut from the forequarters – the only consumable parts of the animal, according to Jewish religious law – than did those who could purchase meat from the hindquarters.[2]

Kosher slaughtering first became a public issue in 1923, when a proposal for an outright ban was introduced in the Sejm. The primary explanation for the bill was that the Jews had instituted the practice of kosher slaughtering in order to take over the meat market, allowing them in turn to exploit the Polish population economically and maintain their own communities. Supporters also charged that *shehita* was both inhumane and unhygienic and not a matter of religious law at all. The bill was referred to committee but never returned to the Sejm floor for action.[3] In 1928 the issue was raised again, this time by the Polish Society for the Protection of Animals, which was under Endek influence. This campaign, too, appeared to employ the humanitarian argument merely as a cover for an attack upon the Jewish role in the meat industry. Indeed, once it became clear that elimination or even restriction of kosher slaughtering would not serve the interests of Polish farmers or consumers, the Society's campaign flickered and died.[4]

By 1935, however, the time was ripe for a new assault on *shehita*, and the Society took up the issue once again. This time the guiding spirit of the attack was Father Stanisław Trzeciak, whose pamphlet, *Kosher Slaughtering*

According to the Bible and the Talmud, appeared the same year.[5] In it Trzeciak sought to prove that shehita was not based upon biblical law at all but was merely a reflection of basic Jewish cruelty. His arguments were readily absorbed by many sectors of Polish society,[6] even though a number of apologetic tracts were published on the Jewish side emphasizing the humanitarian character of kosher slaughtering and its biblical basis.[7] Another work by a rabbi from Częstochowa pointed out that the outlawing of kosher slaughtering would conflict with the constitution of 1935.[8]

Such attempts at rebuttal proved ineffective. In July 1935 the question of *shehita* was placed on the agenda of the Congress of Municipal Associations despite protests from Jewish delegates that the matter did not belong within the purview of such an organization.[9] Finally, during the latter half of the year, the government itself was drawn into the controversy. The Ministry of Agriculture prepared a bill requiring all dairies and factories producing milk products to obtain licenses from local farm bureaus — organizations in which Jews had virtually no representation. The avowed purpose of the bill was to insure the maintenance of sanitary standards, but in fact its real aim was to eliminate the Jews from the dairy industry. For this reason, Jews in Poland referred to the legislation as the "milk decree."[10] It was passed by both houses of the Polish parliament and recorded in the official register on May 6, 1936.[11]

At the same time that the government was pushing for passage of the milk decree, Sanacja deputy Janina Prystor introduced a bill in the Sejm calling for a complete ban upon *shehita*, to begin on January 1, 1937.[12] Despite the government's opposition to its original formulation, the bill was moved along the procedural road to adoption with considerable dispatch. In fact, several municipal governments, evidently taking their cue from the Sejm's deliberations and not even waiting for Prystor's bill to be passed, enacted local ordinances banning *shehita* from all areas under their jurisdictions.[13] The proposal also found wide support in the press, which repeated the old arguments about the allegedly inhumane and unsanitary nature of kosher slaughtering and about how Poles were forced to pay higher prices for kosher meat, thus indirectly supporting the Jewish communities (and the community-supported ritual slaughterers) financially.[14]

The bill was introduced on February 7, 1936, but at the end of February 1936 the director of the government press bureau announced that the government had not yet decided what stance it would adopt on the matter. According to him, the problem of kosher slaughtering had three aspects — a humanitarian one, a legal-religious one (stemming from the fact that Jewish community boards were legally responsible for supplying kosher meat to their constituents and that other religious bodies in Poland sustained themselves with government financial aid), and an economic one (from the perspective of which absolute abolition of kosher slaughtering would not benefit the state).[15] By March 15, on the eve of the scheduled parliamentary debate over Prystor's motion, Prime Minister Kościałkowski told Deputy Foreign Minister Jan Szembek that he was adamantly opposed to the bill and that Prystor's motion was merely an attempt to cultivate popularity. According to Szembek, however, the prime minister felt unable to express his opposition publicly:

[Kościałkowski stated that] even though the proposed law conflicts with the constitution, the government must confine itself to suggesting amendments, for no jurist will be found who would dare to find the law unconstitutional in the face of the antisemitic sentiments of most of the public. The Sejm has become so terrorized (*steroryzowany*) that if a deputy were to vote against the bill he would be met with the general accusation that he had taken a bribe from the Jews. Under such conditions there is no doubt that the law will also be confirmed by the Senat. Raising the matter of *sheḥita* is a policy that helps the Endeks greatly; at the same time it represents disassociation from the principle of tolerance that has been preserved in the Polish tradition, which is liable to create difficulties in our relations with other countries, where we are exposed to a hostile attitude on the part of liberal centers and Jews. This might even lead to the influx of foreign capital into Poland being stopped.[16]

Szembek's record of his conversation with the prime minister shows that the government allowed itself to be dragged into competition with Endecja over antisemitic sentiments but was sensitive to the reactions of Jewish organizations abroad.[17]

Indeed, some segments of Polish Jewry had been trying to rally support from Jews throughout the world to form a united front against the proposed law. To that end, a meeting of the Committee to Protect Kosher Slaughtering took place in Warsaw on February 16, 1936 with 250 persons in attendance, including the Jewish parliamentary representatives and delegates from various Jewish communities and organizations outside of Poland.[18] It seems that most Jewish organizations, for all their sensitivity to the entreaties of their coreligionists, did not know how to utilize the government's sensitivity to foreign public opinion. To be sure, the World Federation of Polish Jews and the American Jewish Committee did try to intervene, and the Joint Foreign Committee of the Board of Deputies of British Jews and the Anglo-Jewish Association actually sent a delegation to Polish Ambassador Edward Rac- zyński to protest the situation.[19] But for the most part Jewish leaders, even those who appreciated the gravity of the situation, had no effective plans for intervention.

Of special note in this regard is a letter written on March 10, 1936 by Yit- shak Gruenbaum to Nahum Goldmann, who served at the time as the Jew- ish Agency for Palestine's envoy to the League of Nations.[20] Gruenbaum re- garded the condition of Polish Jewry as a matter of grave concern, a matter made tangible by the *"sheḥita* decree."[21] In his opinion, the proposal to elim- inate kosher slaughtering was not aimed solely against the Jews but in- tended also to undermine the position of the Polish government.[22] "If we do not succeed in averting the evil decree," he wrote, "we shall reach a cata- strophic situation similar to that in Germany, with the difference that in Germany there are 600,000 Jews and in Poland 3 million."[23] Thus Gruen- baum called for "exceptional action." He suggested that Goldmann consider approaching the Pope for intervention and a positive statement about kosher slaughtering. He also recommended involving Stephen Wise, presi- dent of the American Jewish Congress. Beyond these, he was unable to pro- pose any specific measures that might influence both the Polish government and Polish public opinion.

Nor was Goldmann's response more definitive. He noted that Wise was already planning a major protest meeting by American Jews for March 22 and was contemplating sending a Jewish delegation from the United States for talks with the Polish government.[24] With regard to the Vatican, Gold- mann did not believe it possible to enlist its aid.[25]

Moreover, not all segments of Polish Jewry were convinced of the advis- ability of turning to Jews abroad for assistance. In Agudas Yisroel, for exam- ple, some thought had been given to calling upon Jews throughout the world to observe a day of fasting in protest over the "evil shehita decree," but "for local political reasons that do not permit us to raise our voice through- out the world," its leaders decided to abandon this plan.[26] Those "local politi- cal reasons" had to do with the party's traditional support for Sanacja. Agu- das Yisroel did not want to anger the Kościałkowski government, which itself had misgivings about the bill, even though the proposed law would most di- rectly affect the orthodox Jews who constituted the party's primary con- stituency. Thus the party's spiritual leader, Rabbi Haim Ozer Grudzanski, believed that the episode would end in a government-initiated compromise, in which kosher slaughtering would be permitted but limited to the amount of meat that could actually be consumed by the Jews themselves. In his opinion, the real purpose of the proposed legislation was to take the meat business out of Jewish hands.[27]

Indeed, the government did push toward such a compromise. At the debate over the proposed law in the Sejm plenum on March 17, 1936 (after the bill had been passed by the Administrative Committee twelve days earlier), Agriculture Minister Juliusz Poniatowski stated that he recognized two sound reasons for seeking to abolish kosher slaughtering — the desire to see animals slaughtered in a "more humane" fashion and the desire to bring about a restructuring of the meat industry. However, because the constitution of Poland required that Jews be able to obtain meat prepared according to their religious requirements, the government could not assent to the outright elimination of *shehita*. He declared, therefore, that the government opposed a total ban on kosher slaughtering and recommended that a paragraph be added to the proposal guaranteeing that the religious needs of minority groups would continue to be met.[28]

The following day the Sejm's Administrative Committee approved an amended version of the bill permitting a limited supply of kosher meat to be provided to Jews, Muslims, and Karaites. It also permitted kosher slaughtering of meat for export.[29] This revised proposal was returned to the Sejm plenum on March 20, where, after animated debate, it was approved and passed on to the Senat. According to the version finally adopted at this session, the government was to be empowered to regulate the supply of cattle to kosher slaughterers, and jurisdictions in which Jews numbered less than three percent of the total population were to be permitted to outlaw kosher slaughtering altogether.[30] The Senat enacted the bill into law on March 27, with the provision that it take effect beginning January 1, 1937.[31]

The *shehita* episode generated certain changes in the political behavior of Polish Jewry. For one thing, it promoted cooperation between the Jewish and Ukrainian parliamentary representations. In all votes on the issue in the Sejm and Senat, the Ukrainian delegates sided with the Jews.[32] The leader of the large Ukrainian national party, UNDO, Sejm Deputy Stefan Baran, maintained that the tumult over kosher slaughtering was actually distracting the attention of the Polish public from more fundamental political, ethnic, and economic problems.[33] In his view, even though the bill's initiators defended it on humanitarian grounds, the issue could undoubtedly never have been raised had an infrastructure of antisemitism not already existed among the Polish population. On another occasion Baran explained the Ukrainian vote as an expression of the Ukrainians' refusal to acquiesce in the establishment of a precedent of government intervention in the religious life of one of the country's minorities.[34] Both Jews and Ukrainians were evidently threatened by the rising influence of extreme nationalist elements within the Sanacja camp.

The adoption of the limited ban on kosher slaughtering also served to further alienate Jews from the regime. Even though it had anticipated the outcome that eventually ensued, Agudas Yisroel felt betrayed by the Sanacja, with which it had previously loyally cooperated.[35] During the debate in the Sejm that preceded final approval, Leyb Mincberg declared that the true purpose of the anti-*shehita* law was not to solve a humanitarian problem or even an agrarian one, but to diminish the stature of the Jew, to make him appear despicable, and to drive him from his position in the economy. To his mind, such a law would never have been enacted while Piłsudski was alive. The bill now being approved, he proclaimed, "creates a situation in which Jews are placed beyond the pale of the law; it is the local version of the Nurnberg Laws."[36] Thus a deep chasm was opened between two former political allies; Agudas Yisroel decided henceforth to adopt an aggressive anti-government line.[37]

Indeed, Jews continued to fight the *shehita* restrictions even after the adoption of the law. Protest delegations to the authorities were organized, displays explaining kosher slaughtering were set up, special press conferences were called, and demonstrations were organized in some communities.[38] On March 20, 1936, the Rabbinical Council of Poland proclaimed that during the seven weeks following the first day of Passover, Jews would eat no meat at all.[39] Even the socialist, antireligious Bund loudly condemned the new law, stating that it had been enacted in order to ignite the fire of Jew-hatred throughout Poland.[40] Thus virtually all segments of Polish Jewry, from the most orthodox to the most secular, expressed vigorous opposition to attempts to restrict or outlaw kosher slaughtering. Such attempts represented not only an attack upon freedom of religious expression but also on the livelihood of tens of thousands of Jews and the ability of communities to provide essential services to its members.[41] Even more, they represented a threat to the Jews' formal equality before the law.[42] The compromise achieved in 1936 helped to mitigate these consequences to a small extent, but the situation was hardly satisfactory from the Jewish point of view.

Jews quickly felt the economic hardships that the law engendered. In reviewing the first ten months of the restrictions on kosher slaughtering, *Nasz*

Przegląd reported that all the Jews' fears had been realized and that the ban had adversely affected the ability of thousands of Jewish families to support themselves.[43] According to the newspaper, the price of kosher meat had risen, its consumption had declined sharply, and the incomes of both local governmental authorities and the Jewish communities had diminished. In many smaller towns, kosher slaughtering had been eliminated altogether, and those communities were left without a way to meet their expenditures.[44]

The government, however, evaluated the effects of the law differently. A report by the Ministry of Agriculture noted that the allotment of kosher meat for the first third of 1937 had not been used up. The report concluded that a large portion of the Jewish public did not really require kosher meat and that it would soon be possible to further decrease the amount of kosher slaughtering allowed.[45] Thus the government was disinclined to sympathize with Jewish complaints of hardship. In fact, the only Jewish senior official in the Polish Interior Ministry, Aleksander Hafftka, was reportedly dismissed from his position because of his participation in the Committee for the Protection of Kosher Slaughtering, which had been founded on the initiative of the Jewish Community Council of Warsaw.[46]

Nevertheless, those who had initially advocated a total ban on kosher slaughtering were dissatisfied with what they regarded as their limited achievement, and in 1937 they renewed their offensive. This time, moreover, the government camp, OZON, took part in the struggle to eliminate kosher slaughtering altogether. Claiming that the current law had created chaos in the meat market, OZON Deputy Juliusz Dudziński introduced a bill at a session of the Sejm on February 1, 1938 calling for repeal of the section of the original law that had permitted limited kosher slaughtering under government supervision.[47]

The Administrative Committee of the Sejm approved Dudziński's proposal and called for the complete elimination of *shehita*, even though Agriculture Minister Poniatowski had warned once again of the adverse effect such a step would have on the Polish economy.[48] The Jewish caucus in the Sejm protested the bill as unconstitutional, but to no avail, and a delegation from Agudas Yisroel to Prime Minister Składkowski was unable to prevent the proposal from being brought to the Sejm floor.[49] In fact, when debate on the bill began in the Sejm plenum, on March 25, 1938, the presidium determined that the proposal was not in conflict with the constitution.

During the debate the argument that kosher slaughtering was inhumane was not heard at all, and despite another warning from the government that outlawing *shehita* altogether would do the entire country economic damage, the bill was passed by a large majority. Only the Jewish and Ukrainian delegates voted against it, together with a small number of Poles.[50] And only the fact that the bill was referred to the Senat too late for it to be placed on that body's agenda for its winter session prevented it from becoming law immediately.[51]

The renewal of the efforts to place a total ban upon kosher slaughtering created a storm within Polish Jewry.[52] Even the Bund, despite its socialist, antireligious orientation, felt compelled, in *Naye Folkstsaytung*, to come to the defense of an orthodox Jewish religious practice: "We carry on a bitter struggle against our own clericalism; we are for true religious tolerance, but precisely because of this we oppose a ban on *shehita*." Moreover, the newspaper pointed out, "this ban takes the means of livelihood away from masses of Jewish workers, whose right to work and to life must be preserved." Further, it declared that in the matter of *shehita* the antisemitic attitude of the great majority of the Sejm had prevailed over the interests of the country.[53]

Agudas Yisroel wanted the Bund and all other Jewish parties to display an even stronger reaction. This party's newspaper complained that the Jewish public had yet to carry on a serious, united struggle against the *shehita* decree; no organization had initiated any concrete action in opposition to it.[54] As a result, the leading rabbis of Agudas Yisroel decided on April 24, 1938 to call upon all Jewish political parties jointly to instruct the country's Jews not to eat meat should the new bill become law.

The call may have had some effect. On March 27 representatives of the larger Jewish communities gathered in Warsaw, together with the Jewish parliamentary caucus, in order to discuss various responses.[55] After consulting with rabbis and hasidic leaders, they decided to proclaim March 31, 1938 as a public fast day and to institute a "meatless month."[56] In addition, on March 30 the parliamentary caucus brought representatives of all of the Zionist parties together with those of Agudas Yisroel and the Folkists; the assembled leaders decided to establish a "United Committee for the Defense of Jewish Rights in Poland," which was to arrange for common action against the *shehita* decree.[57]

The government appears to have been concerned about the sharp Jewish reaction. The Foreign Ministry instructed Ambassador Raczyński in London to inform the British press that the Sejm had enacted an amendment to the kosher slaughtering law against the government's inclination and to stress that the purpose of the amendment, as had been made clear during the debate over it, was not to restrict Jews' ability to practice their religion but to eliminate an exploitative economic monopoly that had been in Jewish hands. The instruction further pointed out that kosher slaughtering had been eliminated in Switzerland and Saxony even before World War I and later in Sweden and Romania.[58]

These declarations of opposition to a ban on kosher slaughtering notwithstanding, the government placed a bill empowering the minister of agriculture to permit the sale of meat only by agricultural cooperatives or by licensed merchants on the agenda of a special session of the Sejm called in June 1938.[59] Evidently it hoped that such a law would result in the removal of the meat trade from Jewish hands, thereby achieving the ban's economic goals without the necessity for adopting specifically anti-Jewish legislation. This law was not enacted, but in early December 1938 Dudziński, who in the meantime had left OZON,[60] again introduced a bill calling for the outright elimination of all kosher slaughtering.[61] This time the government supported the idea during the debate in the Sejm Administrative Committee, asking only that the total ban go into effect only at the end of 1943.[62] Two Jewish deputies, Sommerstein and Trockenheim, attempted to dissuade the committee from approving the proposal, but to no avail: the bill was adopted, with an amendment introduced by OZON Deputy Stanisław Leopold making the ban fully effective from December 31, 1942.[63]

This step called forth further protests from Jewish bodies. A special rabbinical council declared a fast for the day when the bill was to be debated in the Sejm plenum, as well as a ban upon the consumption of meat from March 14 to 30, 1939. All Jewish butchers were called upon to close their shops during this period, and *shohatim* (ritual slaughterers) were forbidden from slaughtering any meat.[64] The Jewish labor parties – the Bund and the two wings of Po'alei-Tsiyon – joined in the call to abstain from eating meat during this time[65] – an action praised by Agudas Yisroel, who stressed the need for solidarity among all Jews in the face of the impending new decree.[66]

The authorities appear to have been irritated by these Jewish actions, for they forbade all newspapers to publicize any calls to refrain from eating meat.[67] In any event, the Sejm plenum approved the ban, according to a report of the Administrative Committee on March 22.[68] The Senat was slated to debate the bill on May 11, but its deliberation was postponed until its fall session.[69] In the meantime, war broke out, so that in the end a total ban on kosher slaughtering was never officially enacted.[70]

The extended debate over the elimination of kosher slaughtering indicates once again just how influenced the Polish government was by popular antisemitic feeling. The government allowed the tide of this feeling, as expressed in the Sejm, to determine the course of its policy, rather than acting in what it considered to be the best interests of the country. Indeed, much of the debate over *shehita* was conducted during a period of political crisis brought about by the deterioration of relations with Germany. More than at any other time, Poland needed both internal unity and the good will and concrete support of the West. The ban upon *shehita*, clearly attacking the religious freedom and legal equality of ten percent of the population, was likely to bring about neither.

The elimination of kosher slaughtering was not the only proposed law intending to imapair the Jews' political and economic position. Beginning in 1937, many Polish political leaders lent their support to increasing efforts by trade unions and professional organizations to exclude Jews from their ranks. In the spring of that year, Justice Minister Witold Grabowski visited Germany, where he discussed the possibility of introducing antisemitic legislation similar to the Nazi Nurnberg Laws in Germany.[71] In the wake of his visit, the practice of excluding those who were of Jewish descent from membership in professional organizations became more common. In May 1937 the national convention of the Polish Medical Association adopted a so-called Aryan paragraph by a vote of 140 to 103.[72] The doctors were followed in the same month by the Polish Bar Association, which adopted a resolution calling for the imposition of a *numerus clausus* for Jewish attorneys.[73] Warning against the large numerical advantage enjoyed by Jews, the government organ *Gazeta Polska* wrote, "The situation in the legal profession demands radical changes; attorneys as a body must serve the interests of the Polish people and must demonstrate Polish values in their spiritual life."[74]

The adoption of Aryan paragraphs by the professional associations demonstrated the extent to which racist motifs had been absorbed within Polish antisemitism. Although many supporters were reluctant to acknowledge the racist foundations of such restrictions publicly (largely because the Catholic church refused to consider Catholics born of Jewish parents Jewish), more and more came to agree with the Endek Jędrzej Giertych, who maintained that "baptism can turn a Jew only into a Christian, not into a Pole, and such converts ought to be restricted in their rights just like their Jewish brethren."[75] Thus in January 1938 the general assembly of the Wilno journalists association decided to add a provision to its by-laws stating that membership in the association was restricted to those who were neither Jews nor "of Jewish origin."[76] An identical formula was adopted by the employees of Bank Polski, the state's central financial institution, in April

1938.[77] The Association of Secondary School Teachers, meeting in Kraków in March 1938, resolved to recommend to its board of directors that members "of Semitic origin" be removed from the association's ranks. And the association also directed a request to the government to enact legislation permitting only "Aryan" Polish teachers to teach Polish language, literature, and history in Jewish schools throughout the country.[78]

The pressure of these precedents forced the government to act. On May 4, 1938, the minister of justice was granted indefinite authority to close off the rolls of licensed attorneys and of those studying for admission to the bar in various parts of the country.[79] On June 10 the minister did indeed close the rolls in seven appellate jurisdictions for a period of seven years, although he retained the right to grant a number of exceptions each year.[80] Although the new law applied in theory to non-Jews as well, it was clear that non-Jews were likely to be granted exceptions.[81]

During the same period, other laws and administrative regulations were enacted, which, although they did not specifically mention Jews, were directed primarily against them. One was the Citizenship Law of March 1938, which empowered the authorities to revoke the citizenship of any Polish citizen who had resided abroad for five years and had not maintained "contact with the country."[82] Another was a law forbidding the acquisition of real property located within fifty kilometers of the country's borders without prior government approval. In practice no sale of property in which one of the parties was a Jew was approved, even if the transaction involved the transfer of property from one Jew to another.[83] Finally, a law regulating the manufacture and sale of religious items, enacted on March 25, 1938, forbade members of one faith from dealing in the sacred objects of another. In effect, this law was to interfere with the livelihood of Jews who dealt in Christian religious objects.[84]

Another serious manifestation of the government's antisemitic legal policy was the marked growth from 1937 to 1938 in the number of trials conducted against Jews for "insulting the Polish nation" — trials in which arbitrary and severe sentences were often handed down. In 1937 alone, some seven thousand such trials were held.[85] Jews clearly saw themselves as victims of injustice in light of the reluctance of the judiciary to take a firm stand against pogroms.[86] From the floor of the Sejm, Emil Sommerstein accused the courts of fanning the flames of antisemitism in the country by failing to remain indifferent to the religion of the accused in dispensing sentences, noting that those charged with violent acts against Jews were often lightly punished.[87]

In addition to these indirect attacks, there were clear signs that government circles were considering legislation that would rescind the clauses of the 1935 constitution guaranteeing Jews equality before the law. To begin with, the government showed considerable interest in the anti-Jewish legislation enacted in Romania and Hungary, at one point sending a secret delegation to Hungary to investigate whether that country's laws against the Jews might be applicable in Poland as well.[88] In January 1938, when the Sejm considered the budget of the Interior Ministry, Deputy Bronisław Wojciechowski openly demanded that the government take an example from the manner in which Romania's avowedly antisemitic premier, Octavian Goga, was dealing with his Jews. Wojciechowski called for the enactment of limitations upon Jewish civil rights, to be followed by the expulsion of several hundred thousand "foreign" Jews who had come to Poland from Russia following the close of the First World War.[89] In October 1938, the weekly publication *Zespół*, the voice of more moderate government circles associated with Agriculture Minister Poniatowski, called for the enactment of a law defining a Jew as "a person who belonged or belongs to the Mosaic religion or ... whose father or mother belonged to the Mosaic religion" and limiting the civil rights of all who fit this definition — including the rights to vote, obtain government employment, and serve as officers in the army.[90] In addition, the journal suggested that the government establish emigration quotas for Jews and that Jews be required to pay increased state and municipal taxes should those quotas not be met. Exceptions were to be made only for those pronounced by special courts to have "proven by their lives that they possess emotional and sociocultural characteristics typical of the Polish people."

If such a law could be proposed by the moderate wing of the ruling group, how much more pronounced was the desire of OZON (which in May 1938 enacted its Thirteen Theses on the Jewish Question) to enact anti-Jewish legislation.[91] However, the adverse changes in Poland's relations with Germany in the latter half of 1938 necessitated postponing plans in this direction. Those in power became convinced that although there was an urgent need to pass anti-Jewish laws in Poland, it would be advisable to wait for more propitious circumstances internally and abroad before doing so.[92] The growing threat of war with Germany caused the government to recognize its dependence upon the approval of the West, which could be expected to frown upon any action indicating that Jews were not to be regarded as equal citizens of Poland.

Nevertheless, it is clear that by the beginning of 1939 large segments of the

Polish public and the Polish government were primed – by both the Nazi Nürnberg Laws and OZON's desire to compete with Endecja – to accept legislation that contradicted the promises of equality in the 1935 constitution. Especially important in this regard was the position of Foreign Minister Beck. In a meeting with Wiktor Tomir Drymmer, director of the consular Branch of the Foreign Ministry (the branch responsible, among other things, for carrying out the policy of encouraging Jewish emigration from Poland), Beck stated that although the time was not right for discriminatory anti-Jewish legislation, it was advisable to apply internal pressure upon the Jews through "an appropriate administrative policy." He expressly favored "carrying out a radical purge in the administration and in the state's economic apparatus."[93]

Despite censorship restrictions that at times impeded its ability to deliver information and analysis concerning the transition to anti-Jewish policies on a racial basis,[94] the Jewish press did succeed in conveying a sense of the new danger now facing Jews. It pointed out, for example, that the new exclusionary practices of Polish professional associations were directed not against Jews alone but also against people of "Jewish origin."[95] It also attempted to explain to the Polish public and government that the Citizenship Law of 1938 would merely make it more difficult for Jews to emigrate, both because other governments would become more reluctant to admit Polish Jews and because they would become more hesitant to leave Poland, knowing that they would not be able to return.[96] Perhaps most incisively, Moshe Kleinbaum, analyzing in *Haynt* the government's dilemma regarding anti-Jewish legislation, pointed out that in the final analysis the position of the Jews in Poland would be determined largely by the ongoing development of the relations between that country and Nazi Germany.[97]

Once again the problem preventing Polish Jewry from mounting an effective defense against the increasing attacks upon its civil status was not one of information or understanding. It was rather the paucity of effective weapons at its disposal. Jewish organizations abroad were becoming increasingly concerned with the plight of Jews in Germany and devoting more and more resources to aiding that community. As a result the Jews of Poland were thrown back entirely upon their own resources, which, when put to the test, proved meager indeed. For example, few within the Polish community paid attention to the grievances of Jewish professional associations, who held meetings protesting the exclusion of Jews from the legal and medical professions. Or to three hundred recent Jewish law school graduates who went on a hunger strike in 1938 to call attention to their inability to gain admission to the bar.[98] Jewish political leaders such as Sommerstein and Mincberg spoke out regularly in the Sejm against the injustices to which Jews were routinely subjected.[99] But the parliamentary representatives were not only ignored by their Polish colleagues. They found themselves subject to increasing criticism from within the Jewish community.

7
The Failure of Jewish Leadership in Poland

The difficult struggles that Polish Jewry faced after 1935 caused significant changes in the internal arrangement of political forces within the Jewish community. These changes were graphically revealed during the election campaigns of the Jewish communal governing bodies in the second half of 1936.

Following a longstanding practice in many European countries, Polish Jews were organized in legally-constituted corporations known by them as *kehilot* (communities).[1] The legal status of these communities, their areas of authority, and their manner of operation were regulated by a government statute enacted on October 14, 1927 and amended on March 6, 1928, wherein the communities were defined as autonomous organizations exercising particular religious and social functions. Their tasks were to provide rabbinical services and maintain religious institutions, cemeteries, and Jewish religious schools. They were also responsible for supplying Jews with kosher meat and operating social welfare agencies for those in need. The communities were to be governed by elected boards, which were authorized to levy taxes upon all those benefiting from community services.[2] All who belonged to the "Mosaic faith" were required to belong to a Jewish community and for all practical purposes could not withdraw from it.[3]

On October 24, 1930, Minister of Religion and Education Sławomir Czerwiński issued an ordinance regulating elections to all communal boards and giving his ministry responsibility for supervising the electoral process. Supervision of the community boards on the district level was to remain in the hands of the district governor and on the provincial level in the hands of the provincial governor. The community boards were to be elected for a four-year term. Larger communities would be governed by a broadly-based council and by a smaller administrative committee. The right to vote was to be confined to males above the age of twenty-five who had resided for at least one year within the jurisdiction of the community. Moreover, a further order of the Ministry of Religion and Education of September 9, 1931 gave the district governor the authority to approve, reject, or alter the community budget.[4] Over the years the authorities frequently took advantage of the powers that this ordinance bestowed upon them: they dissolved community councils whose composition was not to their liking and replaced them with their own appointees. Such a step was taken, for example, in Lwów in

January 1935 and again in February 1935, and in Wilno on June 17, 1935.[5]

The authorities also set the dates for elections to the community councils; some, including Warsaw's, were instructed to hold elections in September 1936. Unlike previous campaigns, this one aroused considerable anticipation among the Jewish population. In years past, many groups, including the Bund, some Zionist circles, and secular intellectuals, often paid little or no attention to communal elections or even boycotted them, leaving decisive influence to the orthodox religious parties. In 1936, however, the elections were regarded as a sort of referendum over the manner in which all of the various parties proposed to deal with the increasingly difficult situation Polish Jewry faced.[6]

The Bund took an especially noteworthy interest in this election. Its strength had grown throughout Poland during the previous year, particularly among Jewish trade unions. The strike it had organized on March 17, 1936 in response to the Przytyk pogrom[7] had evolved into a demonstration embracing all segments of the Jewish population, raising the Bund's prestige considerably in the eyes of the Jewish public.[8] Still, the Bund Central Committee had initially decided, on July 4, 1936, against taking part in the elections, in conformity with past practice.[9] However, this time the party's rank-and-file put pressure upon the leadership, and on July 29 the Party Council resolved to enter the fray.[10]

This decision was of the utmost importance, for it turned the communal elections into a full-fledged internal Jewish political contest. Other Jewish parties quickly followed the Bund's lead and devoted all their resources to demonstrating their electoral appeal among the Jewish public. This development in turn gave the Polish authorities a significant stake in the outcome of the elections, which threatened to turn the community councils into platforms for the Jews' external political battles (as, indeed, the Bund explicitly desired). Of course, the authorities, together with the traditional community leadership, wished to see the communities confine their activities exclusively to religious and social realms.

The election campaign to the Warsaw community council developed into a contest among three principal groups — the so-called National Bloc (composed of the General Zionist factions *Al HaMishmar* and *Et Livnot* and the Association of Jewish Merchants), Agudas Yisroel, and the Bund. Of the three, the Bund was most successful: it received 15 of 50 seats on the council (with 10,767 votes out of 40,475 total votes cast),[11] as opposed to 10 for Agudas

Yisroel, 9 for the National Bloc, and no more than 3 for any other list.[12] Five Bund members were selected for the council's fifteen-member Executive Committee, along with five from Agudas Yisroel, three from the National Bloc, and two from other Zionist parties.

The Bund's impressive Warsaw victory aroused a variety of reactions in the Jewish public. The newspaper *Haynt* declared that neither the Zionists nor Agudas Yisroel had a mandate to speak for the Jewish masses.[13] The organ of Agudas Yisroel expressed astonishment that large numbers of Jews had been taken in, as it were, by Bund propaganda and that they had authorized the Jewish socialist party to represent them in the governing body of a Jewish religious community.[14] And the Bund's own newspaper proclaimed a revolution on the Jewish street in response to the failed communal administration in Warsaw, an administration "led by Agudas Yisroel and their Zionist accomplices."[15]

The Bund triumph was indeed of major significance, for it signaled the growing activism of the party's members and supporters and the impotence of the numerous other Jewish political groups. Voters looked upon the Zionists with suspicion, noting the personal and tactical divisions among them and sensing that some of their recent moves toward unification had been made solely for electoral purposes. Neither the Zionists nor Agudas Yisroel appeared to Jewish voters to have correctly interpreted Sanacja's recent proclivity for antisemitic policies. In contrast, the Bund had demonstrated unity and strength in its successful organization and execution of the March strike.

Sensing a change in the Jewish political alignment, the Polish authorities refused to recognize the results of the election. On September 21, 1936 they suspended the new community board's first meeting, on the grounds that it had conducted a political discussion and thereby deviated from the areas of authority granted the community by the law. Finally, on January 5, 1937, they dissolved the board altogether, after the parties represented in it could not agree on a candidate for board president.[16]

In other communities, however, the Bund did not fare nearly as well. In Wilno it received only five seats on the community board, in contrast to nine for the various Zionist parties;[17] in Lublin it tied with Agudas Yisroel, eight seats to eight.[18] In fact, in the 97 cities and towns in central Poland outside of Warsaw in which communal elections were held in 1936, the Bund finished well behind Agudas Yisroel, the General Zionists, and several other groups in the total number of votes received.[19]

Another indication of changing political attitudes among Polish Jewry was provided by the elections to the city council in Łódź, held on September 27, 1936. Łódź was Poland's second largest city and second largest Jewish community as well, with Jews making up about one-third of its total population. The 1936 municipal elections were especially important because they represented the first opportunity for gauging the relative strength of the various political forces after the death of Piłsudski.[20] Jews were anxious to know where the various segments of the Polish community stood on the Jewish question. Moreover, the Jewish vote stood to play a decisive role in determining who would control the city council.

During the previous (1934) elections to the Łódź city council, the Endek National Party had scored a massive victory, assuming an absolute majority (39 of 72 seats) and ending six years of socialist dominance. The Sanacja list and Agudas Yisroel had won ten seats each, with seven more going to a combined list of PPS, the Bund, and German socialists.[21] In the interval, the city council had become a center for extremist Endek agitation and dissolved by order of the interior minister on July 2, 1935.[22] New elections were not scheduled until over a year later.

In its campaign literature, the National Party included for the first time an explicit call for the revocation of Jewish political rights in Poland.[23] It even went so far as to try to intimidate Jewish voters by publishing leaflets in Yiddish threatening those who tried to go to the polls.[24] In response to such threats and at the request of the local Bund leadership, some sixty members of the Bund militia from Warsaw were dispatched to Łódź close to election day, where they joined local forces in setting up armed patrols throughout the city.[25] Noting this response, the Endeks refrained from entering hostilities.

PPS had participated in a common list with the Bund during the previous elections but refused this time to do so, arguing that it could combat the Endeks more effectively with a list of its own. Still, PPS claimed to represent both Polish and Jewish trade unions. Having included several Jewish candidates on its slate, it appealed to Jewish voters to support it. These actions caused considerable tension between PPS and the Bund.[26] On the Jewish side, the General Zionists joined together with Mizrahi and several other groups to form a united list, and Agudas Yisroel did the same with the Folkspartay, the Revisionists, and Jewish artisan associations.

The results of the elections were a triumph for the socialists and a major defeat for the Endeks. PPS and its associates received 34 seats, representing 95,000 votes, while the National Party fell to 27 seats (78,000 votes). The Bund, together with Left Po'alei-Tsiyon, polled over 23,000 votes and won six seats, with three for the bloc led by Agudas Yisroel and two for the one led by the General Zionists. Sanacja did not receive a single seat.[27]

Jews were on the whole quite satisfied with these results. *Nasz Przegląd* wrote that the Endek camp, which had regarded the elections as a referendum on antisemitism, had been soundly defeated.[28] Bund spokesmen declared that the elections had demonstrated the ideological bankruptcy of the Jewish bourgeois parties, who had not yet perceived that their previous dependence upon Sanacja had to be replaced by dependence upon the Polish socialists. They were quick to point out that their bloc had garnered more seats than all of the other Jewish electoral lists combined. However, the Bund complained about PPS's efforts to win Jewish voters to its side.[29]

In this connection, it is interesting to note that the Endek organ estimated that in the Łódź municipal elections, seventy percent of the Poles voted for the National Party, whereas 80,000 out of 130,000 Jewish votes went to PPS.[30] These figures seem highly exaggerated; however, there is no doubt that many Jews did indeed decide to support the Polish socialist list, believing that only a socialist victory could put an end to Endek rule in the city and make a take a strong stand against the "pogromist" policies of Endecja. Thus it appears that PPS's insistence upon maintaining a separate list from the Bund was justified. In fact, middle class Jewish voters may have been more willing to vote for PPS as a defensive move against Endecja than to identify themselves with the Marxist socialist program of the Bund.[31] In the end, PPS and the Bund were able to overcome the differences that had divided them during the election campaign and in December signed a cooperation agreement.[32]

The new alignment of political forces among the Jewish public that was demonstrated during the communal and municipal elections of September 1936 had implications for the organizational structure of Polish Jewry. The Jewish parliamentary representation chosen in the 1935 elections, which numbered four Sejm deputies and two senators, actually represented only a part of the Zionist camp and Agudas Yisroel. At the time of their election they constituted the sole political address to which Jews beset by pogroms and official discrimination could turn. However, large segments of the Jewish public did not recognize these representatives as their spokesmen – a fact that impaired the effectiveness of their efforts and their credibility when they attempted to speak in the name of Polish Jewry as a whole. Indeed, various Jewish parties frequently demanded that the Jewish parliamentary representatives resign their positions to protest the legislature's non-representative character and hostile attitude toward Jews.

Recognizing this lack of cohesive representation, the Zionist Federation of Congress Poland initiated discussions in May 1936 with the Zionist Federations of Eastern and Western Galicia for the purpose of establishing a representative body for all of Polish Jewry, including non-Zionists.[33] However, nothing came of the idea. It was revived a year later, as both the establishment of the World Jewish Congress in 1936 and the formation of OZON in early 1937 quickened Jewish recognition of the need for united countrywide representation. Discussions were held about summoning a Congress for Polish Jewish Self-Help, which would establish an elected body to speak for all segments of Polish Jewry.[34] Efforts to organize such a Congress, however, were plagued with difficulties from the outset. Agudas Yisroel, as an orthodox religious party recognizing only the rabbinate as the legitimate authority in Jewish life, refused to acknowledge a democratically elected body as its representative.[35] The Bund also objected to the idea, arguing that as a class-based party it could not participate in a nonclass-based, all-Jewish representative body.

Still, most Jewish organizations felt a need for unity. On June 16, 1937 the Jewish parliamentary caucus joined with a number of Zionist parties and representatives of Jewish economic organizations to form a Provisional Representation of Polish Jewry (*Tymczasowa Reprezentacja Żydostwa Polskiego*), which Agudas Yisroel also joined.[36] The organ of the Eastern Galician Zionists viewed the Provisional Representation as the first step toward closing the political ranks of the Jews of Poland. However, it admitted that a complete representation encompassing all parties was a utopian dream at this stage.[37] Others argued that the Provisional Representation actually impeded the establishment of a complete representation, largely because it included Agudas Yisroel, which could be expected to block any move toward democratization. The Provisional Representation answered this charge by declaring that it did not intend to work against the establishment of a Polish Jewish Congress and that most of the organizations represented were already taking part in the preparations for this all-inclusive body. However, until it could be established, the Provisional Representation indicated its intention to coordinate the Jewish public's activities in its fight for equality.[38]

Moreover, despite the objections of Agudas Yisroel and the Bund, preparations for a Congress for Polish Jewish Self-Help proceeded apace. The leaders of the various Zionist parties in Poland, with the exception of the Revisionists, were the leading force behind this venture and were assisted by the World Jewish Congress. In early July 1937 an organizing committee for such a Congress was formed, led by Sejm deputy Yehoshua Gottlieb, Moshe Kleinbaum, Noah Prylucki, Anshel Reiss, Henryk Rosmarin, and Aryeh Tartakower, with Baruch Cukierman, director of public relations for the World Jewish Congress, as executive director.[39] In October this committee issued a public call to the Jews of Poland to aid in establishing a uniform representative organization to fight against antisemitism, for democracy, and for self-help and economic rehabilitation.[40] A procedure for elections was decided upon, and elections were set for February 27, 1938, with the Congress slated to convene on March 13.[41]

In the end, however, the Congress idea foundered on the rock of internal Jewish disunity. Many proponents of the plan argued that convening the proposed Congress would be pointless without Agudas Yisroel and the Bund. Such sentiments were particularly strong among the Zionists of East and West Galicia, who felt that the current Jewish parliamentary representation, which included Agudas Yisroel, was more representative than the Congress stood to be.[42] These two regions also feared that the Zionists of Congress Poland, especially the parties of the Zionist Left and *Al HaMishmar*, would dominate the Congress. As a result the Central Committees of both Galician Zionist Federations demanded that plans for the elections to the Congress be permitted to go forward only after at least 500,000 voter's cards had been purchased and a formula for distributing seats had been adopted that would prevent the Zionist Left from becoming the dominant force.[43] In the meantime efforts to find a formula that would allow Agudas Yisroel to participate[44] were unsuccessful.[45] The Bund, too, continued in its unrelenting opposition to the idea of an all-Jewish Congress, which it saw as essentially a Zionist front.[46] Eventually even the Folkspartay, whose leader, Noah Prylucki, was one of the members of the organizing committee, concluded that the Zionists intended to use the Congress to promote mass Jewish emigration from Poland, an idea that the Folkspartay, along with the Bund, adamantly opposed.[47]

Given this mounting resistance to the Congress proposal, many Zionist proponents of the idea began to question whether it made sense to go ahead with the elections as planned. *Nasz Przegląd*, for example, wrote that since the Folkspartay had decided not to participate, only the Zionists remained in the running, and the Zionists certainly did not require a new representation for themselves.[48] In the meantime, the newspaper argued, the Jewish parliamentary caucus was capable of representing the interests of Polish Jewry. Still, the Warsaw leadership of the organizing committee would not give in and intensified its efforts to turn its idea into reality.[49] In late February 1938 a delegation from the organizing committee even met with the director of the Political Department of the Interior Ministry, informing him of the plans for the Congress and the anticipated timetable for its convening.[50]

That timetable, however, was not to be met. The Bund redoubled its propaganda efforts against the Self-Help Congress idea and raised once again its alternative plan for a Congress of Jewish Workers.[51] Under the Bund's influence, the association of Jewish trade unions also adopted a negative attitude toward the Self-Help Congress.[52] So too did the association of Jewish merchants.[53] The Congress organizers thus found that they needed more time to rebuild public support for their program and delayed the planned elections until April.[54] But by the end of that month even Moshe Kleinbaum came to the conclusion that the Self-Help Congress could not be forced upon an unwilling Jewish public,[55] and the idea effectively died.

Thus, despite their perceived need for greater unity, Jewish organizations in Poland proved incapable of overcoming internal disagreements precisely at a time when Polish Jewry was being subjected to a concerted attack by the regime in the form of the total ban on kosher slaughtering,[56] the new citizenship law,[57] and the effective removal of Jews from the legal profession.[58] To be sure, in early April 1938 a coalition of Jewish groups, including the Zionist parties, Agudas Yisroel, the Folkspartay, and several Jewish economic organizations, published a call to the Jews of Poland to close ranks in the face of the waves of antisemitism flooding the country. But the distribution of this call was prohibited by the authorities following its appearance,[59] and in any case it gave no more than lip service to the idea of unity. Ironically, only a few days earlier the Jewish parliamentary caucus, led by Sommerstein, had tried to interfere with the plans for a Congress, for fear that such a Congress might become a political power among the Jews, rivaling its own.[60]

These developments illustrate the extent of the disunity that plagued a Polish Jewry unable to overcome a fierce loyalty to its traditional pattern of separate organizations and create a common front against antisemitism. Even the Zionist camp was plagued by internal division and unable to take the lead in uniting a significant portion of Polish Jewry in the wake of the publication of the Thirteen Theses of OZON in May 1938. To be sure, Moshe Kleinbaum urged the Zionists in this direction with a major article in *Haynt*, where he argued for the summoning of an interparty coordinating committee for Polish Jewry, from Agudas Yisroel on the right to Po'alei-Tsiyon on the left, which would agree on a minimum program of "a defensive political and economic struggle."[61] He maintained that the Zionists could provide the great central idea necessary for drawing the Jews of Poland closer toward unity. Whereas the ideas of the Bund and Agudas Yisroel addressed themselves in divisive fashion to only one segment of the Jewish people, Zionism addressed itself to all segments. He thus suggested that Zionists work to consolidate their own ranks; once they were unified they could then work in stages toward creating an all-encompassing organizational framework for the Jews of Poland. However, the upcoming elections to the Sejm and the city councils caused Jewish internal divisions to be emphasized sharply once again, with even the Zionists battling over the problem of their political orientation and even whether Jews ought to vote in the elections at all.[62]

Meanwhile the Bund began to work vigorously in the summer of 1938 to establish a Congress of Jewish Workers — whose purpose was to discuss the struggle against antisemitism.[63] The organizing committee for this Congress met for the first time on July 12 and in subsequent weeks organized numerous meetings throughout Poland where the idea would be explained.[64] The Zionists viewed these efforts as working against Jewish unity; to their minds they represented an attempt to exploit the atmosphere of desperation and bitterness among the Jewish public in order to produce gains for the party.[65] And indeed, the platform prepared for the Congress was directed against forces within the Jewish community no less than against the major foci of antisemitism. The Bund stressed that both Agudas Yisroel and the Zionists were long-time supporters of the Sanacja; as such, it claimed, "Zionist emigrationism" had actually strengthened the country's antisemitic forces. Thus the fight against "emigrationism" and its Jewish supporters was regarded as the primary subject for the proposed Congress to consider.[66]

In the Jewish press, the Bund came under criticism from the eminent Jewish historian Shimon Dubnow for what he termed its isolationist politics and its separation from the Jewish community as a whole. Dubnow charged that the Bund was not prepared to work together even with other democratic and socialist elements among the Jewish public. Although he was not a Zionist and had long fought against the negative aspects of Zionism, he was amazed by the hostility that the Bund showed toward this movement, which he claimed the majority of the Jewish people supported and appreciated for its wonderful work in building Palestine. He argued that the Bund was in error for regarding itself as a part not of the Jewish people but of the Jewish proletariat. And although its ranks may have grown recently, he predicted that its future strength would depend on its abandoning this attitude of isolation and its joining together with other democratic and progressive elements of the Jewish people.[67]

Dubnow's criticism was rebuffed in the same newspaper by Bund leader Henryk Erlich (who was also Dubnow's son-in-law). Erlich held that the Bund was the largest political force among Polish Jewry and that its position as such was not a transient phenomenon. He also vigorously refuted the claim that the Bund did not regard itself as an organic part of the Jewish people. On the contrary, in his view it best represented the Jews' true interests, as witnessed by the mass demonstrations it had organized in March 1936 and October 1937. Although the Bund was concerned with the problems of all Jews, not merely of Jewish workers, in his view that concern did not obligate them to collaborate with the reactionaries of Agudas Yisroel and the Revisionist movement. He viewed the Zionists as a whole as allies of the antisemites, for any worsening of conditions for Jews ultimately served the Zionists' interests. Thus, the Bund could not look upon the Zionists, who justified antisemitism on historical grounds, as partners in the struggle against the reactionary forces in Poland.[68]

Actually, it appears that Bund leaders were well aware that their party's recent growth stemmed from increasing antisemitism on one hand and a sharp reduction of possibilities for emigration, especially to Palestine, on the other. In this context, their opposition to an all-Jewish Congress seems to have reflected their fear that it was a Zionist trap, intended to slow the Bund's expansion. The organizational fragmentation of Polish Jewry at a time of severe crisis served their party's interests and contributed to the strengthening of its influence among the public.

The Bund's plans for a Congress of Jewish Workers, however, also came to naught. The authorities forbade its convening "for reasons of public security," and in late September 1938 the Bund ceased to publicize its plans. Its official organ expressed the party's anger, claiming that the Congress of Jewish Workers had been outlawed because it stood a chance for success, whereas plans for an all-Jewish Congress had been allowed to proceed because there was no chance they would ever be realized.[69]

In reality, however, it appears that the Bund's idea of a Jewish Workers' Congress was itself motivated by fear of the potential internal political effects of an all-Jewish Congress and was designed to undermine efforts to bring it about. The Bund's work against the all-Jewish Congress, together with the negative stance of Agudas Yisroel toward the idea that delegates to the Congress should be elected democratically, ultimately defeated the Congress concept. This political infighting exposed to the Jewish public in Poland and abroad, as well as to the Polish community and authorities, just how weak Polish Jewish leadership really was. This exposure, in turn, undoubtedly contributed to a mounting sense of impotence among Polish Jews and encouraged antisemitic forces to continue their attacks.

If the Jewish parties were more interested in testing their strength against each other than in uniting for common defense, they were given the opportunity to do so in late 1938 and in 1939. As described in chapter two above, on September 13, 1938 President Mościcki dissolved the Sejm and Senat, which had been elected in 1935 for a five-year term. Actually OZON, which had not existed as a party at the time of the last elections, was the driving force behind this move, because it wanted to increase its standing in parliament. In addition, the supporters of Mościcki and Rydz-Śmigły hoped once and for all to eliminate the influence of the right-wing Piłsudskist faction, which as late as January 1938 had managed to secure the election of their leader, Sławek, to the office of speaker of the Sejm by a decisive majority.[70] As in 1935 the major opposition parties — Endecja, PPS, the Peasant Party, and the (*Stronnictwo Pracy*) Labor Party — announced that they would boycott the new elections, although they approved of the dissolution of parliament. They based their refusal to take part in the elections on the claim that the electoral statute did not permit their candidates to be elected freely.[71]

The elections, which were held on November 6, 1938, resulted in the return of 166 deputies from OZON out of 208 total deputies elected. Also elected were 19 Ukrainians associated with the Ukrainian nationalist party UNDO, 5 Jews, and one Belorussian. OZON's great accomplishment in these elections lay in the 67 percent voter turnout — voters had evidently been influenced by the statement of the primate of the Polish Catholic church, Cardinal Hlond, that boycotting the elections was an unpatriotic act. Moreover, the dissemination of partisan propaganda had been prohibited during this campaign (in contrast to 1935) under threat of two years' imprisonment, and censorship of newspapers had been tightened. The election was also held following the Munich conference, which had resulted, *inter alia*, in the transfer of a piece of Czechoslovak territory to Poland — which enhanced the prestige of the regime in the eyes of broad segments of the Polish public. These facts undoubtedly account for OZON's resounding victory, which was viewed with great satisfaction in government circles.[72]

The dissolution of parliament was regarded by the Jewish public calmly, for the legislature had been responsible for the passage of a number of anti-Jewish laws. Zionist circles that had not agreed to take part in the 1935 elections now demonstrated a readiness to reexamine their position, especially in light of the promise that the next Sejm would consider changes in the electoral ordinance.[73] Still, some Zionist leaders from Congress Poland were hesitant. Kleinbaum, for example, remained against participation, because the democratic elements of the Polish community, led by the socialists, were not taking part. On the other hand, he granted that there were serious reasons for participating: he believed that as Poland's external situation worsened, the government would take a more favorable stand on many internal issues, including the electoral ordinance and the Jewish question. He concluded that the governing body of the Zionist Federation of Congress Poland faced a difficult decision regarding its attitude toward the elections.[74]

Kleinbaum's comments indicate that the prospect of a change in the electoral ordinance was regarded by the Zionists of *Al HaMishmar* as a fundamental turning point in the government's approach to domestic policy. He also expressed implicitly a feeling that, in light of past experience and in the conditions prevailing in Poland at the time, the importance of a Jewish parliamentary representation should not be overlooked, especially given a hostile OZON regime. Such a representation, some Zionists believed, could look out for Jewish interests; therefore they argued that the Zionists should not automatically follow the Bund into identifying with the approach taken by the Polish left-wing opposition.

The Zionist Federations of East and West Galicia approved participation in the elections, urging voters in districts where there were no Jewish candidates to vote for Poles sympathetic to their demand for full civic equality.[75] Agudas Yisroel, Mizrahi, the Zionist *Et Livnot* faction, the Revisionists, the Jewish Merchants Association, and the Jewish Small Business Association all adopted similar stands. On the other hand, the Bund, the Folkspartay, and both the left and right factions of Po'alei-Tsiyon resolved to boycott the elections. In the end the Zionist Federation of Congress Poland did likewise, because, as its leaders explained, the elections were to be conducted according to the old electoral ordinance, with candidates selected by electoral colleges appointed by the authorities — a system that made it impossible to present candidates other than those acceptable to the regime. The Zionist Federation of Congress Poland argued further that the abstention of the Polish democratic camp from the elections would in any case insure the absolute rule of OZON and antisemitic circles in the Sejm, making Zionist participation of virtually no value.[76]

Of the five Jews who were elected to the Sejm in the 1938 elections, two were from Warsaw — Shlomo Seidenman, an attorney representing *Et Livnot*, and Jakub Trockenheim of Agudas Yisroel, who had served as a senator during the previous parliamentary term. A second deputy from Agudas Yisroel,

Leyb Mincberg, was elected in Łódź. The two remaining Jewish deputies represented the Zionist Federations of East and West Galicia — Emil Sommerstein from Lwów and Yitshak Schwarzbart from Kraków. In addition, two Jews were appointed senators — Rabbi Izaak Rubinstein of Wilno and the vice-president of the Organization of Jewish Veterans of Polish War of Independence, Zdzisław Konopka-Żmigryder.

As it happened, none of the Jewish parties adopted an attitude toward participation in the elections of 1938 different from the one it had held regarding the elections of 1935. However, the parties that opposed participation adopted a much quieter tone in expressing their opposition. This change was noticeable, though, among the Polish opposition parties as well, a fact that suggests that the Jewish parties were influenced in this direction by their Polish counterparts. Indeed, in late 1938, as a result of changes that occurred in the OZON leadership following the resignation of Adam Koc, the regime began to show greater consideration for the opposition, and there was even talk of the possibility that some opposition leaders in exile abroad might be able to return to Poland. Indeed, it seemed that the time might be ripe for the government and the opposition to turn over a new leaf in relations between them.

Such was not the case, however, with regard to the government's Jewish policy. Even the changes in the OZON leadership and the cessation of close cooperation between the government camp and Falanga and extreme Endek elements did not change the camp's fundamentally antisemitic orientation. In fact, OZON's new leaders were anxious to show that any liberal tendencies they had would have no bearing upon the Jews. As a result, Jewish elements, such as Agudas Yisroel and the assimilationists, who had supported BBWR in 1935, believing it to be committed to equality for all Polish citizens, did not identify themselves with the government in 1938.

In any event, one outcome of the supposedly greater consideration shown by the government for the Polish opposition parties was the setting of democratic elections to the local municipal councils throughout the country in December 1938. These elections were the first in many years in which groups representing the entire Polish political spectrum participated. For this reason their importance extended far beyond the local level.[77] In this context they also provided the Jewish parties with a further arena for testing their strength.

On December 18, elections took place in four major cities (Warsaw, Łódź, Kraków, and Poznań) and in 492 provincial towns in the southern and western parts of the country. In general they witnessed an increase in the strength of the opposition parties, in particular of PPS in Warsaw, Łódź, and Kraków and of the National Party in the western regions. Nowhere did OZON receive an absolute majority, and it enjoyed relative success only in Warsaw, where, together with other progovernment groups, it received 40 seats, compared to 27 for PPS, 8 for the National Party, and 5 for ONR.[78]

The Jewish vote in Warsaw was also significant. The Bund and Jewish trade union slates received 17 seats (representing 61.7 percent of all votes cast for Jewish electoral lists); an alliance of the *Et Livnot* Zionists, Agudas Yisroel, Mizrahi, the Revisionists, and the Jewish Merchants Association took two seats; and another alliance of the *Al HaMishmar* Zionists and the right wing of Po'alei-Tsiyon returned one delegate.[79] In other words, representatives of Jewish parties held 20 percent of the seats on the Warsaw city council.

Jewish lists also won significant numbers of seats in Łódź and Kraków. In Łódź, the Bund, together with the left wing of Po'alei-Tsiyon and the Jewish trade unions, won 11 seats, the same number as OZON but 7 less than the National Party, while other Jewish lists added six more representatives to the Jewish total. PPS dominated the voting in Łódź with 33 seats; an additional five were won by German ethnic lists. In Kraków, Jewish parties returned 13 of 72 delegates, as opposed to 24 for PPS, 23 for an OZON-Labor Party alliance, and 12 for the National Party. Among the Jewish lists, the Bund and the assimilationists received 2 seats each, with the remainder going to the Zionist bloc, Agudas Yisroel, and independent slates.[80]

In commenting on the election results, OZON argued that no political conclusions could be drawn from them.[81] In contrast, Mieczysław Niedziałkowski, editor of the PPS newspaper *Robotnik*, saw far-reaching significance in them, especially insofar as they refuted the nationalist and OZON contention that PPS had grown stronger thanks to the Jewish vote. "We are not at all ashamed of the votes of Jewish socialists or democrats," he wrote, "but the victory came thanks to the votes of the masses of Polish workers."[82]

An interesting reaction to the election results came from the German ambassador in Warsaw. He saw in them a demonstration of serious opposition to that same regime that had viewed the parliamentary elections held but a short time earlier as a great victory. The German report placed special emphasis upon the achievements of PPS in Warsaw, Łódź, Kraków, and in various provincial cities, arguing that the party had benefited from many Communist and Jewish votes. It also noted a radicalization within the Jewish public, which allegedly had transferred many votes from the bourgeois parties to the Marxist Bund. Thus it foresaw the possibility of an agreement between the government and Endecja, despite the tradition of competition and hatred between them.[83]

For the Jews, the most significant result of the election was the absolute majority of Jewish votes won by the Bund in Poland's two largest Jewish communities, Warsaw and Łódź. This result represented a continuation of the strengthening of the Bund that had been noticeable in the elections to the Warsaw Jewish community board and to the Łódź city council in September 1936. Yitshak Gruenbaum viewed the Bund victory as a catastrophe for all Jewish parties that had taken part in the parliamentary elections, as well as for all branches of the Zionist movement. In his view, the Jewish masses in Poland had expressed opposition to the antisemitic Polish government, although most of those who had voted Bund were far from being ideological Bundists.[84]

Kleinbaum, on the other hand, did not view the results as a massive rejection of the idea of Zionism as a national liberation movement (an idea that undoubtedly a large percentage of those who had voted for the Bund list endorsed), but simply as a refusal to entrust the struggle for equal rights for Jews in Poland to the Zionists. He also expressed satisfaction with the results of the elections in Warsaw, Łódź, and Kraków, which proved, to his mind, that there existed a strong Polish democratic camp upon which Jewish opposition to antisemitic aggression could depend.[85] For its part, the Bund newspaper noted that the party's victory had "exceeded all expectations" even though the Bund's campaign had been hindered by numerous encumbrances.[86] In a later article it termed December 18, 1938 "a historic day" in which the masses of Jewish voters in Poland had given the Bund authorization to speak for them.[87]

Indeed, support for the Bund had increase dramatically since 1936, while that for the Zionists remained more or less constant and that for Agudas Yisroel declined.[88] There is no doubt that these results reflected Jewish attitudes throughout the country, and they appear to have influenced the results of the elections in other localities during the first half of 1939. In these elections, too, the Bund registered dramatic gains.[89] In May 1939, when Poland's diplomatic situation appeared precarious, the Bund received 10 of 17 Jewish mandates in Wilno (as compared with 26 for the National Party, 19 for OZON, 9 for PPS, 5 for the Zionist-led Jewish National Bloc, and 2 for Right Po'alei-Tsiyon). In Lublin during the same month, the Bund received 8 of 9 Jewish seats, 10 of 15 in Białystok, 9 of 11 in Grodno, 7 of 9 in Radom, and 5 of 6 in Zamość. One exception to the Bund's dominance in these elections was Lwów, where the party did not obtain a single seat on the city council against 16 seats won by the Jewish National Bloc. In fact, the Jewish National Bloc did quite well in Lwów, even compared to non-Jewish parties: OZON received 23 seats, Endecja 22, and PPS only 9.[90]

On the whole, the results of the municipal elections were favorable to Jewish interests. The rise in PPS strength undoubtedly served as a brake upon the antisemitic momentum fostered by OZON and Endecja. This rise was especially noteworthy because the entire municipal election campaign had been characterized by antisemitic agitation accompanied at times by terror. This agitation was carried out both by the National Party and by OZON, and it encompassed even the western parts of the country, where there were few Jews. In Gdynia, for example, Endecja embarked upon a campaign to intimidate Jewish voters and to prevent them from voting, even though no Jewish list was standing for election. The authorities made no attempt to put a stop to the agitation in this town, which was in an area that had become the focus of a major crisis in Polish-German relations.[91]

The Jewish press and public figures from all camps devoted much attention to analyzing the results of the elections. *Haynt* wrote that there could be no argument that the electoral results represented a tremendous victory for the Bund and a great defeat for the Zionist parties.[92] The newspaper viewed the results as an indication that the national consciousness of many segments of Polish Jewry had been significantly weakened and that assimilationist tendencies, albeit in modified form, were once again on the march. It termed the Bund slogan that Jews still had a future in Poland an illusion and called upon the Zionist movement to renew its struggle against this "dangerous assimilation ... that wears a veneer of Jewish diaspora nationalism and makes use of ostensibly nationalist phrases." Indeed, support for the organized Zionist movement appeared to be decreasing throughout Poland. Whereas some 206,000 Polish Jews cast votes for delegates to the Nineteenth Zionist Congress in 1935, only 116,000 voted for delegates to the Twentieth in 1937 and 141,000 for the Twenty-First in 1939.[93]

Zionist emissaries from Palestine who were in Poland at the time interpreted the Bund's victory as an expression of the Jews' will "to hold on" in Poland. They regarded the vote for the Bund not as an expression of agreement with that party's ideas but as a protest vote against antisemitism and a recognition that the Bund had been paying special attention to the problems plaguing Polish Jewry in the here-and-now.[94]

The Bund continued throughout the first half of 1939 to dispute this Zionist analysis of the election results. Against *Haynt*'s claim that the Bund spread illusions about the future of the Jews in Poland, *Folkstsaytung* argued that in fact "Zionism brought the illusion of Palestine" to the Jewish street. The election results, it maintained, represented not merely a one-time defeat for the Zionists but a complete rejection of it, after a lengthy struggle.[95]

Indeed, in this internal debate the Zionist side appeared to be continually on the defensive against the Bund — which, interestingly, generally refrained from attacking the Zionist idea in principle, preferring instead to focus upon practical points. Bund leaders argued that the proposed Zionist solution to the problems of Polish Jewry had been proven an illusion in light of the closing of the gates of immigration to Palestine. Further, they claimed, a common interest existed between Zionist aims and the anti-Jewish policy of the Polish government. Jointly promoting Jewish emigration from the country necessitated practical cooperation as well. Such practical cooperation, according to the Bund, was not only unacceptable on principle; it also gave legitimacy to the view that since Jews were foreigners in Poland, discrimination against them was acceptable. Finally, Bund spokesmen contended that the Zionist focus on Palestine distracted the attention of Jews from their problems in Poland and weakened the battle for their rights and livelihood there.

It appears that such arguments found a receptive ear among many Jewish voters who did not subscribe to the Bund's combination of national and class ideology at all. Moreover, a comparative analysis of election results reveals that many who voted for the Bund in the municipal elections of 1938–39 had not heeded the party's call to boycott the November 1938 elections to the Sejm and had voted for Jewish candidates representing the Bund's rivals. Evidently these voters wished to see a strong Jewish representation in the Polish Sejm but, when given a choice, preferred the unity within the ranks of the Bund — its leadership, its initiative, its concentration upon the Polish domestic scene, and its absolute opposition to any cooperation with a hostile regime — to the divisiveness within the Zionist camp.

Certainly, too, the crisis of public confidence in the Zionist leadership was a reflection of the drastic reduction in the number of immigration certificates made available by the British mandatory authorities — a reduction that had begun in 1936 and culminated with the White Paper of May 1939, placing an absolute ceiling upon the entry of Jews into the country. The Zionist movement was unable to alter this situation at a time when pressure upon the gates of Palestine was heavier than it had ever been before. Voters were prepared to reward the Bund for its consistent willingness to engage antisemitic forces in battle, and they protested against the notion of "emigrationism"[96] — an idea that militated against any initiative by the Polish public that might lead to productive, long-term Polish-Jewish coexistence. On the other hand, it must be recalled that the Bund's strength grew primarily in those areas where it had been strong before. It was not able to significantly penetrate such large areas as Galicia (Lwów and Kraków), Wołyń, and Zagłębie (Sosnowiec), where the Zionists were historically strong.[97]

In the final analysis, however, the results of the elections point once again to the Jewish masses' mounting sense of catastrophe, engendered both by their daily struggle for existence and by the absence of suitable destinations for emigration.

8

Ukrainians and Germans in Poland: Fluctuating Relations and Anti-Jewish Agitation

Relations between Polish Jewry and the country's largest ethnic minority, the Ukrainians, fluctuated in the interwar years.[1] There had been a period of parliamentary cooperation between the two groups during the 1920s, when, at the initiative of Yitshak Gruenbaum, a Minorities Bloc had included representatives of many Jewish and Ukrainian parties in a single electoral list. However, the bloc had ceased to exist before the 1930 parliamentary elections, largely because Ukrainians had been reluctant to stand for election once again under its banner. The radical Ukrainian nationalist party OUN, outlawed in Poland, maintained a center in Berlin and was responsible for the assassination of Polish Interior Minister Bronisław Pieracki in June 1934. It conducted strong antisemitic propaganda and organized attacks upon Jews, as, for example, in the village riots in the Sokal area in April 1933.[2] At a time when the Polish government's repression of the Ukrainian minority under the so-called pacification program was at its height,[3] the principal organ of Endecja expressed the wish to carry out joint anti-Jewish actions with the Ukrainians as a means of developing Ukrainian confidence in and loyalty toward Poland.[4]

Although the Weimar regime in Germany supported the struggle of the Ukrainians of Eastern Poland to a significant extent, it did not wish to be conspicuous in its support for the extreme ambitions of OUN and asked the Ukrainian party's leader, Eugen Konovalets, to leave Germany.[5] However, since the 1920s, Ukrainian nationalists had developed close connections with the Nazi party, even though members of that party had varying ideas of how to deal with the Ukrainian problem. Following the Nazi accession to power in 1933, Konovalets returned to Berlin to direct OUN headquarters.[6] Nevertheless, the German regime took care not to demonstrate support for a Ukrainian anti-Polish struggle — sensitive as they were to the correct relations between Germany and Poland after the signing of the nonaggression pact between the two countries in 1934. Never during the 1930s did Hitler promise to support the establishment of a greater Ukrainian state.[7]

In 1935 a period of "normalization" began between the Ukrainians and the Polish government. The largest Ukrainian party, UNDO, took part in that year's parliamentary elections and reached an agreement with the authorities concerning its electoral activity. Concurrently, antisemitic agitation increased among the Ukrainian population. The Ukrainian leadership did not encourage this development, but it does appear to have condoned it in silence.

In general, UNDO adopted a formally correct stance on the Jewish question in its statements intended for public consumption. The Ukrainian representatives in the Sejm and Senat, however, voted with their Jewish colleagues against the limitation of kosher slaughtering, no doubt out of fear that a ban would create a precedent for government interference in the internal affairs of other national minorities. Because of this action, the Ukrainians came under fire in a portion of the Endek press, which saw in their vote an unpatriotic renewal of Ukrainian-Jewish cooperation against the Polish majority.[8]

Still, on the practical level, Jews living in areas of heavy Ukrainian concentration were subject to a boycott of their businesses by the local population. To be sure, Ukrainian spokesmen denied any fundamental hostility toward Jews. One of the leaders of UNDO, Sejm deputy Stefan Baran, stated in an interview by *Haynt* that the source of all misunderstandings lay in economic rather than political considerations, especially in the different occupational structures of the two minorities. Expressing hope for an improvement in Ukrainian-Jewish relations, he claimed that the masses of Ukrainians in Poland were not influenced by the huge wave of antisemitism in the country.[9] Similarly, the Ukrainian Senator Stanisław Łuckyj told British Consul Frank Savery that the Ukrainians in Poland were not antisemites — adding, however, that there were too many Jews in Eastern Galicia.[10] In fact, in virtually all declarations by UNDO leaders on the Jewish question during this period, opposition to antisemitism in principle was accompanied by justification of an economic or even a political struggle against the Jews.

Indeed, the upsurge of antisemitism in Poland after 1935 and the spreading of Nazi propaganda, to which the radical OUN contributed, did not leave the rank and file of UNDO unaffected. The leadership of that party was well aware of the attitudes spreading among the Ukrainian public due to the penetration of members of OUN into the more moderate legal Ukrainian organizations.[11]

This process was noted by the Jewish press. Hillel Zeidman wrote in the organ of Agudas Yisroel about the increasing Ukrainian antisemitism which, in his view, stemmed from both the economic boycott and antisemitic propaganda and was inciting those in Ukrainian settlements to commit acts of violence against Jews. The Jewish response to such Ukrainian actions was, in his view, passive and fearful. Concerned with general problems, the Jewish leadership did not take the time to extend aid to rural Jews living in areas of Ukrainian settlement. He also charged that the development of the Jewish cooperative movement was being neglected by the Jewish leadership: in every respect coexistence with the other minority was not receiving proper attention from the Jewish side.[12]

Moshe Kleinbaum also devoted considerable space to comparing Jewish and Ukrainian interests and their influence upon the two minorities' mutual relations. In an article entitled "The Polish-Ukrainian-Jewish Triangle," he examined differing interests and orientations among Ukrainians and Jews,[13] arguing that the Ukrainians, as a territorial minority, viewed themselves as part of a rightfully independent Ukrainian nation standing opposite Poland, whereas the Jewish minority desired only civic equality within the Polish state. In his opinion, the two groups shared the desire for the realization of full civil rights. Their other interests, however, not only did not coincide but frequently clashed, especially in the economic and diplomatic realms. With regard to the latter, he observed that many Ukrainians felt compelled by their antagonism toward Russia to adopt a pro-German — hence anti-Jewish — orientation. Nevertheless, he saw room for Ukrainian-Jewish cooperation. Even though Poles tended to view such cooperation as anti-Polish, in reality it was nothing of the kind. As he wrote, "It is a struggle for internal balance, for internal order, and for internal coalescence within the state, which should lead to a strengthing of [Poland's] position internationally." This struggle depended as well, he stated, on the democratic forces among the Poles.

At the same time that Ukrainian-Jewish relations were undergoing adjustment, similar changes were occurring in Jewish relations with Poland's German minority. That minority enjoyed considerable economic importance, especially in the western provinces, even as it maintained strong political ties with Germany. Ethnic Germans possessed large landed estates in Pomorze and Silesia and industrial plants in Upper Silesia and the Bielsko region. German-owned banks provided credit to German enterprises and economic organizations in Poland, and a widespread network of German credit and savings cooperatives provided a healthy base for the German minority's intensive economic activity. A significant concentration of Germans could be found in the city of Łódź and its periphery. There were also many German settlements in the province of Wołyń in the east.[14]

The 1920s were marked by joint initiatives for collaboration and coordination of political positions between the Jewish and German minorities in Poland, especially in the parliamentary arena, where each group worked to strengthen both its own status and the status of all minorities. However, even these limited initiatives were opposed by various factions among both Germans and Jews. During the 1930s the political organizations of the Germans in Poland were for the most part thoroughly infused with Nazi influence. In fact, the Nazification of these organizations was essentially complete by 1935 and accompanied by growing aloofness, estrangement, and hostility between Germans and Jews in Poland.

Some German parties in Silesia, Poznań, and Central and Eastern Poland were under Nazi influence even before Hitler's accession to power. The German Youth Party (*Jungdeutsche Partei* – JDP), founded in Bielsko in 1931 under the leadership of Richard Wiesner, was a Nazi party from the beginning, confining its membership to those who could prove Aryan descent for at least three generations. Although there was a certain amount of competition between the younger and older German parties, both displayed an affinity for Nazism[15] and argued that the Polish authorities discriminated against them on both a political and an economic basis. Such discrimination, they warned, would have an adverse effect on relations between Poland and Germany.[16] To be sure, they declared their loyalty to the Polish state and took care not to distribute Nazi or antisemitic literature publicly. Nevertheless, despite the officially friendly relations between the two countries, symbolized by the nonaggression pact of 1934, the *Jungdeutsche Partei* maintained anti-Polish underground cells that carried on espionage and sabotage activities under the direction of German diplomatic offices in Poland. The authorities in Germany were of the opinion that competition among various German parties contributed to the greater activization of the German minority.[17]

The Jewish public does not appear to have been sufficiently aware of what was happening among the German minority following the Nazi accession to power. The Jewish press did not devote much space to the increasing affinity of Poland's ethnic Germans for Nazi ideology or to their efforts to advance German interests in Poland. One reason may have been that the German parties maintained an appearance of moderation to those outside the community. Nevertheless, in July 1935 the Bund newspaper published an article by an anonymous German author, "On the Hitler Movement in Poland," which claimed that all German organizations in Poland had become Nazified and benefited from financial support from Berlin. The article further contended that these organizations had succeeded in drawing in the majority of ethnic German workers in Poland.[18]

More important for the Jews of Poland than what was happening among the country's German minority, however, was Poland's new friendship with Germany and its effect upon Polish public opinion, especially with regard to the Jewish question. Two voices from Wilno, the university professor Władysław Studnicki and the editor of the conservative newspaper *Słowo*, Stanisław Cat-Mackiewicz, represented pro-German opinion among the Poles. The positive attitudes of both men toward Germany were reflected in their antisemitism, which became more extreme from year to year. Studnicki held that Poland could not count on the aid of the Western powers and had therefore to initiate the formation of a bloc with Germany and other countries aimed at eastward expansion, mainly against the Soviet Union.[19] With regard to the Jewish question, he denied the possibility of any solution based on assimilation and favored instead a gradual removal of the Jews from Poland – looking positively upon the spread of Zionist and territorialist ideas among them.[20] He also approved of the strengthening of the economic position of the German minority in the country as a way of helping to bring about the "de-Jewification of Poland (*odżydzenie Polski*)."[21] Mackiewicz also held radically antisemitic views. Whereas, he claimed, he favored the "assimilation of peoples kindred to us," he opposed the assimilation of Jews. Declaring unashamedly, "We are racists (*jesteśmy rasistami*)," he denied a place in Polish society even to Jews who converted to Christianity.[22]

This nexus of pro-German orientation and antisemitism proved problematic for the Endek camp, which as a whole wavered between identification with the Nazi regime's views on the Jewish question and its own view of Germany as Poland's primary enemy.[23] As the principal Endek newspaper wrote, "The Polish national camp will not turn its attention from the Jewish problem in order to concentrate it exclusively upon the great enemy, Hitler."[24] This newspaper also reacted enthusiastically to the idea expressed in the Nazi press in 1936 that it would not be enough if all Jews were to leave Germany; they would also have to be removed from the neighboring countries from which they might threaten Germany in the future.[25] In 1935 the National Party adopted the position that the Hitler regime benefited Poland by its attitude to Jews; therefore Poland had an interest in preserving the regime in Germany, even as it fought the German danger to Poland at the same time. The party held that thanks to Hitler, Poland's two principal enemies, Germany and the Jews, had begun to fight with one another.[26] Various Polish elements even accused Jews residing in the western part of the country, particularly in Silesia, of being a vanguard of German colonization because they spoke German and exhibited German cultural characteristics.[27]

The Jewish press railed against the connection between the government's pro-German policy and the spread of antisemitism in the Sanacja camp. It also saw the radicalization of antisemitism within Endecja as a direct result of its opposition to the government on the one hand and the influence of German antisemitism on the other. *Nasz Przegląd* wrote that "antisemitism in Poland marches hand in hand with the Hitlerite orientation."[28]

In an article written in 1938, Moshe Kleinbaum pointed to the signing of the Polish-German nonaggression pact four years earlier as the beginning of the decline of Polish Jewry; antisemitism had become the bridge spanning the abyss of a thousand years of hatred and mistrust between the Polish and German peoples. He perceived a danger of Nazi penetration into Poland with the help of the ethnic German organizations, who were demanding the right to conduct unrestricted pro-Nazi propaganda throughout the country.[29]

The nonagression pact strengthened Polish-German ties in other areas as well, at times to Jewish detriment. On November 4, 1935, for example, an economic pact was concluded between the two countries, including an agreement on tariffs and trade. During negotiations, the Germans demanded an end to the anti-German boycott being conducted in Poland under Jewish leadership. Agreeing to this demand, authorities took steps against the Jewish Boycott Committee.[30] The Jewish representatives in the Sejm and Senat thus took a stand against the ratification of the pact.[31]

Between March 1936, when Germany remilitarized the Rheinland, and November 1937, when a German-Polish accord was signed concerning the Polish minority in Germany and the German minority in Poland, a certain cooling of relations between the two countries was noticeable. During this time Poland attempted to strengthen its relations with the countries of Western Europe. Rydz-Śmigły signed the Rambouillet Treaty with France in September 1936, which allotted the French credit for the development of Poland's war industry. Beck also visited Paris and London. Although these developments did not signal a serious change in the direction of Poland's foreign policy,[32] Jewish opinion was encouraged by the government's apparent moves to distance itself from Germany and draw nearer the West. The Jewish parliamentary representatives felt freer to warn about the spread of German antisemitism in Poland, which, they claimed, distracted the country's attention from its security needs and especially from German anti-Polish activities in Gdańsk, which might eventually lead to war.[33]

Indeed, beginning in mid-1938 the German minority in Poland began to step up the pace of anti-Polish activities, in opposition to the spirit of the recently concluded agreement between the two countries. Anti-Polish propaganda and penetration by Germans into economic positions in Poland's western provinces and in Wołyń were encouraged by local German consulates.[34] Nevertheless, with Britain and France unwilling to confront Germany's policy of expansion, Poland sought to take advantage of the international crises brought on by that policy in order to reap political and territorial gains.

The Polish government does not appear to have grasped the full significance of Germany's aggressive foreign policy. Thus, for example, it issued no official protest against Germany's annexation of Austria in March 1938. The Polish government also exploited the international situation in order to provoke a minor "Lithuanian crisis," which forced the Lithuanian government to recognize the boundary between the two countries and to establish diplomatic relations with Poland. Beck looked forward to the dismemberment of Czechoslovakia prefigured in the Sudeten crisis. He saw an opportunity to annex a part of Czechoslovakia (the Transolza area) with a large Polish population and anticipated that the establishment of a semi-independent Slovakia and the transfer of Subcarpathian Ruthenia to Hungary would give Poland and Hungary a common border and permit the establishment of a "third European bloc" that could reduce Soviet influence. The Munich pact did not satisfy Polish demands; only after those demands were included in a Polish ultimatum to the Czechoslovak government did Poland annex the Transolza region.[35]

During 1938 the Polish authorities frequently confiscated Polish and Jewish newspapers that criticized Germany, in particular for articles that called attention to the cruelties perpetrated in German concentration camps or that castigated Hitler as a warmongerer.[36] On October 19, for example, the Jewish newspaper *Haynt* was forced to close because of its publication of stories about the persecution of Jews in Germany and its occupied lands. It was permitted to resume publication only on January 24, 1939.[37] Moreover, government censors frequently blacked out reports carried by the Jewish Telegraphic Agency about the persecution of Jews in Germany.[38]

Despite the declared anti-German stance of the Endek National Party, there were instances of cooperation between its members and activists for the German minority, especially in Poland's western provinces.[39] And by 1938 the party leadership displayed a tendency to moderate its avowed anti-German policy. Some voices urged the leadership to revise the party's platform and take a stronger official stance regarding the Nazi regime's anti-semitism.[40] And from the German side, approval began to be expressed of Roman Dmowski as the one who had liberated Poland from Jewish domination, his anti-German orientation notwithstanding.[41]

As earlier, however, organizations of the German minority and German diplomatic offices in Poland took care during this period not to carry on public anti-Jewish agitation.[42] Evidently they believed that hatred of Jews was sufficiently strong in government circles and among the parties of the right without their efforts — even though an anti-Jewish message was carried by these organizations ever since the Nazi rise to power, when the Nazi party assumed absolute control over most of them.[43]

In the 1938 Sejm elections the German minority did not win a single seat. However, two German representatives, Erwin Hasbach and Maksymilian Wambeck, were appointed to the Senat by the Polish president.[44] After all, following the Munich pact and the annexation of the Sudetenland, Poland had the largest German minority in Europe. These representatives and the ethnic German organizations demanded increasing freedom of action in political, economic, and social spheres. Of the approximately 12,000 German citizens living in Poland in 1938, 1800 were active members of the Polish branch of the Nazi Party (NSDAP-Polen), which among other activities, disbursed funds collected by German charities for unemployed ethnic Germans who were Polish citizens and published a magazine in Warsaw called *Idee und Wille*, through which Nazi antisemitic literature was distributed in Poland.[45]

Voices in the Jewish press in Poland once again warned that close Polish-German ties would have deleterious effects upon Poland's entire domestic situation. Funds for antisemitic agitation and the distribution of anti-Jewish propaganda, they reasoned, must be coming from abroad — indicating an unwarranted foreign involvement in Poland's internal affairs. Further, they noted, Polish public figures had been invited as guests of honor to anti-semitic congresses held by Nazi research institutes.[46] Moshe Kleinbaum commented on these effects from another angle: in early 1939 he wrote that the fate of Polish Jewry was bound decisively to the future orientation of Polish foreign policy. Should Poland decide finally to join the bloc of the Western democracies against Hitler, he forecast, the country would proceed along the road to internal democratization as well — a development that would be reflected positively in its policy toward the Jews.[47]

Nevertheless, it does not appear that the Jewish press made a concerted effort to guide Polish Jews as to how they might work against the penetration of German influence into their country. Neither the newspapers nor political and economic leaders called consistently, for example, for a continuation of the anti-German boycott. In fact, reading the Jewish press of 1938–39, one wonders to what extent Jewish leaders really understood the organizational and ideological changes that had taken place among the German minority and the threat those changes posed to the Jews' political and economic status in the country.

During the year leading up to World War II, developing political relations between Poland and Germany continued to influence that status. The Jewish question was raised in high-level conversations between the leaders of the two countries: for example, in Hitler's meeting with the Polish ambassador in Berlin, Józef Lipski, on September 20, 1938, at the height of the Sudeten crisis; in Lipski's discussion with German Foreign Minister Joachim Ribbentrop on October 24–25; and in Beck's conversation with Hitler on January 5, 1939. In these talks and others, the two countries spoke of possibilities for cooperation in fostering the emigration of Jews.

In fact, on October 24, 1938, Ribbentrop presented Lipski with a German proposal for a cooperative "all-inclusive solution (*Gesamtloesung*)" of the various problems confronting the two countries, including cooperation in colonial matters and in the matter of Jewish emigration.[48] In a fashion typical of the relations between the two countries at the time, Ribbentrop made this proposal to Lipski in the course of discussions on specific territorial issues and *after* the German government had already completed preparations for deporting Jewish citizens of Poland, residing in Germany, back to their country of citizenship.[49] The German foreign minister did not shy away from speaking of the Jews as a problem shared by both countries, a problem that Poland would be able to solve on a grand scale only with German cooperation and assistance. Thus his intent was clear: such assistance could be forthcoming as part of an overall solution of the problems on which the two countries disagreed. The German suggestion would make it easier for the Polish government, looking for a way to get rid of its Jews, to give in to German territorial demands regarding Gdańsk and the Polish Corridor. By the same token, the planned deportation of Polish Jews from Germany served as a reminder to the Polish government that, should it prove stubborn in negotiations, Germany had it in its power to make Poland's Jewish problem even worse.[50]

There was an additional aspect to the involvement of the Jewish question in Polish-German relations. In the spring of 1938, shortly after the annexation of Austria to Germany, the Polish government began to express concern for the fate of the Polish petroleum industry in Galicia, many of whose shares were held by Austrian Jews now subject to German jurisdiction as a result of the *Anschluss*. Aware that the German government was in a position to confiscate this Jewish property and thereby acquire control of the Polish petroleum industry, Lipski advised his government to open secret negotiations with Germany whereby Poland would adopt a "passive attitude" toward the expropriation of the property of Polish Jews living in Germany and Austria in return for a German promise not to deport those Jews to Poland and a commitment to turn their shares in Polish oil companies over to the Polish government.[51] The Polish government thus not only showed no concern for the bitter fate of its Jewish citizens residing in Germany but used them as pawns in their attempt to gain control of certain Jewish property in Austria. In the meantime, however, on April 21, 1938, officials of the Gestapo in Berlin had decided, after consultations with the German Foreign Ministry, to demand that all Jewish Polish citizens in the country leave before the new Polish citizenship law went into effect.[52] As a result, the Polish Foreign Ministry, after consultations with the Ministry of Industry and Commerce, decided to act cautiously with regard to revoking the citizenship of Polish Jews in Germany.[53]

Despite this decision, on October 6, 1938, Polish Interior Minister Składkowski issued an order requiring an endorsement to be placed in all Polish passports issued outside of Poland, attesting to their continued validity. The order was published on October 15 and slated to take effect two weeks later. Polish consulates in Germany, however, refused to enter the necessary stamp in the passports of Jews living in that country, thus effectively revoking their citizenship and denying them the possibility of seeking asylum in Poland from the persecutions in Germany.[54]

In response to the Polish actions, the German government told the Polish government on October 26 that if it went through with its plan to deny its Jewish citizens in Germany the right to enter Poland, Germany would react with the immediate expulsion of Polish Jews as a precautionary measure. The Germans demanded a reply from the Poles the same evening.[55] Evidently the Polish Foreign and Interior Ministries were not in complete agreement on this matter. Beck was not happy that the interior minister had allowed only fifteen days from the publication of his order for the new passport regulation to take effect. Nevertheless, he agreed that it was too late to cancel the order, and he recommended that should Polish Jews be deported from Germany, Poland would have to deport German citizens in retaliation.[56] Lipski, in contrast, did not favor such a step, arguing that it would merely exacerbate relations with Germany and perhaps even lead to the expulsion of Poles living in Westphalia. In the end the ambassador's approach was accepted; the passport order would not be rescinded, but no retaliatory measures against German citizens in Poland would be taken.[57]

The same day that Germany had issued its ultimatum to the Polish government, Reinhard Heydrich, a high-ranking official of the Gestapo, issued an order, with the approval of the Foreign Ministry, compelling Jewish citizens of Poland to leave German territory by October 29 at midnight. At the same time instructions were given for the arrest of a large number of Polish Jews and their transfer to the Polish border. These instructions were carried out on October 28 and 29; between 15,000 and 20,000 Jews, mostly heads of families, were taken into custody and allowed to bring with them a small amount of hand luggage and the sum of 10 *RM* in cash. Most were forced across the Polish border, even though the Polish authorities refused to admit them. It was agreed, however, to postpone the implementation of the passport regulation until November 15.[58] Some 5,500 Jews were brought to the border at Katowice, another 2,500 to Chojnice, and some 6,500 to the town of Zbąszyń.[59] In Katowice the provincial governor, Michał Grażyński, extended assistance to the deportees, and those who had relatives or friends in Poland were given railroad tickets and allowed to proceed further. Similar assistance was given to the Jews in Chojnice, where Jewish organizations also extended aid. In both places, moreover, the local population gave succor to the deportees, and the attitude of the local police was a correct one. In Zbąszyń, however, the situation was different: there the Polish army erected a tent camp on the border and did not allow the deported Jews to proceed.[60]

As decided earlier, the Polish authorities did not take any immediate action in response to the German move,[61] but began on November 2 to negotiate with the Germans over the status of the remaining Jewish Polish citizens in Germany and of those who had already been deported. These negotiations were suspended, however, on November 10, when the seventeen-year-old son of two of the deportees at Zbąszyń, Herszel Grynszpan, took revenge for his parents' plight by assassinating a German diplomat in Paris. This action, in addition to causing a break in German-Polish talks, also provided the excuse for the infamous *Kristallnacht* pogrom.[62]

Negotiations were resumed in December and led to the signing, on January 20, 1939, of an agreement by which the deported Jews would remain in

Poland but be allowed to return to Germany temporarily prior to July 31, 1939 to liquidate their affairs. The Polish government further obligated itself to admit the wives and children of the deportees to Poland before that date. In return, the German government agreed that deportees would be allowed to remove from Germany personal possessions and equipment essential for reestablishing themselves – provided they had been in their possession prior to October 26, 1938. The two governments also agreed to set up a joint account for liquidating assets that would not be transferred to Poland, mainly real estate.[63] The deterioration in relations between the two countries, however, impeded the execution of this agreement. In July 1939, some 3,000-4,000 women and children still awaited an entry visa to Poland,[64] and Jewish Polish citizens who remained in Germany often found the doors of Polish consulates closed to them.[65]

According to German ambassador Moltke, the response of the Polish press to the expulsion of the Jews from Germany to Poland was generally mild, although it expressed reservations over the action of the German government. Moltke believed, however, that Polish public opinion displayed a harsher attitude toward Germany, both on humanitarian grounds and because of mounting anti-German feeling. The German ambassador claimed that the Jews in Poland were taking advantage of the situation in order "to galvanize support vocally" and to step up the organization of aid activities for the refugees.[66]

Składkowski regarded the deportation of Polish Jews from Germany as one sign of growing tension between the two countries.[67] He also justified detaining the Jews in the camp at Zbąszyń for security reasons, because Germany had allegedly planted Nazi agents with the deportees. He noted, however, that the local population had received instructions to assist the Jewish refugees.[68]

The Jewish community immediately organized aid for the deportees. A Central Relief Committee was formed in Warsaw, headed by Moshe Schorr, Rafael Szereszewski, and Henryk Rosmarin. The journalist Samuel Wolkowicz was dispatched by the Committee to Zbąszyń, where, together with the Jewish community of Poznań, he tried to create a framework for life in the camp. In the Sejm, on January 12, 1939, Sommerstein protested the forcible confinement of Jews to the camp, but to no avail.[69] Only after a period of time was the Joint Distribution Committee able to arrange for the necessary supplies to be brought to Zbąszyń. Meanwhile, other Jewish organizations set up health and educational facilities.[70]

The Bund, together with Jewish trade unions, organized a special Workers' Committee (*Komitet Robotniczy*) to assist the deportees. Representatives of Polish workers also participated in the effort.[71] In addition, the World Jewish Congress intervened with the Polish ambassadors in Paris and Washington, demanding that the Jews in Zbąszyń be permitted to enter Poland. A representative of the Congress, Maurice Perlzweig, even went to Warsaw to speak with government officials about the situation.[72]

Perlzweig was assured that the Congress's demands would soon receive positive action. However, in mid-May 1939 3,500 Jews remained in the Zbąszyń camp, living in extremely poor conditions. After seven months, the resources of the Central Relief Committee had been depleted, and little new support was forthcoming. The ominous political developments of mid-1939 served to distract the attention of the Jewish community, and in any case the Polish government forbade further nationwide fundraising activities on the deportees' behalf to preclude competition with its own fundraising efforts for defense against what appeared to be an increasingly probable German air attack.[73] In any case, shortly thereafter the government permitted internees who could prove they had work in Poland or reasonable chances to emigrate to leave the camp.[74] In early June hundreds of these Jews demonstrated outside of the headquarters of the Relief Committee demanding immediate aid for those who had remained behind and threatening a hunger strike. The 1,800 deportees who had been able to proceed to Warsaw also had a most difficult time.[75]

Meanwhile, in May 1939, the German government issued an order that all Jewish Polish citizens remaining in Germany without a valid Polish passport would have to leave by July 31 or face forcible deportation.[76] Even in early June, however, additional groups of Jewish Polish citizens were sent across the border, only to be turned back by Polish border guards.[77] The Jewish press in Poland demanded that the Polish government take reprisal measures against German citizens in the country in order to prevent further deportations.[78]

In the face of this serious situation, the Zionist parties together with Agudas Yisroel and the Folkspartay convened a special meeting in Warsaw on June 26. They resolved to enlist public sympathy for the deportees' plight, to request that all Jewish communities contribute to the relief effort, and to demand a special allocation from the government for assistance to its recently uprooted citizens.[79] The government, however, failed to respond; the camp at Zbąszyń was not liquidated until a few days before the outbreak of war.[80]

On balance, it may be said that the Polish government contributed directly to the sufferings of the deportees, both through its transparent attempts to revoke the citizenship of the Polish Jews in Germany and through its refusal to admit the Jews into Poland once they had been deported. Not only did the Polish government fail to defend the rights of its Jewish citizens living in Germany; it actually indicated its willingness to see their property confiscated, in the hope that it could profit from their tragic situation.

On the other hand, as on so many other occasions, Polish Jewry was not prepared to respond to the crisis as it developed. Despite unquestionable feelings of Jewish solidarity and a proper organization of aid activities in many local communities, it was unable to marshal sufficient resources to mitigate the deportees' suffering except in the short run. The situation demonstrated once again that the Jews of Poland were unaware of the political dimensions of events and lacked a capable leadership to present their demands for assistance effectively before the government and awaken Jews in the country and abroad to the ramifications of the situation. In the end, the deportees remained dependent upon the good will of a few local Jewish communities that were themselves in tight financial straits. Their plight was not enough to impel the Jews of Poland to close ranks.

Developments in German-Polish relations also affected Polish Jewry less directly by influencing the politics of the Ukrainian minority. By 1937 many Ukrainians began to express disappointment with the results of the normalization policy of the previous two years,[81] and in UNDO circles the demand for territorial autonomy was heard with increasing frequency. No doubt this change was encouraged in no small measure by the Nazi propaganda penetrating into Poland, the influence of which was not limited to the German minority alone.[82] At the UNDO convention held on January 4–5, 1938 in Lwów, resolutions were approved calling for an autonomous Ukrainian territorial government, parliament, and militia; for changes in Polish electoral procedure so as to allow entirely free selection of candidates; for an end to settlement by Poles from the western parts of the country in the east; and for the establishment of a Ukrainian university in Lwów.[83]

The final blow to the normalization policy came with the beginning of German territorial expansion in 1938. A large portion of Poland's Ukrainian population now saw in Germany the force that would eventually permit the attainment of Ukrainian national goals. On May 7, 1938 the UNDO Central Committee approved a political proclamation stating explicitly that the normalization policy had not achieved the desired results and that Polish officials had demonstrated opposition to the development of a Ukrainian national life. The party repeated the call for territorial autonomy for the Ukrainian people.[84]

UNDO's attitude toward Poland became even more hostile in the wake of the Munich agreement, following the establishment of an autonomous Ukrainian regime under German tutelage in Subcarpathian Ruthenia. While Ukrainians in Poland looked upon this autonomous territory as a sort of Ukrainian Piedmont,[85] the German government saw it as a bargaining chip in its relations with Poland. In December 1938 the German press began an open and harsh propaganda campaign in favor of the establishment of a Greater Ukraine encompassing, eventually, parts of Poland, the Soviet Union, and Romania.[86] The UNDO leader Wasyl Mudryj told the German ambassador in Warsaw that he no longer believed in the possibility of a Polish-Ukrainian understanding and that his party was placing its hopes in the German government for support for its positions.[87]

This new Ukrainian attitude contributed to Poland's efforts to bring about the annexation of Subcarpathian Ruthenia to Hungary. On October 24, 1938, Lipski asked Ribbentrop to approve such an annexation, on the grounds that Subcarpathian Ruthenia was serving as a base for Communist propaganda.[88] And indeed, in February 1939, after German plans for the complete dismemberment of Czechoslovakia had been finalized and Hungary had formally joined the Axis, Germany decided to append the territory to Hungary, eliminating the Ukrainian autonomy that it had established only a few months earlier.[89] This development caused great disappointment among the Ukrainians of Poland, which the Polish government attempted to exploit. In April 1939 Składkowski met with Mudryj and Luckyj about improving mutual relations, promising that in the future the Ukrainians of Poland would receive autonomy.[90]

The development of the Polish government's relations with the Ukrainian minority exerted great influence upon the attitudes of both parties toward the Jewish question. Heretofore, whatever opposition UNDO leaders demonstrated to antisemitism stemmed primarily from their concern that, as a precedent, it would justify anti-Ukrainian discrimination in the future. This appears to have been the principal reason for the stance of the Ukrainian Sejm deputies in the debate over kosher slaughtering.[91] Similarly, following the pogrom in Brześć in May 1937, Stefan Baran published an article in the Ukrainian newspaper *Dilo* entitled "After the Jews Will Come Our Turn."[92] In the matter of ghetto benches, Ukrainian and Belorussian students at Wilno University expressed solidarity with their Jewish classmates, fearing that a "day without Jews" might lead eventually to a "day without Ukraini-ans."[93] However, UNDO maintained that the Ukrainians favored separation in the universities and argued that the Jewish struggle against segregated lecture halls was evidence of their strong tendency to seek full assimilation and to push into foreign surroundings.[94]

Articles in the Ukrainian press in summer of 1937 further illuminated Ukrainian attitudes toward the Jewish question. One of the leaders of UNDO, Włodzimierz Kuźmowycz, turned directly to the Polish Jewish community in the pages of *Dilo* with a proposal for political cooperation between the two minorities. In such cooperation he saw the creation of a potential political force constituting perhaps one third of Poland's popula-tion.[95] It may be, however, that this attitude reflected disappointment with the policy of normalization of relations with the Polish government and in-direct warning to the government and the recently-formed OZON to recon-sider their policy toward the Ukrainians, rather than a true desire for close cooperation with the Jews. This conclusion is suggested by another article in *Dilo* that same month, stating that "our approach to the Jews stems from clear political calculation and cultural humanism, so that under the present circumstances we view them as a natural ally." The article declared further that the Ukrainians would fight against violent antisemitism but would not give up their economic struggle and would defend themselves "against the poison of Communism, which the Jews are injecting into our village life."[96]

This distinction between anti-Jewish violence and a nonviolent eco-nomic campaign against the Jews echoed Składkowski's *owszem* speech of June 1936. Just as that speech had been ineffective in restraining radical ex-pressions of antisemitism on the part of some Poles, the same policy was unlikely to provide a serious basis for cooperation between Jews and Ukrainians.

In addition to accusing Jews of spreading Communism, UNDO spokes-men charged them with strengthening the process of Polonization in terri-tories with a Ukrainian majority. They also maintained that in the Ukrain-ian territories ruled by the Soviet Union, Jews had long served as agents of Russification. Nevertheless, they refused an Endek offer of Polish-Ukrainian cooperation against the Jews.[97] Concerned about the encouragement the government gave to Polish merchants from the western part of the country to move eastward, Ukrainians understood that if such movement grew stronger, it would eventually injure Ukrainians no less than Jews, both polit-ically and economically.[98]

From the Jewish perspective, Ukrainian offers of cooperation complicated

Jewish relations with the government. In July 1937, Moshe Kleinbaum rebutted the argument, widespread in Polish circles, that the common struggle of Jews and Ukrainians for equal rights undermined the interests of the Polish state by demonstrating that the two minorities had opposing ideas regarding both domestic and foreign policy.[99] In his opinion Jews were oriented, as it were, along an axis joining London, Paris, and Washington; and in Poland itself their struggle was not with the Polish people but only with certain Polish political parties. He believed that the Jewish minority, lacking a territorial base, needed to ally itself with democratic political forces in the country working against the regime in power. In contrast, Ukrainian policy had a territorial goal — the establishment of an independent Eastern Ukraine with its capital at Kiev. This difference, he believed, made it difficult for Jews and Ukrainians to adopt a common political position. Nevertheless, he saw no basis for Ukrainian-Jewish conflict. He proposed that instead of two sides of the Polish-Ukrainian-Jewish triangle fighting against the third, the democratic elements of all three needed to struggle together for the realization of the constitution's promise of equality.

By the end of 1938, in the wake of the Munich accords, an increase in pro-German tendencies among UNDO put a stop to all declarations of Ukrainian-Jewish cooperation by party leaders. Ironically, this development appears to have resulted in a moderation of the Polish government's anti-Jewish drive. German ambassador Moltke reported to Berlin that "Poland cannot operate simultaneously against both Ukrainians and Jews" and that therefore the enactment of the anti-Jewish legislation prepared by OZON had been put off.[100] Moshe Kleinbaum shared this view.[101] To his mind, the mounting Polish-German tension had made it necessary for the government, and eventually even for OZON, to oppose the attempts of Sejm deputies Kienć and Stoch to introduce anti-Jewish bills. Still, he argued, the situation was far from what it should be: unity based on common perception of a mutual German threat rather than restrained aggression in pursuing what remained an anti-Jewish policy.

The effects of the latest developments in Polish-German and Polish-Ukrainian relations upon the future of Polish Jewry was also the subject of a memorandum received toward the end of 1938 by the chairman of the European office of the Joint Distribution Committee, Morris Troper.[102] The report argued that these developments created a favorable conjuncture for the Jews of Poland but that in the absence of a Jewish political leadership worthy of the name there was no possibility of exploiting the situation to strengthen the Jewish position. It criticized the leaders of the various Jewish parties sharply, calling them "provincial people" who were not capable of evaluating the internal situation in Poland in the context of developments in the international diplomatic arena. It held further that the Jews would soon have to take a clear stand with regard to the Ukrainian demand for territorial autonomy; should they remain neutral, they would merely incur the wrath of both Ukrainians and Poles. The author of the report recommended that the Jews side with the Polish government, not only because the Ukrainians were receiving support from Germany but because he believed that, in the absence of a reliable local Jewish leadership, Jewish organizations in Britain and the United States would have to take over direction of the fight for Jewish equality in the country. They could do so effectively, he argued, only by making the case before Polish diplomatic representatives abroad that Jews were the only national minority in Poland that remained loyal to the state.

In reality, the author of this report was only partially correct. Many Jewish leaders in Poland did in fact understand the situation in the context of international diplomatic developments, and the Jewish press was full of cogent analyses of the implications of the changes in Polish-German relations for the Jews. However, none of these analyses convinced them to form a unified political representation capable of conducting a single, independent Jewish policy. After the Munich crisis and the deterioration of Polish-German relations, there was no possibility for Polish Jews to adopt any position other than one of complete loyalty to Poland. And in such a situation, that loyalty had to be unconditional.

9
Jewish Emigration: Efforts and Realities

As we have seen, after Piłsudski's death the Polish government lacked widespread public support. Although Poland's economic situation began to improve substantially after 1935, rural areas were still in much distress, and their problems demanded solution. However, instead of introducing a much-needed agrarian reform, the government found it more convenient to divert the public's attention by focusing concern on the Jewish question. Its principal solution to that problem was mass emigration of Jews from the country — which it advocated both domestically, to Poles and Jews alike, and internationally, in various international fora.[1] Unfortunately, it raised this idea to the level of top priority precisely at the time when the gates of potential destinations for the intended emigrants were almost entirely shut.

Nevertheless, the government continued to pursue this solution. It also used the Jewish problem as a lever for justifying its demands for overseas colonies and mandatory territories.[2] On August 2, 1936 it issued an official announcement stating that an answer to the Polish Jewish question would be possible only after Poland was awarded colonies in virtually unsettled territories in South Africa and South America and calling upon the League of Nations to take up this issue "at the soonest possible moment."[3] Indeed, in their reports during this time, French diplomatic representatives in Warsaw and Berlin voiced their suspicion that Poland was coordinating its colonial demands with Germany and that the Jewish issue was serving merely as an excuse to raise those demands.[4] Thus for the first time Poland presented Jewish emigration as an international problem demanding consideration by the League, the Western powers, international Jewish organizations, and Jewish financiers. In doing so, it deviated from the approach taken by previous Polish governments, which had held that the Polish Jewish question was an internal Polish matter in which outside elements had no right to interfere. This principle had been invoked as recently as September 1934, in Beck's abrogation of Poland's obligations under the Minorities Treaty of 1919.[5]

In taking this approach, the government tried to pressure the colonial powers into opening the gates of their colonies for mass settlement by Jews. However, not only did these demands not bring about a liberalization in the admission of Jews into these territories; they generally resulted in heightened immigration restrictions. And to the extent that international bodies attempted to find destinations to which Jews could emigrate, they were generally concerned with the problem of Jewish refugees from Nazi Germany and not with the Polish Jewish problem.

At the time, the primary realistic destination for Jewish emigration from Poland was British Mandatory Palestine, but in 1936 the British government reduced the number of entry visas given to Jews. In response, the Polish government tried both to induce Britain to rescind the immigration restrictions and to locate alternative destinations.[6] In international fora, it pointed out that their campaign for Jewish emigration was predicated not on antisemitism but on objective social and economic factors.[7] To make its case more convincing, it endeavored to enlist the assistance of international Jewish organizations such as the World Jewish Congress and the Jewish Agency for Palestine. To that end, government officials met in Geneva during the second half of 1936 with Nahum Goldmann, the representative of both organizations, and suggested the possibility of settling Polish Jews on the island of Madagascar. Although the Poles suggested that the World Jewish Congress approach the French government, which controlled the island, about this possibility,[8] they did not wait for the WJC to do so. When Beck stopped in Paris on his way from Geneva to Warsaw in October 1936, he spoke with French prime minister Leon Blum about the Madagascar possibility. Blum agreed to permit a Polish delegation to visit the island to determine the feasibility of the idea.[9]

Accordingly, in late 1936 the Polish government appointed an investigating committee consisting of Mieczysław Lepecki, vice-president of the International Society for Colonization; Leon Alter, director of the Jewish Emigrant Aid Society of Poland; and the agronomist Shlomo Dyk. The committee departed for Madagascar in 1937 and returned to Poland thirteen weeks later.[10] Its findings were announced in December 1937: only the central area of Madagascar was suitable for "white settlement," to be based mainly upon agriculture, and even its suitability depended upon prior development of transportation and the creation of satisfactory sanitary conditions.[11]

Over all, the Polish government maintained that Palestine was the most realistic place for resettlement of masses of Polish Jews. Thus it sought to assist the Jewish Agency to further Zionist political demands and increase Jewish immigration into the country. Polish representatives spoke about the matter in the League of Nations and with the British government — not as a purely Middle Eastern problem but also as a domestic concern of Poland and other Central and East European countries with large Jewish populations.[12] Aware of the prospect of drastic reductions in the number of Jews allowed into Palestine, Polish ambassador Raczyński in London was instructed as early as April 1936 to press the British government not to introduce such reductions, so that Poland would not have to raise the problem with the Political Committee of the League of Nations.[13] Raczyński, however, was not successful in this effort.[14]

In general, Polish public opinion was widely supportive of the government's efforts, seeing in its Jewish emigration goal an essential step toward improving Poland's economic and social conditions and toward mitigating antisemitic pressures. Although some arrived at this conclusion through rational analysis, for others it was simply an expression of their hatred of Jews. The latter, influenced by Endek propaganda, believed that Jews should be forced to quit the country en masse through stepped up anti-Jewish discrimination, intensification of the boycott, antisemitic legislation, and physical violence. The British embassy in Warsaw, which frequently reported about the Polish public's attitudes toward the emigration question – and especially toward Zionism and Palestine – noted in September 1936 that emigration was the only solution to the Jewish question that found wide support among Polish political parties of different orientations. According to the report, the only disagreement was over the methods by which emigration should be encouraged. Endecja did not recoil from programs for expelling the Jews from Poland altogether, whereas supporters of the government argued that Jews merely posed a barrier to Poland's national economic progress and therefore had a duty to leave the country en masse. For this reason, the report indicated, government circles were supportive of Zionism.[15]

These attitudes were reflected in the Polish press, where the stance of Endek newspapers on the issue did not differ substantially from that of Sanacja organs; all enthusiastically supported the drive to increase the exit of Jews from the country to all possible destinations, and all welcomed Jewish-initiated plans for emigration. In August 1936 the newspaper of the National Party wrote, "If Jews do not wish to leave Poland and prefer to convert it into "Judeo-Polonia," then they must be forced to do so by political means."[16] In another issue the newspaper claimed that "in order for the Jews to leave it is not enough to locate destinations for them; it is necessary . . . to revoke the Jews' political rights and to take away their livelihood in order to make them interested in emigrating."[17] By the same token the quasi-governmental organ *Gazeta Polska* wondered why the majority of the Jewish public opposed emigration plans, blaming the Jewish leadership for this opposition. The newspaper expressed the opinion that Jewish emigration should be funded by the same wealthy Jews throughout the world who assisted Jewish immigration to Palestine.[18]

The emigration concept was also supported at the third congress of the Peasant Party, held in December 1935, where resolutions called for granting equal rights to all national minorities in the country. However, they stated specifically that, in contrast to the Slavic minorities, Jews were to be regarded as a foreign element in Poland. The Jewish question was to be solved, according to the congress resolutions, by their mass emigration to Palestine and to other territories that would be made available to them through international agreement.[19]

In light of the decline in their economic situation, the economic boycott against them, the discriminatory policy conducted by the government, and the mounting agitation and violence against them from 1935 on, more and more Jews, losing hope that their situation would improve and fearing what the morrow might bring, were indeed ready to leave the country. However, there were few places for them to go. Almost all Jewish emigration after 1935 was directed overseas; there was virtually no migration of Polish Jews to other countries on the European continent.[20] France and Belgium, the primary destinations of Polish emigrants during this period, required only agricultural and industrial laborers and mineworkers, occupations in which few Jews were involved.[21]

The internal Jewish debate over the issue was a furious one: should Jewish organizations actively oppose the government's encouragement of emigration or should they take advantage of the government's willingness to help Jews find suitable sites for resettlement. On one side stood the parties that vigorously opposed all "emigrationist" propaganda — the Bund, Agudas Yisroel, the Folkspartay, and the assimilationists. On the other stood the Zionist parties. However, even within the Zionist camp, which had begun losing influence among the Jewish masses, there was considerable disunity. Factions fought with one another over the question of whether to accept Polish governmental assistance on behalf of increased immigration allowances to Palestine without first being assured that the Jews' status as equal citizens of the Polish state would not be impaired by cooperating with an emigration scheme. They were also divided over how to relate to the government's interest in possible territories for Jewish resettlement other than Palestine, with many questioning whether cooperation in this direction would not be tantamount to admitting the bankruptcy of the Zionist idea. Some worried that their pursuit of an "emigrationist" policy, together with the government and Jewish organizations abroad, in the absence of realistic possibilities for mass Jewish resettlement, would lead only to heightened antisemitic agitation in the country and in the end strengthen the hand of the regime's enemies on the right. As a result, many Zionist circles adopted an "antiemigrationist" posture and tried to avoid giving any appearance of cooperating with the government.[22]

At the center of the Zionist debate in 1936 stood two towering figures in the movement – Yitshak Gruenbaum, at the time already a member of the Jewish Agency Executive in Jerusalem, and Vladimir (Ze'ev) Jabotinsky, leader of the Revisionist Party's New Zionist Organization, which had seceded from the World Zionist Organization and the Jewish Agency one year earlier.[23] On August 2, 1936 Gruenbaum, on a visit to Poland, summoned a press conference for Polish journalists in Warsaw to present his view of the situation in light of recent developments. In his opinion, antisemitism was becoming a major force in Poland; many Poles, including veteran officers, were struggling to establish businesses and looked upon Jewish peddler stands as desirable objects to take over. Because of the growing pressure upon Jewish sources of livelihood, the Jewish masses would have to leave Poland for Palestine sooner or later.[24]

Gruenbaum's remarks elicited sharp responses in the Jewish press, not only in the newspapers of the Bund and Agudas Yisroel, but even in Zionist publications. *Chwila*, for example, pointed out that antisemitic newspapers supported Gruenbaum's statements while Jewish public opinion in Poland opposed them.[25] Similarly, *Nasz Przegląd* noted that the Endek organ *Warszawski Dziennik Narodowy* gave prominence to Gruenbaum's remarks.[26] The Bund newspaper, *Folkstsaytung*, was even stronger in its criticism. It reminded its readers that in 1927, during a visit to the United States, Gruenbaum, at that time a Sejm deputy, had declared that there were "a million superfluous Jews in Poland." Such words could only fan the flames of antisemitism; in fact, they suggested that antisemitism was actually the fault of the Jews.[27] Indeed, the organ of the Folkspartay, *Folkistishe Bleter*, expressed the opinion that Jewish spokesmen who declared that Jews ought to leave the country were responsible in no small measure for the increasing antisemitism in Poland.[28]

Gruenbaum, however, stuck to his position, insisting that in light of Poland's economic situation, Jews ought to publicly acknowledge the necessity of emigration. He believed, in opposition to his critics, that such an acknowledgment would actually strengthen their political and legal status in the country. In any case, he argued, Jews were in full agreement with the

Polish government in this matter, and they should not be taken aback by the thought of cooperation.[29]

Far greater than the controversy over Gruenbaum's remarks, however, was the one caused a month later by the publication of Jabotinsky's so-called Evacuation Plan, published as a supplement to the conservative Polish newspaper *Czas* in its edition of September 8, 1936. The supplement contained articles by Jabotinsky, Jan Krakowski (a pseudonym for Jan Bader, a Revisionist leader from Kraków), and Josef Schechtman, chairman of the branch of the New Zionist Organization presidium established the previous June, as well as a statement of support for the program from the editors of *Czas*.[30] Jabotinsky wrote that tremendous pressures upon the Jews were endangering their existence, pressures that could be grouped under the name of "the antisemitism of objective facts." Jews thus required, in his words, control over "one corner of the world, in Palestine," where they could undertake "settlement under international supervision." He spoke of the need to "organize systematic mass emigration of Jews from all countries in which they live, a true exodus of those Jews who wish to leave." One and a half million Jews needed to leave Europe over the next ten years, he declared, especially from Poland, Romania, Subcarpathian Ruthenia, Austria, the Baltic States, and the Third Reich. These Jews would form the basis for the establishment of a Jewish state in Palestine on both sides of the Jordan River.[31]

The day after the appearance of the *Czas* supplement, Jabotinsky called a press conference and outlined the details of his program. Of the million and a half Jews whose emigration he sought, 750,000 were to come from Poland — 75,000 each year for the next ten years. These emigrants were to be between the ages of 20–39, the primary childbearing years, so that the loss of population would be extensive and lasting. His goal, he declared, was to reduce the number of Jews in a given country to the point where that country would no longer be interested in further reducing the number. This goal was what he meant when he spoke of "evacuating" the Jews of Europe. Additionally, he suggested that it might be necessary to transfer the mandate over Palestine from Britain to countries more interested in accomplishing this end.[32]

Jabotinsky remained in Poland until November 10, responding to heavy criticism of his program from the Jewish public — which was particularly upset by his use of the term "evacuation."[33] In an interview in *Nasz Przegląd*, Jabotinsky explained that he called only for voluntary emigration, not expulsion. His program did not mean that he was prepared to forget the demand for equal rights for Jews in the countries from which they would leave. In fact, he stressed, he would refuse to negotiate with antisemitic governments, which he defined as those that, in their constitutions, had abrogated the principle of civic equality for Jews.[34]

Even before he announced the evacuation plan publicly, Jabotinsky had been in close contact with the Polish authorities, seeking to enlist their assistance in furthering his program. In London he had discussed the idea with Raczyński, and in June and July 1936, in Warsaw and in Geneva, he had met twice with Beck. In addition, a representative of the New Zionist Organization, Jacob de Haas, discussed the idea with the Polish ambassador in Washington, Jerzy Potocki. The government followed up on these earlier contacts once the evacuation program was made public. The day after the appearance of the *Czas* supplement, Michał Łubieński, director of the Polish foreign ministry, invited senior government officials to a meeting at which Jabotinsky explained his plan.[35] On September 11 Jabotinsky met with Prime Minister Składkowski and asked that Poland intervene in the international arena on behalf of mass Jewish immigration to Palestine. In addition, though, he requested that the government issue a simultaneous statement indicating that it intended to scrupulously preserve the Jews' equal rights.[36]

Shortly after these developments, at the session of the League of Nations in Geneva, Beck spoke with Nahum Goldmann about cooperation over emigration. Goldmann insisted, however, that any such cooperation by the Jewish Agency or the World Jewish Congress was conditional upon the government not having any contact with Jabotinsky or his "fantastic program." Goldmann argued that the Revisionists lacked broad public support in Poland, as indicated by the latest elections to the Warsaw Jewish community board, and that by keeping company with them, as it were, the government was reducing its prestige among both Jews and non-Jews. Beck replied that the Polish government did not intend to show the Revisionists any preference over the Jewish Agency.[37] In the meantime, having become acutely aware of the internal conflicts dividing the two rival Zionist organizations, Polish government representatives at the League of Nations, including Deputy Minister of Industry and Commerce Adam Rose and the Poles' permanent delegate to the League, Tytus Komarnicki, spoke of the need for the League to locate alternative territories to Palestine for Jewish resettlement — something that neither of the rival Zionist groups desired.[38]

Meanwhile, the overwhelming majority of the Jewish press continued to criticize Jabotinsky's program, discounting his assurances that his concept of "evacuation" implied only voluntary and not forced emigration and that he did not intend to renounce the struggle for equal rights. Jewish newspapers found it significant that precisely those Polish newspapers most hostile to the Jews, especially those associated with Endecja, greeted the evacuation idea most warmly and defended Jabotinsky against his critics.[39] Even the Warsaw Yiddish paper *Moment*, to which Jabotinsky had been a major contributor since 1932, joined in the attack.[40]

Bitterly disappointed by this response, Jabotinsky sensed that perhaps Polish Jewry was losing interest in the Palestine idea altogether.[41] In actuality, however, his critics were correct: Jabotinsky did not regard the Jewish struggle for equal rights with great seriousness. Nor did he place any great hope in the country's liberal forces. His evacuation plan appeared to him far more realistic than the hopeless effort to preserve a future for the Jews in Poland; in his opinion the Jews of Eastern Europe were on the edge of a catastrophe and ought to have looked upon his program with seriousness if not with enthusiasm. Most of all, he felt he had failed to convey to Polish Jews the gravity of their situation.[42]

Assimilationist circles attacked the idea of Jewish emigration from Poland with particular ferocity, even though they were aware of the recent radicalization of antisemitism in the country. They were especially critical of Jabotinsky's evacuation plan, which they viewed as altogether fanciful. The organization of Jewish war veterans believed that the interest of the Jews would best be served by strengthening their civic and patriotic sense rather than by pursuing programs to "cleanse" the country of them. In their opinion, Poland needed to know that in case of war the Jews could provide 350,000 soldiers, not that they wanted to leave.[43]

Many Jewish critics of the emigration concept did not differentiate between Gruenbaum's and Jabotinsky's approaches. *Folkstsaytung*, for example, wrote that both expressed the basic Zionist idea that Jews were foreigners everywhere. No wonder, the Bund newspaper declared, the calls of both Zionist spokesmen were "warmly received" in Endek circles.[44] The only difference between them, according to the Bund, was that whereas Gruenbaum wished to carry out his exodus quietly, the Revisionists thought it necessary to raise their voices in order to obtain their final goal – a Jewish state. Both men, however, implied that the Poles were the sole owners of the Polish state.[45]

Gruenbaum himself explained the difference between his approach and Jabotinsky's. Whereas he claimed to advocate the emigration of only the excess Jewish population, Jabotinsky spoke about liquidating Polish Jewry altogether. Although the newspaper *Haynt* accepted Gruenbaum's distinction,[46] in truth, if Jabotinsky is to be taken at his word that he did not wish to see Jews forced out of Poland, the two positions were not substantially different. In the diagnosis of the situation of Polish Jewry, the pessimistic prognosis, and the suggested cure through Zionist migration, they essentially agreed. Only in the manner in which they presented their analyses did they differ.

To be sure, the two represented different interpretations of the Zionist idea, reflecting both the movement's goals and the manner in which they were to be obtained. However, many of Gruenbaum's disciples apparently felt their master had strayed from the proper approach to the key problem of emigration, and they dissented from his position. Indeed, many Zionists believed that cooperating with the Polish government would strengthen the government's efforts to separate the issue of Jewish emigration from the general problem of overpopulation in the country and undermine the Jews' status as equal citizens of the state. They worried that public declarations by Jewish leaders about the need for Jews to leave Poland en masse, however much they might serve to dramatize the difficulty of the Jewish position, constituted an acceptance of the Jews' inferior status in the country. Further, they felt that such declarations were especially dangerous when there did not appear to be any realistic possibility of carrying out a mass emigration program.

Zionists also had difficulty determining where they stood with regard to mass Jewish emigration to destinations other than Palestine.[47] A controversy developed when word began to circulate that Nahum Goldmann and a Zionist leader in France, Marc Jarblum, were holding discussions with the French authorities about Madagascar as a site for Jewish colonization, in accordance with Beck's suggestions along those lines. Goldmann claimed that the World Jewish Congress was merely investigating a theoretical possibility, without taking any stand on the idea one way or the other.[48] In the name of the Jewish Agency, Yitshak Gruenbaum explained to Beck in October 1936 that previous efforts to resettle Jews, especially in agricultural settlements, had been successful only in Palestine, because of the motivating force of Zionist ideology. Jewish migration to other locations had generally gravitated toward industrialized countries. The Jewish Agency, he stated, had no objection to migrations to new sites, as long as their initiators did not approach Jewish individuals and institutions with requests for financial assistance in carrying them out.[49]

For the Bund, too, the idea of emigration presented problems. One of the party's publications stated that the Bund did not oppose emigration per se; it merely objected to the attempt to present emigration as the solution to all of the problems confronting Polish Jewry.[50] Such propaganda diverted Jews' attention from their immediate problems and made them "passive and apolitical." Still, at Bund conferences during 1936, the emigration issue was hotly debated, with many representatives demanding a change in the party's position.[51] It was especially important to Bund leaders that PPS identify with their stand on the issue; for this reason the Bund's daily newspaper was furious with the editor of the PPS organ, Mieczysław Niedziałkowki, for expressing support in a newspaper interview for Jewish emigration and the establishment of a Jewish national home in Palestine. The Bund newspaper reminded Niedziałkowski that "the Zionist movement has taken it upon itself to settle people in a home that is for the most part occupied by others, in order to take control of all of it with the assistance of the house superintendent."[52]

The Communist Party of Poland approached the Bund in November 1936 with a proposal to collaborate in fighting antisemitism and the evacuation program. This proposal was connected with KPP's demand to place these items on the agenda of the Congress of Jewish Trade Unions, slated for December 1936.[53] The Jewish Communists argued, especially at that time, that the leaders of the Zionists and Agudas Yisroel in Poland were merely helping the regime realize its desire to get rid of the Jews and send them to various colonies; neither party, they claimed, was advancing the war against antisemitsm and "the pogrom government."[54]

The Bund hoped to exploit the increasing restrictions upon the entry of Jewish emigrants from Poland into other countries in general and the drastic diminution of entry permits into Palestine in particular in order to increase its strength significantly. The tremendous gap between the political and economic pressures being placed upon Jews to leave the country and the absence of suitable destinations convinced many that the Zionists simply did not have a practical way of dealing constructively with their immediate situation. This feeling, together with the negative impression created among many Jews by the suggestion of certain Zionist leaders that they should cooperate with the hostile Polish government, contributed substantially, without a doubt, to the Bund's victories in communal and municipal elections during the years before the outbreak of war.

Some of the complexities of Zionist cooperation with the government were revealed during the negotiations over the so-called Clearing Agreement in

1936. Zionist spokesmen wished to enter into an arrangement with the Polish authorities by which Jews emigrating to Palestine would be allowed to transfer currency there for the purpose of investment. They also sought to obtain favorable regulations for taking monies held by various Zionist funds in Poland out of the country. A Jewish Agency delegation headed by Yitshak Gruenbaum proposed the establishment of a corporation to be known as the Society for Strengthening Polish-Palestinian Commerce, which would serve as a clearing house for payments for Polish exports to Palestine and for currency transfers between the two countries. The Jewish Agency tried to convince the Polish authorities to offer Polish merchandise for sale in Palestine at a discount, so that it could compete effectively with imports from other countries.[55]

The Polish government, however, made its acceptance of the Jewish Agency's proposal conditional upon certain extraneous demands, including one requiring the Jewish Agency to allocate fifty percent of all immigrant visas to Palestine to Jews from Poland and to permit Polish officials to take part in their distribution.[56] Government spokesmen charged that the Jewish Agency had been allocating too many visas to people who would not engage in agriculture in Palestine and who were thus liable to return to Poland at the first opportunity.

The Jewish negotiators replied that they were not at liberty to agree to these conditions.[57] In fact, they did not wish to agree to them. Gruenbaum wrote to Jerusalem that in his opinion Polish officials would use any power given them over the distribution of immigrant visas in order to assign those visas to members of the Revisionist youth movement, Betar. He also speculated that the demand that fifty percent of all immigrant visas be given to Polish Jews echoed Jabotinsky's evacuation plan, in which half of the proposed 1.5 million Jewish evacuees were to come from Poland.[58]

At first the Poles appeared willing to drop their political demands; indeed, on November 7, 1936 both sides agreed to the general outlines of a Clearing Agreement.[59] Less than a week later, however, the Polish negotiators notified Gruenbaum that the government would not honor the agreement unless its political conditions regarding immigration visas were met.[60] This development necessitated a further round of negotiations, which ended only on March 5, 1937 with the signing of the final agreement. This agreement stipulated a regulation of the allocation of immigrant certificates to Jews possessing capital in accordance with the status of Polish exports to Palestine: the total amount of foreign currency acquired by Poland as a result of its exports to Palestine and funds sent by Jews in Palestine to their relatives in Poland was always to balance the amount of foreign currency removed from Poland by Jews moving to Palestine and expended in Poland on imports from that country. A joint Polish-Jewish commission was to supervise the agreement, which was scheduled to go into effect the following May 1. The duration of the agreement was not fixed, although each party retained the right to abrogate it on three months' notice.[61]

At the same time, Polish and Zionist leaders were cooperating on another front as well. Agents of the underground Jewish defense force in Palestine, Haganah, were engaged in purchasing weapons secretly from the Polish government, and the Polish army provided training for Haganah personnel. In September 1936 Haganah agent Yehuda Tennenbaum (Arazi) made contact with senior Polish officers in charge of arms exports, who agreed to supply him on condition that he present himself as an independent arms dealer. Tennenbaum was also in contact with Polish military intelligence, and Poland's deputy foreign minister, Mirosław Arciszewski, knew of his mission and agreed to assist him should he encounter any difficulties.[62] Similarly, the Revisionist New Zionist Organization sought to acquire arms from the Poles at this time as well.[63]

Polish efforts to encourage Jewish emigration became even more intense from 1937 to 1939. In early 1937 the Sanacja organ criticized some Polish Jewish leaders for their negative attitudes toward emigration to countries other than Palestine. At the same time it praised Jewish organizations abroad for seeking alternative destinations for resettlement: the French colonies, the Dominican Republic, Ecuador, Cyprus, Uganda, and other British overseas territories. It also expressed a willingness to discuss even the efforts of the the Agroid Company to facilitate the emigration of Polish Jews willing to engage in agriculture to Birobidzhan. In sum, the newspaper saw many possible destinations for Jewish emigration from Poland.[64]

Since Britain did not look with favor upon Polish involvement in the Palestine problem, and the investigating commission dispatched to Madagascar was not at all optimistic about prospects for settlement on that island,[65] the government explored other avenues. One involved wealthy Jewish financiers in the United States such as Bernard Baruch and Felix Warburg, who had approached the Polish ambassador in Washington, Jerzy Potocki, with several suggestions for dealing with the Jewish problem through investments in Polish industry and agriculture and in Jewish resettlement schemes. In early June 1937 Potocki reported these possibilities to U.S. Secretary of State Cordell Hull, adding that the problem of Jewish emigration from Poland had become especially acute as of late, owing to an upsurge in antisemitism among the lower classes of the Polish population.[66]

During the summer of 1937 Baruch, who was then in Paris, held several talks with the Polish ambassador to France, Juliusz Łukasiewicz, on projected credits for Poland; he also raised the issue of funding Jewish emigration from the country.[67] And in late 1937 and early 1938 Potocki discussed the Jewish emigration issue on several occasions with President Roosevelt.[68] These talks appeared promising, for in November 1937 the U.S. ambassador to France, William Bullitt, traveled to Warsaw to inform Beck, among other things, that Roosevelt was prepared to assist Poland in dealing with its Jewish problem, mainly by aiding Jewish emigration to the countries of South America.[69]

The prospects raised in these discussions, however, ultimately came to naught. In mid-1938 Poland was disappointed by Roosevelt's call for an international conference at Evian, France, to discuss the problem of refugees from Nazi Germany — without consideration of the problem of Jewish emigration from Eastern Europe at the same time.[70] In response to what it regarded as a slight, the Polish government threatened to intensify its antisemitism in the country as a means of pressuring the Western nations into dealing with Poland's Jewish problem along the lines of internationally-organized emigration. This tactic was noticeable especially in Raczyński's discussions with British officials.[71] However, not only did it not succeed in creating alternative destinations for Jewish resettlement; it appears to have made governments more reluctant to admit Polish Jews into their borders — a conclusion suggested by the steadily diminishing numbers of Jewish emigrants from Poland between 1936 and the outbreak of war.

Despairing of Western cooperation, the Polish government looked to Germany. Polish Ambassador Lipski in Berlin was encouraged by Hitler's promise that, after the disposition of the Sudeten issue, the Third Reich would demand overseas colonies, which could be used to solve the Jewish problem not only in Germany but in Poland, Hungary, and Romania as well. Lipski told Hitler that "if he can find such a solution we shall build him a beautiful monument in Warsaw."[72] However, Polish-German relations quickly developed in another direction altogether, to the point where in late October the two governments clashed over the status of Jewish Polish citizens in Germany.[73]

By late 1938, then, it appeared that the Poles needed to direct their efforts to draw international attention to the Polish Jewish problem toward the Western powers. Once again they attempted to gain a hearing from the

Intergovernmental Committee on Refugees, set up at Evian for dealing on an ongoing basis with the problems of refugees from Germany. They insisted that the Polish Jews deported from Germany and detained at the Zbąszyń camp were actually refugees from Hitler and thus proper objects of the Committee's concern. Deliberations on this matter proceeded for several months, and in July 1939 the Committee finally agreed to Poland's demand.[74]

Meanwhile, Potocki, on orders from Beck, continued to discuss the emigration issue with Bernard Baruch and other American Jewish financiers. This time he proposed that a "supplemental Jewish homeland" be created in the Portuguese African colony of Angola.[75] Roosevelt showed interest in the idea, most likely to deflect pressure from several sources to open the gates of the United States to increased immigration from Eastern Europe. Like previous proposals, however, nothing came of it.[76]

Despite its notable lack of success, by the end of 1938 the emigration idea was the only approach to the Jewish question that the Polish government was prepared to consider. Its position was summarized by Składkowski on January 23, 1939 in response to an interpellation in the Sejm a month earlier by OZON leader Skwarczyński inquiring what steps the government was taking to reduce the number of Jews in the country. Składkowski replied that the government was not prepared to concede that possibilities for resettlement would open only when Jews faced a catastrophe. He hoped that soon other governments as well as Jewish organizations would work together with Poland toward mass emigration.[77] Significantly, the prime minister made no mention of any internal solutions to the problem.

In early 1939 the Polish Foreign Ministry held intensive discussions under Beck's direction to create internal pressures within Polish Jewry to encourage them to emigrate en masse. Various proposals, none of which ever received official approval, were offered, including a further revision of the citizenship law that would have revoked the citizenship of some one-half million "Jewish migrants (*napływowi Żydzi*)," the imposition of a special "emigration tax upon Jews (*żydowski podatek emigracyjny*)," and the appointment of a commissioner for Jewish emigration within the Foreign Ministry.[78]

Another aspect of the government's approach was revealed in a secret report dated December 29, 1938, received by the European office of the Joint Distribution Committee. It indicated that the Foreign Ministry had summoned representatives of the Polish press to a meeting at which the newspapers were instructed to devote significant space to the emigration issue. The Foreign Office reportedly asked the newspapers to stress that the government would not continue its tolerant policy toward Jews if that policy was interpreted as a sign that Jews were welcome to stay in the country. It was noted further that Germany was succeeding in getting rid of its Jews with international cooperation precisely because of its cruel policy toward them.[79]

Obviously responding to this directive, the editor of *Gazeta Polska*, Bogusław Miedziński, wrote that there could be no solution to the Jewish problem in Poland other than emigration. Basing his stand not on economic arguments but rather on the charge that ninety percent of all Communists in Poland were Jews, he declared that these Jewish Communists should be regarded as open enemies of the Polish people and their state. Moreover, even the more conservative portions of the Jewish community constitued a foreign body in Poland and did not look upon the country as their homeland.[80] The newspaper also publicized the threats of Polish diplomats engaged in negotiations over the emigration question: i.e., if that problem were not included on the agenda of the various conferences dealing with the refugee issue, tendencies within Poland to seek a solution to the Jewish question along German lines would become stronger.[81]

The government preferred, however, to advance the emigration idea with Jewish cooperation. Nevertheless, most Jewish organizations were not prepared to give it. Jewish opposition continued to be regularly expressed in the Jewish press.[82] The 1937 convention of the Zionist Federation of Congress Poland also enacted a resolution castigating the government's emigration plans as well as the notion that conditions might be created that would force masses of Jews out of the country.[83] And in the Sejm, deputies explained the Jews' attitude toward the issue repeatedly. In February 1937, for example, Izaak Rubinstein linked the government's interest in emigration to domestic and foreign propaganda purposes rather than genuine concern for dealing with the Jewish question constructively.[84] In other speeches Jewish Sejm deputies warned that by using antisemitism as an incentive for emigration the government would merely make potential receiving countries restrict the number of Jews allowed to enter their territories even further. "Emigrationism," they argued, was not only unconstitutional; it was unrealistic and damaged the country.

Still, Jewish attitudes toward emigration did not remain entirely static.[85] A certain change in tone was noticeable even in the Bund, which previously had raised opposition to the government's emigration plans to the level of principle, maintaining that, although it did not oppose Jews leaving the country, it did not regard such departure as a way to solve the Jewish problem.[86] In April 1937, however, Bund leader Henryk Erlich wrote that his party "understood well that if destinations of possibilities for emigration for the Jewish masses existed, tens of thousands, perhaps even hundreds of thousands, of Jews would leave. But where will they go?... We Bundists do not deny the need for masses of Jews to emigrate, but we do deny that that need applies to Jews only." According to Erlich, the Bund hoped to work together with all Polish workers and peasants to create a situation in which none — Poles, Ukrainians, or Jews — would be superfluous.[87]

Erlich's colleague Wiktor Alter also wrote an important article on emigration immediately after the publication of OZON's Thirteen Theses on the Jewish question. In it he stressed that the Bund had always fought against "Palestinism" but not against Palestine, against "emigrationism" but not against emigration. "To put it simply," he wrote, "we are Jews, and we did not need to discover Jerusalem because of antisemitism." For this reason, he stated, the Bund sought to lead the political struggle of the Jews in Poland.[88]

The Bund had to defend its stand against ideological allies as well. PPS member Jan Borski published a pamphlet entitled *The Jewish Question and Socialism*, in which he argued that even if a socialist regime were established in Poland, the Jewish question would only be solved by a territorial solution.[89] The Bund conducted a campaign against Borski's view. It criticized the PPS newspaper, *Robotnik*, for defending Borski's right to express such an opinion and condemned the official party apparatus for distributing his pamphlet. Their actions, the Bund claimed, placed a PPS stamp of approval, as it were, upon Borski's approach in the eyes of Polish workers.[90]

Moshe Kleinbaum, expressing the position of what he termed the "democratic Zionists" on the emigration question, engaged the Bund in argument over its response to Borski. Kleinbaum took issue with what he regarded as the Bund's assumption that anyone who called for increased Jewish emigration from the country was automatically an antisemite. PPS, in his view, was not an antisemitic body, yet it understood that socialism would not solve the problems of Polish Jewry. On the other hand, he stressed, democratic Zionists rejected Jabotinsky's "evacuationist" concept, which negated any possibility of Jewish life outside of Palestine and was prepared to accept any initiative for emigration, even if that initiative was connected with extreme antisemitism. Democratic Zionism, according to Kleinbaum, necessitated a synthesis between mass Jewish immigration to Palestine — with the ensuing struggle for a Jewish homeland there — on the one hand and a fight for a democratic regime in Poland and elsewhere on the other.[91]

In the face of increasing restrictions upon immigration to Palestine, however, the Zionist movement found its standing among Polish Jewry

severely damaged. Emissaries of Jewish organizations in Palestine who visited Poland in 1937 reported that members of the Zionist parties were becoming apathetic about the movement's goals and languishing in an atmosphere of despair. One of them wrote, "The Jews need to find a way out of
their distress immediately, not at the proverbial end of days."[92] The Polish
Zionist leadership came in for criticism for its alleged failure to initiate political action or even to organize the Jewish public to protest its condition.
The Zionists, according to such evaluations, had nothing to say to the masses
of Polish Jews.[93]

The restrictions upon immigration to Palestine encouraged the Jewish
Agency to maintain continuous close contact with the Polish government
regarding Britain's Palestine policy. In July 1937 Chaim Weizmann, president
of the World Zionist Organization, met several times with Raczyński in
London and asked that the Polish government apply pressure upon Britain
to increase the amount of territory allocated to a future Jewish state under
the plan for the partition of Palestine that the British were then considering.
Weizmann maintained that if the Jewish Agency were given greater control
over Palestine's immigration policy, 100,000 Jews would leave Poland for
Palestine within a year.[94] On September 12, Weizmann and Nahum Goldmann met with Beck in Geneva prior to the Polish foreign minister's scheduled address to the Council of the League of Nations. Weizmann asked Beck
for support for the partition plan, explaining that should it be accepted, the
mass emigration of Jews from Eastern Europe could begin. Beck consented,
citing common interests between his government and the Zionists.[95] Goldmann asked again for Polish intervention with the British government in
early 1938, after the British authorities had imposed a ceiling of 8,000 Jewish
immigrants until March 31, 1938, when they were scheduled to make a final
determination as to whether the partition scheme was feasible. Polish representatives agreed on this occasion as well; indeed, Beck met with British
Foreign Minister Anthony Eden in Geneva on this matter, although to no
avail.[96] Finally, Polish spokesmen told Goldmann that if the gates of Palestine remained closed, the Polish government's interest in the Zionist movement would decrease, and the government would have to look for alternative destinations for Jewish emigration.[97]

The government also carried on simultaneous discussions on this issue
with the New Zionist Organization, which opposed the partition of Palestine. In mid-1937 the New Zionists issued a statement praising the Polish
government's position on Jewish emigration, with the sole reservation that
the government ought to stop looking at other territories and concentrate

all of its attention upon Palestine.[98] In mid-October Jabotinsky and Schechtman met with Beck and with heads of departments in the Foreign Ministry and urged the government to take a stand against partition.[99] At the end of the month the two Revisionist leaders met with Rydz-Śmigły, a meeting that marked the first time that the marshal had ever received a Jewish spokesman. Jabotinsky spoke mainly about the internal situation in Poland, emphasizing that Polish interventions on behalf of a Jewish Palestine would lose their effectiveness if the Polish government continued its antisemitic policy. Rydz was somewhat apologetic, claiming that he was not familiar "with all of the intricacies of domestic policy," and Jabotinsky emerged from the meeting with the feeling that the prognosis for Polish Jewry was "extremely black."[100]

Nevertheless, the influence of the Revisionists upon the Polish government appears to have been quite strong. Even at this time of extreme restrictions upon Jewish immigration to Palestine, the Polish government approached Weizmann with a request that the Jewish Agency assign more immigration certificates to those in the Revisionist movement. Raczyński was asked to explain to the Zionist leader that despite all of the "tactical" differences between him and Jabotinsky, it was in his movement's interest to see more Jewish "fighting elements" in Palestine, which the Revisionists could purportedly provide.[101] In the contacts between representatives of the Jewish Agency and the Polish government in Geneva in 1938, Nahum Goldmann, responding to Gruenbaum's entreaties, tried to interfere with the close relations developing between the Poles and the Revisionists.[102]

The problem was discussed by Goldmann with Tadeusz Gwiazdoski, deputy director of the Political Department of the Polish Foreign Ministry, on September 23, 1938. The Jewish leader expressed astonishment over the frequent contacts between the highest echelons of the Polish leadership and Jabotinsky when the Revisionist movement did not, in his words, represent any significant force in Poland and could not provide either an alternative destination or financial assistance for would-be emigrants. Gwiazdoski replied that Foreign Minister Beck realized that the Revisionists were without influence: support for the movement, he explained, stemmed from an emotional affinity on the part of some Foreign Ministry officials with backgrounds in the Polish Legions of World War I for Jabotinsky's style. He indicated further that should plans to partition Palestine reach fruition, Poland would support them, for such a development would make it easier for many Jews to immigrate to that country. In practical matters, he emphasized, the government regarded the Jewish Agency as the representative of world

Jewry and did not incline toward the Revisionist position.[103]

By the end of 1938 Jabotinsky felt that the time was ripe for a new initiative on his part. He spoke with U.S. ambassadors Drexel-Biddle in Warsaw and Kennedy in London about the possibility of simply bringing one million Jews to Palestine all at once and placing a *fait accompli* before the world.[104] In his report on these discussions he concluded that "Washington is ripe for a bold proposal" and recommended going ahead with the plan.[105] In this connection he called for the convening of what he called a "Zion Sejm" in Warsaw, at which representatives of all Eastern European Jewish communities would meet to discuss their rescue through the establishment of a Jewish state in Palestine. He planned for the Zion Sejm to ratify the program of immediate immigration of one million Jews and to appoint delegations to be sent to various governments, including the United States and the British mandatory authority. The draft of the call to the Zion Sejm, which Jabotinsky submitted to the Polish government with a request for support, also included a condemnation of forced emigration. Jabotinsky proposed that the Zion Sejm serve as an advisory body to the Polish government on Palestine affairs.[106] At first the Polish government showed interest in the proposal, but with political conditions worsening in the summer of 1939 it decided not to allow any political demonstrations, of which the Zion-Sejm was regarded as an example.[107]

Interestingly, on this occasion, in contrast to 1936, Jabotinsky's plans aroused no storm at all. Jewish public opinion evidently regarded these new proposals as an extention of his evacuation idea. In any case, the victory of the Bund in the municipal elections of 1938–39 demonstrated that more and more Jews viewed all mass emigration schemes as illusory and dangerous in the current context and preferred to wage their struggle in the Polish domestic political arena. Jabotinsky was a popular figure among Polish Jews because of his rhetorical ability and inspiring personality, but his movement and programs remained without strong public support.

The ambivalence that Jews displayed in coming to terms with the government on the emigration issue led the authorities to take a new approach in soliciting Jewish cooperation — especially after the influx of deportees from Germany made the matter even more acute. In November 1938 Maksymilian Friede, a Jewish commercial court judge, was approached by the government with a mandate to form a Committee for Jewish Colonization Affairs. Its mission would be to make contact with the Intergovernmental Commission on Refugees in London and to influence that body, with the assistance of Jewish organizations abroad, to incorporate the problem of Polish Jewry into its purview. This committee, under the chairmanship of Moshe Schorr, was to warn the international body that should it prove unresponsive, the Polish government would not be able to withstand the pressures brought upon it by those who supported and perpetrated acts of antisemitic violence. It was also to maintain contact with Daniel Wolf, a wealthy Jew from The Hague with business interests in Poland, who had displayed an interest in the problems of Jewish emigration. Finally, it was to create branches and conduct a fundraising campaign among Polish Jews throughout the country, with the goal of collecting 3,000,000 zł. for the organization of the anticipated Jewish exodus.[108]

The formation of the Colonization Committee, which was charged with exploring possibilities for Jewish settlement outside of Palestine as well, encountered severe criticism from a sizeable portion of the Jewish public. Most of this criticism was directed against Zionist figures who had agreed to join the committee without receiving authorization for such action from any Zionist body. Some argued that the committee was simply a "blind tool" in the hands of the Polish authorities, especially the Foreign Ministry.[109] In early January 1939, Jewish newspapers published a statement by various Zionist parties and organizations expressing their absolute objection to the Colonization Committee.[110] The Zionist Federation of West Galicia, which had not joined in this statement, objected nevertheless to the committee's existence and activities.[111] At the same time, Agudas Yisroel criticized the Zionist leaders for their objections, which in their view stemmed primarily from Zionist fears that their own fundraising efforts would be hurt by the committee's entry into the fundraising field.[112]

The public debate notwithstanding, the Colonization Committee sent a memorandum explaining its formation, its purposes, and its activities to Lord Winterton, chairman of the Intergovernmental Commission on Refugees. They pointed out the importance of increasing the volume of Jewish emigration from Poland, arguing that by doing so the commission could help weaken the basis of anti-Jewish propaganda there. The memorandum suggested that the Commission address itself first to the problems created by the expulsion of thousands of Polish citizens from Germany. It maintained that Palestine should be the primary destination for Jewish migrants, with other territories entering into consideration only should Palestine prove unable to accommodate all those seeking to enter. Finally, the Colonization Committee expressed its willingness to cooperate with international agencies in all matters related to the occupational retraining and colonization of Jews.[113] At the same time, the committee also discussed with the Polish government representatives the possibility of dispatching delegations to various countries to develop contacts with Jewish and non-Jewish organizations that might further its ideas.[114]

To that end, the government dispatched a delegation of the committee to London in January 1939 to meet with representatives of the Jewish Agency and World Jewish Congress — including Chaim Weizmann, Nahum Goldmann, and Stephen Wise. The Board of Deputies of British Jews and representatives of the Joint Distribution Committee also received the delegation, as did Lord Winterton and the executive director of the Intergovernmental Commission, George Rublee.[115] The World Jewish Congress had already decided, on January 14, to concern itself with the emigration issue and to summon an all-Jewish conference on the matter, to which representatives of the four principal countries encouraging Jewish emigration — Poland, Romania, Hungary, and Czechoslovakia — would be invited.[116] The Joint Distribution Committee, on the other hand, thought it best not to give in to the Polish government's pressure and thus opposed the Colonization Committee's activities.[117] It was able to foil plans for a similar delegation to visit the United States, on the grounds that the U.S. government had no concrete proposals regarding Polish Jewish emigration and becoming involved in emigration might endanger the JDC's practical work in Poland.[118]

In the end, the Colonization Committee's delegation did not achieve any significant result. Nor did the committee's behind-the-scenes negotiations with Daniel Wolf. Wolf had offered to raise £10,000,000 for a project to resettle 50,000 Polish Jews annually. After consultations with Jewish leaders in other countries, however, the committee concluded that it ought not embark upon such a venture without first securing a suitable destination for the emigrants.[119]

Curiously, for all of its efforts to augment Jewish emigration from the country, the Polish government placed serious roadblocks in the way of implementing the Clearing Agreement, the one project on which it had reached a formal accord with a major Jewish organization and which was intended to facilitate the entry of wealthy Jews into Palestine outside of the immigration quotas imposed by the mandatory authorities.[120] It appears that the government was sensitive to a possible adverse reaction to the arrangement on the part of both the British government and the Arabs of Palestine.[121] Some Jewish elements who opposed the agreement also tried to subvert it, with the result that, within months of its inauguration, the Polish government was seeking to have it modified.[122] Finally, in May 1938 the government announced that it was withdrawing from the agreement altogether as of August 1. Negotiations were subsequently held about a new one,[123] but they soon came to naught – a result, at least in part, of pressure by the Revisionists upon the Polish government not to enter into any agreement that recognized the Jewish Agency as the sole spokesman for Jewish interests in Palestine.[124]

In the meantime, though, the government was continuing to assist both the Haganah and the Revisionist-associated National Military Organization (*Irgun Tseva'i Le'umi*, or *Etsel*) in the training of soldiers and in arms procurement.[125] Yehuda Tennenbaum (Arazi), the Haganah agent, was joined in February 1937 by Katriel Katz; the two worked closely with Polish staff officers until the months before the outbreak of war.[126] The arms that they purchased were financed in part by Daniel Wolf, who pledged to contribute £100,000 to the Polish treasury.[127] Wealthy Polish Jews who wished to transfer their funds to Palestine would also pay for the arms, to be reimbursed upon their resettlement.[128]

However, in July 1939, apparently in response to British pressure, the Polish general staff abruptly put a stop to Haganah arms purchases. Training courses for Haganah soldiers, on the other hand, continued virtually until the outbreak of war. On June 16, 1939 a course for future Haganah instructors was opened at Zielonka, near Warsaw, with opening ceremonies attended by representatives of the Foreign, Interior, and Military Affairs Ministries and of Zionist bodies. The government does not seem to have been terribly concerned about keeping this course secret, for it opened it to selected visiting dignitaries and journalists, including Yitshak Gruenbaum. When the course came to an end on July 16, its graduates were certified as military instructors and permitted to conduct their own training courses for future soldiers, including full military maneuvers and practice with live ammunition, at any of the various Zionist training farms in Poland except those along the Soviet border.[129]

Parallel to these efforts the Polish Foreign Ministry – especially its Consular Department, which was in charge of emigration programs – endeavored to assist *Etsel*. In addition to training soldiers and aid in procuring arms, this assistance also involved encouragement of attempts to bring Jews to Palestine surreptitiously, without regard for the British-imposed immigration quotas. *Etsel*'s special representative in Poland, Avraham Stern, maintained regular contact with Wiktor Drymmer of the Consular Department. With Beck's approval more than 200,000 *zł*. ($40,000) in cash and armaments were allocated to *Etsel* from the Consular Department's budget.[130] In addition, in April 1939 the Polish government agreed to sell *Etsel* the ship *Pułaski* for use in transporting illegal immigrants to Palestine, even though it reneged on its offer shortly thereafter.[131] At the same time a course for twenty-six *Etsel* instructors from Palestine was given by Polish officers at Andrychów in southwestern Poland. Following the completion of the course several graduates remained in Poland to organize their own training courses for future soldiers.[132]

Despite this practical assistance, however, the government's motives remained suspect in the minds of most Jews: although the authorities made vocal demands in the international community for the solution of the Polish Jewish problem, they failed to realize the provisions of civic equality contained in the April 1935 constitution. Although the bulk of Polish Jewry understood the urgent necessity for many Jews to emigrate, to Palestine or to any other possible destination, Jews distinguished that necessity from "emigrationism," which they recognized only as a political imperative, demanding their removal from Poland because they were a foreign body in that country. Indeed, the government's repeated calls for Jewish emigration not only did not result in the opening of any new sites for resettlement, but actually endangered the position of Jews in Poland by making their continued presence appear illegitimate. As a result, more and more Polish Jews transferred their allegiance from the Zionist parties, which appeared incapable of achieving positive results, to the Bund, whose insistence on dealing with the immediate problems of Polish Jewry in Poland alone, through cooperation with PPS and other progressive forces among the Polish public, appeared a more realistic approach. Undoubtedly, had it been possible to bring a large number of Jews to Palestine during the years prior to the outbreak of war, the political allegiances of Polish Jews would have been distributed differently. However, even to pursue that possibility, the Zionists could not have avoided negotiating and even cooperating with the Polish government in a way that a majority of the Jewish public condemned. The Zionists were thus caught in a vicious circle. But in the end the same could be said about Polish Jewry as a whole.

10
Toward War

The half year between the final dismemberment of Czechoslovakia in March 1939 and the outbreak of World War II on September 1 was marked by a Polish rapprochement with Britain and France in response to the drastic deterioration in Polish-German relations. The Polish public witnessed the collapse of the principal thrust of the foreign policy formulated in 1934 by Piłsudski and developed by Beck, which was based upon Polish consultation with and at times even cooperation with Germany. Now it appeared that the turn had come for Poland to fall victim to German desires for expansion, and war seemed likely.

This new situation placed the Jewish question in Poland in a new light, for Germany was rapidly becoming the common enemy of both the Poles and the Jews. The Jews thus became the only national minority in the country whose loyalty could be counted upon under present circumstances,[1] and after the liquidation of Czechoslovakia Jewish newspapers expressed the feeling that Poles and Jews shared a common fate and that Jews throughout the world had a vital interest in the preservation of a strong and independent Poland.[2] Aware of this relationship, the Germans tried to drive a wedge between the Polish government and the Jews. In a conversation with Ambassador Lipski in Berlin on March 21, 1939, German Foreign Minister Ribbentrop warned that Poland was in danger of "Bolshevization" and that "the Jewish element" was the only part of Poland's population interested in helping this process along. Although Lipski replied that no Polish patriot would cooperate with the Soviets,[3] unlike in previous conversations the Polish ambassador had held with German officials, he did not respond to Ribbentrop's statements about the Jews.

The German government continued to encourage Polish-German cooperation against the Soviet Union as a vital interest of Polish foreign policy, arguing that Bolshevization would be more costly to Poland than the concessions it would have to make to preserve good relations with Germany. Trying to get this message across to the Polish public as relations between the two countries were deteriorating, the Germans also portrayed the Polish-British rapprochement as a "Jewish policy." This tactic was illustrated in a letter sent by the director of the German *Institut fuer Rassenforschung* at Leipzig University to the German Foreign Office on May 4, 1939. The writer advised promulgating the idea among Poles that "the Jewish plutocracy" had taken over Poland and was aiming to bring the country closer to Britain. Such a message, he ventured, would create among the Polish public insecurity and doubt about the correctness of Polish foreign policy and might also destroy any feelings of national unity on the eve of war.[4] All means to achieve this end were regarded as acceptable, even if they resulted in strengthening the hand of the traditionally anti-German Endecja. The antisemitic argument was thus made to fit all circumstances, no matter whether German propaganda raised the spectre of a "Jewish plutocracy" in Poland – an argument used to protest the growing rapprochement of Poland with Britain and France – or spoke of the "Bolshevization" of Poland under Jewish direction – an argument used to counteract opposition to Germany's demands.

How effective were these German efforts to influence Polish public opinion by raising the spectre of Judaization? In late March 1939 a joint conference was held by representatives of PPS and the so-called Democratic Clubs, made up of people who had left the Sanacja fold in 1937 on the charge that Sanacja's present leaders had betrayed the true legacy of Piłsudski. Holding antisemitic propaganda to be an antipatriotic act serving German interest consciously or unconsciously and injuring Poland's security, the conference condemned antisemitic propaganda in the country as paving the way to Hitlerism. It demanded that the constitutional guarantees of civic equality for all citizens be implemented to the fullest.[5]

On April 16, 1939 the Democratic Clubs formed themselves into a new Democratic Party (*Stronnictwo Demokratyczne*), with Mieczysław Michałowicz at its head. The new party's founding platform regarded the Jewish question as a lure for antidemocratic support – exploiting the Jewish population's faulty occupational structure and the lack of suitable sites to which to direct Jewish emigrants. All manifestations of violence against Jews were condemned, as were plans for the enactment of anti-Jewish legislation or for forcing Jews to leave the country.[6] The Jewish press welcomed the formation of the new party as "an idea whose time had come," noting that it would pull select (if small) circles from the Sanacja camp. An article in *Haynt*, for example, expressed the hope that the current world situation would cause the party to emerge as a potent political force capable of galvanizing all of the country's democratic elements.[7]

Actually, it is possible to discern a certain slowdown in the pace of antisemitic attacks during March and April 1939. Observers who followed the Endek and OZON press during these months noted a "lowering of the tone" with regard to the Jewish question, although they did not regard this development as a significant turning point.[8] On the other hand, during the same months antisemitic propaganda continued to be distributed, and calls for the Polonization of the country's political, economic, and social life continued to be heard.[9] Moreover, just as administrative pressures were being applied against the German minority in the western part of the country, the Jewish press complained loudly about numerous instances in which Jews in Silesia — including the cities of Chorzów, Katowice, and Bielsko — had been driven from the border area by order of the local authorities.[10]

Endek circles claimed that the Jews were not prepared to fight against Germany but only against Hitlerism, whereas Polish interests were to fight Germany but not necessarily to put an end to Hitler's rule.[11] The National Party's newspaper wrote that "the Jews must be warned against the belief that the will to get rid of them in Poland has been weakened."[12] According to later issues of the newspaper, the Jews were fighting for a new alignment of forces in Europe in order to strengthen Jewry, whereas Endecja was committed to struggle for the continued independence of a Greater Poland.[13]

These charges of Jewish lack of patriotism were answered vigorously by former Sejm deputy Apolinary Hartglas, who argued that Jews did not need to be ashamed that they did not hate the German people. On the contrary, their hatred of the Nazi regime was an expression of their Polish patriotism: Nazism was responsible for Germany's aggressive policy against Poland, so that it was precisely the ideological affinity of Endecja and other Jew-haters for Hitlerism that stood to weaken the sense of patriotism in the country in time of war.[14] Many among the Jews understood that recent Polish-German tensions were what had brought about the lessening of pressure by the ruling party to enact anti-Jewish legislation, and they realized that the antisemites, still regarding the Jews as greater enemies of Poland than the Germans, were sorry that the troublesome international situation made it an unpropitious time for spreading this message aggressively.[15]

Indeed, during the summer of 1939 the National Party launched a barrage of new antisemitic propaganda. Evidently the party feared that spreading anti-German sentiment would lead to a further weakening of antisemitism, which in turn would threaten the continued development of the party. At the same time, the Endeks renewed their calls to fire Jewish municipal workers and remove Jews from chambers of commerce throughout the country.[16] The OZON organ *Gazeta Polska* accused the National Party of carrying on an internal conspiracy that weakened the country's leadership significantly.

The newspaper charged that according to the National Party, obedience to the authorities was to be given only conditionally.[17] It also accused the party of having established a hierarchically-organized, violent underground group, which, acting in accordance with party directives, had, among other things, instigated anti-Jewish riots in colleges and universities.[18]

Heightened antisemitic propaganda came from certain Polish business and professional associations as well. The meeting of the Association of Polish Merchants in March 1939 approved the sending of a memorandum to the minister of industry and trade demanding that the business permits of a sizeable portion of Jewish-owned enterprises not be renewed. In effect, this meant that the number of Jewish-owned businesses would eventually be reduced to ten percent (the percentage of Jews in the Polish population overall).[19] Further, in July 1939 the Merchants Association of Poznań decided, with the support of the local chamber of commerce, to demand that the government require differential labelling for products made by Polish and Jewish businesses.[20]

Similarly, the Union of Engineers' Organizations had resolved to include an "Aryan paragraph" in its bylaws, meaning that no Jew, spouse of a Jew, or person of Jewish descent could be a member of the association.[21] And during all this time pickets remained on guard to enforce the anti-Jewish boycott and to distribute antisemitic handbills.[22] In March 1939 Jewish stalls in a number of towns were attacked on market day, and many Jews were severely beaten.[23] In conferences held in the spring of 1939, OZON's Young Poland League spoke of the need to prepare Polish youth to replace Jews in industry and commerce,[24] and the state Foreign Trade Council withheld import licenses not only from certain Jewish importers but even from a number of Jews who had converted to Christianity.[25]

Endek University students also continued their antisemitic campaign during this period, giving it at times an even more extreme expression than before. Their violent activities were not always confined to the university campus. For example, on May 3, 1939, Falanga students went out into the streets of Warsaw and in the name of patriotism shouted slogans condemning Germans and Jews, attacking the Jews until a group of Jewish porters offered physical resistance.[26]

In essence, OZON and Endecja were able during this period to cooperate on virtually all matters pertaining to Jews. An example of this trend was the resolution adopted by the Warsaw City Council on April 4, 1939. The majority of OZON delegates joined with their counterparts from the National

Party and ONR to form a 47-vote majority forbidding Jewish council members from serving on municipal draft boards on the grounds that Jews should not be trusted with military matters.[27]

All the while Germany continued to use the Jewish issue to combat mounting Polish anti-German feeling. In response to a call for Poles to boycott German goods,[28] the German Chamber of Commerce wrote to its counterpart in Warsaw, "We do not wish to believe that this action has anything in common with the boycott that Jews have waged against Germany for many years."[29] German radio stations, especially in Breslau, Gleiwitz, and Koenigsberg, broadcast Polish-language programs arguing that Poland was playing into the hands of the Jews by adopting an anti-German policy.[30] Even though the OZON newspaper *Gazeta Polska* warned that the purpose of these programs was to persuade Polish listeners that the Jews were the common enemies of both Germans and Poles,[31] the broadcasts, which reportedly included daily readings from the Endek press,[32] struck a responsive chord among the Polish public, according to German representatives in Poland.[33]

Thus a certain ambivalence characterized government and OZON attitudes toward the Jewish question. While both parties condemned violent political antisemitism, neither was willing even in these circumstances to disavow economic antisemitism. Only the former was regarded as a Nazi propaganda tool, and OZON publications castigated Endecja for aiding and abetting the Germans by spreading antisemitic propaganda. At the same time, those same publications cast doubt upon Jewish expressions of patriotism, which they regarded as opportunistic. In their view, Jews deserved no credit for the "natural" hatred of Hitler.

During the months before the outbreak of war, the focus of public discussion about Polish Jewry appears to have moved away from the emigration issue.[34] Nevertheless, in April 1939, in preparation for Beck's planned visit to London, the Polish government asked that the Jewish question be placed on the agenda of the foreign minister's meetings with British officials.[35] On the eve of Beck's departure, the British Embassy in Warsaw sent the Foreign Office a background paper on the situation of Polish Jewry at the beginning of 1939. The paper declared that the Polish public was hostile to the Jews and that the government was under pressure to initiate anti-Jewish legislation. Personally, it said, the Polish foreign minister opposed the antisemitic tendencies within the government, but public pressure would eventually force the ruling party to abrogate Jewish civic equality if a site could not be found for absorbing at least the annual natural increase of the Jewish population in the country, which by then had reached 40,000.[36]

The Foreign Office, in turn, expressed the fear that Poland would take an example from Germany and come to the conclusion that cruelty to the Jews was the best way to induce other countries to cooperate in efforts to facilitate their emigration.[37] One wonders how, at such a fateful hour, both governments found the time to devote to idle discussions about the problem of Jewish emigration. Nevertheless, at the conclusion of Beck's visit, on April 6, 1939, a joint Polish-British communique announced that the problem of the emigration of Polish Jewry would be taken up in any international effort to solve the Jewish question.[38]

Following Beck's visit, Raczyński submitted a memorandum to the British permanent undersecretary for foreign affairs, Alexander Cadogan, in which he asked that, in light of the British government's latest White Paper on Palestine of May 1939, according to which the entry of Jews into the country was to be limited to 25,000 refugees and 50,000 additional immigrants over the next five years before being suspended altogether, 45 percent of the remaining places for immigrants be assigned to Jews from Poland. He asked further that Polish Jewish citizens who were expelled from Germany in October 1938 be considered eligible to enter Palestine under the quota of 25,000 refugees, and that Britain allocate an alternate territory within the British empire in which Polish Jews could be resettled according to the same terms that the British government was prepared to offer refugees from Germany.[39] In formulating the response to Raczyński's wishes, the Foreign Office consulted the Colonial Office, which suggested making a positive answer conditional upon Poland's agreement to cooperate with Britain in the struggle against illegal Jewish immigration to Palestine.[40]

The talks between Poland and Britain caused Germany to abrogate its 1934 nonaggression pact with Poland on April 28, 1939. After that day, the Polish government's foreign policy fell more into line with the thinking of the opposition parties, as the gathering emergency mitigated interparty rivalry.[41] Exiled leaders of PPS and the Peasant Party were now permitted to return to Poland, an act that reflected a general closing of ranks in the country.[42] Nevertheless, antisemitic propaganda reached new heights of intensity during the campaign for subscriptions to the state air defense loan, which began on April 5 and ended on May 6. Circles close to the government, as well as the Endek press, accused the Jews of shirking their national duty by their poor subscription rate to the loan.[43] The OZON organ *Gazeta Polska* complained particularly about insufficient contributions from Jewish industrialists in the Białystok region and from Jews in the provinces of Kielce, Lublin, Nowogródek, Wilno, and Wołyń. Castigating the alleged gap between the Jews' words and their deeds,[44] the newspaper claimed that only Jews in the Kraków province had contributed their fair share. The Endek press even suggested that, because Jews allegedly controlled eighty percent of Poland's capital, they should be forced to make a mandatory "contribution" to the country's defense, with responsibility for collection being placed upon the heads of the Jewish communities.[45]

In actuality, it appears that the charges of insufficient Jewish subscription were groundless. In general, data classifying loan subscribers according to their religious or ethnic identity were lacking. Nevertheless, according to provisional estimates made by the Association of Jewish Merchants, Jews purchased 130 million *zł.* in loan subscriptions out of a total of 400 million *zł.* sold.[46] Jewish cooperative banks contributed 21 million *zł.* to the loan campaign, as opposed to 11 million *zł.* in contributions from all other cooperative banks.[47] All segments of the Jewish community took an active role in the fundraising drive, at a time when 600,000 Jews (almost 20 percent of the total Jewish population) were entirely dependent upon the assistance of Jewish charities and a similar number received partial assistance.[48] Jewish newspapers published photographs of letters by leading rabbis calling upon the Jewish community to fulfill its duty to Poland.[49] Indeed, at the conclusion of the campaign, the OZON newspaper *Kurier Poranny* admitted that the Jews had subscribed to the defense loan in accordance with their abilities.[50] Endecja, in contrast, continued to agitate on this matter, and echoes of such agitation found their way into the Sejm.[51]

Even during this critical period, the Jews continued to defend their positions in the Polish economy. In May 1939 the first nationwide meeting of the branches of the Jewish Economic Committee took place in Warsaw. Resolving to search for new sources of livelihood for Jews and to work for the occupational retraining of the Polish Jewish masses, the convention called for the establishment of a central credit agency for Polish Jewry.[52] The Jewish Colonization Committee also renewed its activities, with Maksymilian Friede making another trip to London to meet with the Intergovernmental Commission on Refugees.[53] There, Friede told Jewish representatives that even though the situation for Jews in Poland had recently improved, they must still not forget the need for many Jews to emigrate from the country.[54]

During this time some Jewish leaders called for the various Jewish parties to reach a greater degree of understanding among themselves in order to advance the Jewish struggle for civic equality and to increase understanding of the Jewish situation among broader segments of the Polish populace.[55] However, the final round of municipal elections that took place in May-June 1939 accentuated not Jewish unity but rather the differences between the Jewish parties. The victory of the Bund in these elections continued to be the subject of debate even after their conclusion, with Bund leader Wiktor Alter continuing to attack the Zionists for a position that allegedly played into the antisemites' hands.[56] Thus at precisely the most critical moment for Polish Jews, internal unity appeared farther away than ever before — without any indication on the horizon that the idea of uniting into a Congress of Polish Jewry might, following the bitter lesson the the failures of former years, be revived.

Ironically, the victorious Bund appears to have been the principal Jewish force opposing internal unification. Although the Joint Distribution Committee had asked Polish Jews to set up a central organization for administering its various activities, the Bund resisted these efforts. In the end the JDC agreed to its creation without the Bund, with a mechanism established whereby the Bund would consult with the central organization on matters affecting it directly.[57] Negotiations leading to formation of the new organization continued throughout the entire summer. They were completed only on the very eve of the war[58] — too late for it to have any effect.

Thus it was left to the Jewish press simply to monitor government and public expressions on Jewish issues. In this connection the press seems to have believed that attitudes were changing for the better. Kleinbaum, for example, commented on Rydz-Śmigły's speech in Kraków of August 6, 1939, in which the marshal declared that the time had come for all citizens to concentrate and to unite their efforts in strengthening mutual cooperation and identification for the sake of the security of the country. Kleinbaum stressed optimistically that on this occasion Rydz-Śmigły had spoken of "citizens (*obywatele*)," whereas in the past it had been more common in discussions of security matters to speak of "native countrymen (*rodacy*)," a term that might be taken as excluding Jews.[59] However, such a change appears to have been superficial, for the quasi-governmental *Gazeta Polska* continued to propagandize in an antisemitic fashion. In the week preceeding the outbreak of war, it published pictures of Jewish merchants on its front page, stressing their ethnic identity and indicating that they had been sent to the internment camp at Bereza Kartuska for profiteering in foodstuffs.[60] The leading Endek newspaper went even further, charging all Jews with illegal traffic in foreign currency and with damaging the value of the Polish *złoty*.[61]

The Ribbentrop-Molotov pact of August 23, 1939 sent shock waves through Polish Jewry. The Bund Central Committee condemned the agreement sharply, charging that it strengthened Hitler's hand and made war more likely. At the same time the Bund expressed its approval of the recently-concluded Anglo-Polish military alliance.[62] The Jewish press, like its Polish counterpart, devoted much attention during the final week of peace to the Polish army's military alert and to its ability to withstand a German attack. Taking care to obey all censorship requirements, it refrained from spreading attitudes of gloom or defeat among Polish Jewry.[63]

The Endek press, in contrast, showed no compunction about using even the Ribbentrop-Molotov pact as an excuse for unbridled antisemitic agitation. Its publications charged that the Jews were behind the rapprochement between Germany and the Soviet Union, which was aimed against Poland, for the Comintern was entirely under Jewish domination.[64] This agitation was accompanied by outbreaks of anti-Jewish violence by mobilized reservists in Warsaw, the identity of whom the authorities strictly forbade disclosure.[65]

Sadly, these new outbursts of antisemitism took place against the background of a massive campaign by Jews to organize volunteer efforts related to the country's defense. On the last day of peace, August 31, 1939, Jews were responsible for digging anti-aircraft pits at 230 sites around Warsaw. Even those recently deported to Poland from Germany lent a hand in the work.[66] But even at this eleventh hour many Poles allowed themselves to be distracted by antisemitic agitation, abetted at times actively or passively by state authorities. The German threat did not result in a coalescence of all Polish citizens in the face of the common enemy; on the contrary, some parties and influential political figures found it expedient to increase internal fragmentation by attacking the one minority group whose loyalty could be counted upon unquestionably. Ironically, perhaps it was because the Jews' loyalty was taken for granted that the government saw no need to protect them from the antisemites, who were trying to make even deeper inroads into the Polish public consciousness. Perhaps these motives help explain the continued enmity of Jews displayed by a notable percentage of the Polish population even during the war years.

For its part, the Jewish public was not able to concentrate upon the German threat in the last days of peace, preoccupied as it was defending itself against the attacks of Polish antisemites. It was, however, poorly equipped for both tasks — fragmented organizationally and with no effective leadership to serve as its authoritative voice, either domestically or internationally. In the municipal election campaign, which continued until mid-1939, it appeared that Polish Jewry was determined simply to go about its business as always, with no reference to the rapidly mounting national emergency. Even during the final month before the war the Bund refused to unite with other Jewish parties in an all-Jewish front, while the Zionist press devoted most of its attention to the struggle against the British White Paper and to the World Zionist Congress, which convened in Geneva on August 21. Polish Jews thus made an inviting target for the Endek antisemites and gave the government no reason to adopt any more than a lukewarm stance toward their postulates. They also gave Jews around the world little cause to turn their full attention to them, to raise their spirits, and to aid them in the trials that would undoubtedly accompany the outbreak of war.

Summation

The final years of Polish Jewry's existence as a major center of Jewish life saw the radicalization of antisemitism, both in Polish society in general and in the ruling circles, where it became an increasingly prominent theme in the country's political life following Piłsudski's death. Although expressing reservations about its more violent manifestations, the government lent it official legitimacy and hardly any segment of the organized Polish community remained untouched by it. The prognosis for Polish Jewry thus appeared bleak, with members of the community enmeshed in a daily struggle for security and survival against powerful and hostile external forces that sought to abrogate their constitutional guarantees of civil equality and force them to leave the country en masse.

The enmity that Jews experienced during this period assumed new forms and drew in no small measure, directly and indirectly, from the example of Nazi Germany. Even during the period of Polish-German confrontation on the eve of World War II, many Poles were impressed by the successes of German foreign policy and by the Nazi regime's ability to solve Germany's Jewish problem. To be sure, Nazi propaganda never agitated directly against the Jews of Poland, but as relations between the two countries deteriorated, it did not hesitate to portray the Jews as the common enemy of Germans and Poles alike.

In the face of these developments, Polish Jews attempted to wage a coordinated and concerted political battle against all forms of antisemitic attack — economic warfare, violent rioting, discriminatory legislation, and hostile administrative practices and regulations. However, they did not succeed.

Of the three primary political groups within Polish Jewry — the Zionists, Agudas Yisroel, and the Bund — only the last was effectively organized and capable of carrying on concerted opposition to anti-Jewish forces. The Bund leadership, moreover, was able to increase its strength by taking advantage of the malaise that plagued the Polish Zionist movement in the face of the effective closure of Palestine to Jewish immigration. But the party was not prepared, for doctrinaire reasons, to join with nonproletarian Jewish groups in an all-Jewish defense. Nor was it satisfied with the manner in which its perceived allies, the progressive Poles, responded to the Jews' need for support. Similarly, Agudas Yisroel, despite its disaffection with the Polish government over the kosher slaughtering controversy, was reluctant to participate in an all-Jewish organizational framework or in an electoral alliance with other

Jewish parties, mainly for fear of damaging the authority of its parliamentary representation. And in the end the Zionists, who had consistently exhorted fellow Jews to join them in forming an all-Jewish representative body, were unable to unite even their own separate federations and parties, even though the differences among them with regard to local Polish issues were mainly tactical.

The Jewish press, too — despite its impressive role in exposing abuses of Jewish rights, even in the face of government restriction that often impeded its work — was unable to forge a unified Jewish organizational framework. This failure is not surprising, for almost all of the Jewish newspapers were closely tied to existing Jewish political parties and necessarily reflected their attitudes and shortcomings.

Perhaps the major reason Polish Jewry was unable to close ranks in the face of the mounting threat to its security at that time was the absence of charismatic and authoritative leadership. The only voice that could officially represent Polish-Jewish interests was the small Jewish parliamentary caucus, which although respected by much of the Jewish public, was not recognized as its legitimate spokesman. The Jewish Sejm and Senat deputies constantly spoke out against the injustices suffered by their charges, but in the parliament they generally did so to deaf ears. Following their parties' directions instead of leading them, they were incapable of wielding any power effectively and usually acted without coordinating their interventions with one another.

As a result, the most effective Jewish battles were fought locally — notably the self-defense organized during the Przytyk pogrom and the stubborn resistance of Jewish university students to the ghetto benches. Although both actions had countrywide implications, they originated at the grass roots level, without direction from above. Perhaps their success lay precisely therein.

This is not to say that Polish Jews did not fight tenaciously against economic and legislative discrimination. On the contrary, they appear to have stood up fairly well to the daily tests they encountered. But no matter how valiantly they fought, they had no chance to alter their situation substantially without creating a new organizational framework, based on a sense of common Jewish destiny and mutual identification. This failure was to seriously impair their ability to confront the grave challenges that lay ahead. Indeed, with the approach of war, many felt they were trapped with no way out — left to face the Nazi onslaught virtually alone.

Abbreviations Used in the Notes

AAN Archiwum Akt Nowych
AH Haganah Archive
AIP Archiwum Instytutu Polskiego
AJCB American Jewish Committee *Bulletin*
AJYB *American Jewish Year Book*
AL Lestschinski Archive
BDBJ Archive of the Board of Deputies of British Jews
CAHJP Central Archives for the History of the Jewish People
CZA Central Zionist Archive
DBFP *Documents on British Foreign Policy*
DGFP *Documents on German Foreign Policy*
FRUS *Foreign Relations of the United States*
HA Histadrut Archives
HIA Hoover Institution Archives
JA Jabotinsky Archive
JTA Jewish Telegraphic Agency
KPP Komunistyczna Partia Polski
LPA Israel Labour Party Archive
MSW Ministerstwo Spraw Wewnętrznych
NA National Archives
ONR Obóz Narodowo-Radykalny
PRO Public Record Office
WA Weizmann Archive
YVA Yad Vashem Archive

Notes

Chapter 1: Background: The Piłsudski Years

1. See Pobóg-Malinowski, *Najnowsza historia*, pp. 180–84; Landau and Tomaszewski, *Zarys historii gospodarczej*, p. 41; Tartakower, "Ma'avakam haKalkali," p. 147.

2. Zweig, *Poland*, p. 30; Polonsky, *Politics*, p. 9.

3. Landau and Tomaszewski, *Zarys historii gospodarczej*, pp. 161, 168.

4. Ibid., p. 240; Mahler, *Yehudei Polin*, pp. 11–13. See also Kagan, "Agrarian Regime."

5. In 1933 there was, however, a slight upturn in industrial output and in agricultural prices. See Landau and Tomaszewski, *Zarys historii gospodarczej*, pp. 58–60, 179. The economic history of interwar Poland is generally divided into four major periods: 1918–1923 (a period of economic reconstruction following the establishment of the Polish state), 1924–1929 (a period of economic expansion), 1930–1935 (the period of the great depression), and 1936–1939 (a post-depression period characterized by increased government intervention in the economy).

6. On the moratorium, enacted in 1932, see Pobóg-Malinowski, *Najnowsza historia* 2:750–51.

7. See Landau and Tomaszewski, *Zarys historii gospodarczej*, pp. 233–41.

8. Polonsky, *Politics*, p. 347.

9. See Leszczyński, "Ekonomishe Entviklung," pp. 718–21; idem., "Vegn a konstruktivn Plan," p. 41; Bronsztejn, *Ludność*, p. 67. Cf. the remarks by Endecja leader Roman Dmowski in Dmowski, *Świat powojenny*, pp. 323–24.

10. See Bronsztejn, *Ludność*, pp. 70–71, 78; Mahler, *Yehudei Polin*, pp. 127, 130, 139.

11. In contrast, 79.5 percent of non-Jewish industrial laborers worked in factories employing twenty workers or more. Bronsztejn, *Ludność*, p. 70. See also Garncarska-Kadary, "Ha-Ovedim," pp. 19–20.

12. Other factors contributed to this process as well. Some state and private factories simply closed their doors to Jewish workers. Jewish factory owners also did not employ many Jewish workers, in large measure because of their fear of the Jewish workers' class consciousness. On the other hand, Jewish workers often preferred to work in petty manufacturing or in artisanry, for by accepting employment in a large industrial enterprise they felt that they were giving up the chance of eventually owning their own shops. See Mahler, *Yehudei Polin*, pp. 56, 90–92.

13. Berenstein, "KPP," p. 4.

14. See Bronsztejn, *Ludność*, pp. 257–59.

15. Gitterman, "Perspektywy," pp. 7–20.

16. CKB (Cekabe) were the abbreviated initials of an organization whose full name was *Centralne Towarzystwo Popierania Kredytu Bezprocentowego i Krzewienia Pracy Produktywnej wśród Ludności Żydowskiej w Polsce* (Central Society for the Support of Free Credit and the Spread of Productive Labor among the Jewish Population of Poland).

17. Szlamowicz, "Oddłużenie," pp. 52–57. See also the minutes of the meeting of the Comité des Delegations Juives, Lucerne, September 4, 1935, CZA — A127/48. A report was presented at this meeting estimating the total outstanding peasant debt to Polish Jewish creditors at 600 million *złotych*, a figure that was certainly too large.

18. Segal, *The New Poland*, p. 146.

19. A copy of the report can be found in CZA — A127/40. See also Schipper, *Dzieje Handlu*, pp. 638–42; Tartakower, "Pauperyzacja," p. 99.

20. Chojnowski, *Piłsudczycy*, pp. 54–55; Polonsky, *Politics*, pp. 238–39. See also Holzer, *Mozaika*, pp. 300–301. This situation gave Piłsudski a certain tactical advantage, for it made BBWR dependent entirely on the marshal as the decisive authority figure. Even the bloc's leaders were military officers (the so-called colonels) subject to Piłsudski's command. Micewski, *Z geografii politycznej*, p. 314. See also Jędruszczak, *Piłsudczycy*, p. 46; Kulesza, *Koncepcje ideowo-polityczne*, pp. 123–30. Note that the term Sanacja was applied to the Piłsudski camp before BBWR was organized.

21. Hartglas, *Na pograniczu dwóch swiatów*, p. 346. See also MSW, *Sprawozdanie*.

22. See Tartakower, "Yidn," pp. 220–24; Hafftka, "Życie," pp. 295–300.

23. On this idea, see Rothschild, *Piłsudski's Coup d'Etat*, p. 244; also Landau, "Ha-Yehudim," pp. iii–iv. Articles in the Polish Jewish press of the period also noted the centrality of the Piłsudski-Dmowski struggle. See, for example, *Haynt*, April 1, 1937 (M. Kleinbaum, "Natsie un Shtat"). On the other hand Terej, *Idee, mity, realia*, pp. 149–50, does not view the struggle as a major theme in interwar Polish history. This view, however, is the exception among historians.

24. The foreign policy perspectives of the two are compared in Bromke, *Politics*, pp. 14–30. For a serious article juxtaposing Dmowski's and Piłsudski's teachings, written by a Nazi scholar, see Maschke, "Dmowski."

25. Pobóg-Malinowski, *Najnowsza historia*, 2:793, noted three phases in the development of Dmowski's sociopolitical outlook — the democratic-parliamentary phase, the phase of sympathy toward fascism, and the Catholic phase. These phases can be used as points of reference for understanding the changes within Endecja as a whole, for as Dmowski moved from phase to phase, he left behind followers who remained faithful to his earlier teaching. Although these people did not cut their ties to Dmowski, they remained ideologically stationary.

26. On OWP see Rudnicki, "Obóz." See also idem, "Narodowa Democracja po przewrocie," pp. 352–69.

27. Jędruszczak, *Ostatnie lata*, p. 35; Wapiński, *Endecja na Pomorzu*, pp. 134–35. See also Terej, *Rzeczywistość*, pp. 10, 13–14, 22–23.

28. Holzer, *Mozaika*, pp. 363, 368. On the intensification of the anti-Jewish activity of OWP and on the camp's growth in general, see the minutes of a speech by Dmowski at the OWP convention in June 1931, in Zielinski, "Reorganizacja," p. 266.

29. Rudnicki, "Program," p. 30; Wapiński, "Endecja," p. 840.

30. Wapiński, *Endecja na Pomorzu*, pp. 105, 129.

31. Dmowski's remarks from articles published in *Gazeta Warszawska*, quoted in Kalicka, *Z zagadnień jednolitego frontu*, p. 52.

32. Niemunis, "Stronnictwo Narodowe," pp. 113–15, 122. See also Terej, *Rzeczywistość*, p. 75; Rudnicki, *Obóz Narodowo-Radykalny*, p. 145; Kowalec, *Narodowa Demokracje*, pp. 136–39.

33. On the circumstances of the founding of ONR see Rudnicki, *Obóz Narodowy Radykalny*, pp. 212–22. See also Terej, *Rzeczywistość*, p. 10.

34. Report on the Jews of Poland prepared for the Comité des Delegations Juifs, Paris, 1934, CZA — A127/40. In response to these attacks, the Jewish socialist party known as the Bund, together with PPS and the Communist Party of Poland, organized self-defense groups. See Kalicka, *Z zagadnień jednolitego frontu*, pp. 323–25, 355; Goldstein, *Tsvantsik Yor*, pp. 228–29;

Rowe, "Jewish Self-Defense," pp. 105–49. The so-called Revisionist Zionists, through their youth movement, Betar, also organized self-defense groups to fight ONR attackers. See *Sefer Betar*, p. 340; *American Jewish Year Book*, 1935, p. 231.

35. It was later discovered that Pieracki had been killed by Ukrainian nationalist extremists.

36. Rudnicki, *Obóz Narodowo-Radykalny*, pp. 252–54.

37. The members of the two groups were also referred to by the names of the groups' founders: members of ONR-Falanga were called *Bepiści* (after the initials of Bolesław Piasecki), while those who belonged to ONR-ABC were known as *Rossmanowcy*, after their leader Henryk Rossman. See Pobóg-Malinowski, *Najnowsza historia*, 2:793–94; Rudnicki, "Program," pp. 39–40.

38. Singer, *Od Witosa*, p. 191.

39. Piłsudski generally refrained from taking part in the public debate over the Jewish question and did not publicly attack Dmowski's position on this issue. See Groth, "Dmowski," pp. 75, 83, 86.

40. This likelihood is demonstrated by the radical downturn in the condition of Polish Jewry following the Marshal's death. On this, see below.

41. It is still not clear whether Piłsudski had planned a preventive war against Germany in 1933; nor is it clear to what extent France's refusal to take an active role in such a campaign induced the marshal to seek rapprochement with his Western neighbor. Polonsky, *Politics*, p. 382 provides a rich bibliography on this question.

42. Immediately following the Nazis' accession to power Polish Jews organized an economic boycott against Germany. The Central Organization of Jewish Merchants resolved in April 1933 to replace German merchandise with merchandise from other sources and established a Central Committee for Economic Action against Hitler (*Centralny Komitet dla Antyhitlerowskiej akcji Gospodarczej*). See *Nasz Przegląd*, April 5, 1933.

43. Moltke to Bülow, April 26, 1933, in *DGFP*, Series C, 1:351 (doc, 192).

44. According to a 1933 German census there were 148,092 Polish citizens resident in Germany, including 56,480 Jews. See Watz, SS Command, to German Foreign Ministry, April 28, 1937, YVA – JM 3235.

45. The Jewish boycott had concerned Moltke almost since its inception. On March 22, 1933 he notified the Foreign Ministry in Berlin that the pro-boycott propaganda being waged by Jewish merchants and newspapers was exploiting Polish-German divisions for the Jews' own purposes and was turning the Poles against Germany. He pointed to a significant change that had come over the Jews of Poland, who had previously regarded Germany as a friend. Cable, Moltke to German Foreign Ministry, March 22, 1933, YVA – JM 2431.

46. Szembek, *Diariusz*, 1:53–55. See also Wojciechowski, *Stosunki*, pp. 35–36. On the importance of this conversation for the development of Polish-German relations, see Mackiewicz, *Historia*, pp. 244–45.

47. Wojciechowski, *Stosunki*, p. 43.

48. Cable, Beck to Wysocki, May 9, 1933, AIP – A11/49/N/2; Szembek, *Diariusz*, 1:66–67.

49. Szembek, *Diariusz*, 1:68–69. Despite the official improvement in relations, secret subversive German organizations had been set up in Poland with the Nazis' accession to power. The activity of these groups revealed the true intentions of the German government toward Poland. See Cygański, *Hitlerowskie organizacje*, p. 182.

50. For details, see Wojciechowski, *Stosunki*, pp. 108–109. In addition to the non-aggression pact, a press accord was signed on February 24, 1934, which obligated the appropriate agencies

in both countries to exert influence upon public opinion in accordance with the spirit of the non-aggression agreement. See Michowicz, *Walka,* p. 73. The pact provided the Poles with an increased sense of security by removing the uncertainty to the permanence of its border with Germany that had been created by the Locarno Pact of 1925.

51. Cables, Moltke to German Foreign Ministry, April 15, 1934 and June 8, 1934, YVA — JM 2431.

52. Cable, Moltke to German Foreign Ministry, July 17, 1934, ibid.

53. *Fun noentn Over,* 1956:151.

54. Singer, *Od Witosa,* pp. 19–20.

55. In response, Jewish merchants organized a "Jewish League for the Protection of Polish Goods." See *AJYB* 1935–36:208, 339. For details on the dispersal of the Central Committee by the authorities and on the operation of the boycott in general, see Melzer, "HaHerem," pp. 149–66.

56. In 1931 Piłsudski and Beck (then the deputy foreign minister and a close confidant of the marshal) had decided to wait for an appropriate moment to renounce Poland's obligations under the treaty and to confront the League of Nations with a fait accompli. Michowicz, *Walka,* pp. 16–23.

57. See Lemański, "Generalizacja," pp. 532–33; Michowicz, *Walka,* pp. 71–76.

58. Michowicz, *Walka,* pp. 115–26.

59. Ibid., pp. 138–41, 155.

60. Grünberg, *Niemcy,* pp. 71–72.

61. See Michowicz, *Walka,* pp. 150–51.

62. *Nowy Dziennik,* February 1, 1934 (O. Thon, "Sukces Dyplomacji Polskiej").

63. See, for example, the editorial in *Dos Yudishe Togblat,* January 30, 1934.

64. *Chwila,* January 29, 1934 (F. Rottenstreich, "Układ z Niemcami").

65. Kleinbaum to Gruenbaum, March 11, 1934, CZA — A127/491/3.

66. *Sprawozdanie Sejmu,* November 6, 1934 (Session 24).

67. See especially O. Thon's interview in *Nowy Dziennik,* September 15, 1934, as well as the editorials in *Haynt,* September 14, 1934, *Nasz Przegląd,* September 15, 1934, and *Naye Folkstsaytung,* September 16, 1934. The newspaper of Agudas Yisroel directed mild criticism against Beck's declaration, claiming that it stood to impair the legal rights of Jews in other Eastern European countries, which were not guaranteed as they were in Poland. *Dos Yudishe Togblat,* September 17, 1934 (D. Flinker, "Tsu Minister Beck's Aroystrit in Zheneva").

68. For details about the alignment of Polish Jewry into parties see Hafftka, "Żydowskie Stronnictwa." On the directions taken by the various parties, see Tartakower, "HaMahshavah," pp. 123–48; Tartakower, "Yidishe Politik," pp. 150–52.

69. See Hafftka, "Żydowskie Stronnictwa," pp. 253–54; Tartakower, "HaMahshavah," pp. 128–29. For a sociological study of the assimilationists, see Heller, "Assimilation;" also Heller, *Destruction,* pp. 183–209.

70. The West Galician federation also encompassed Silesia. Efforts had been made to coordinate the national policies of these three Zionist federations, and in 1934 a United Political Committee was formed for this purpose. The Committee held a number of meetings and then suspended operations. See *Sprawozdanie Egzekutywy.* On previous attempts at coordination and unification see Hafftka, "Żydowskie Stronnictwa," pp. 262–63.

71. Like the General Zionists, Mizrahi was also divided into three separate regional centers. The Revisionists, too (after 1931), maintained three different central committees under

the leadership of a single supreme council. See Hafftka, "Żydowskie Stronnictwa," pp. 261–63. On the beginnings of Zionist organization in Poland, see Mendelsohn *Zionism*, passim.

72. For details on the organizational structure of the Zionist left in Poland, see Hafftka, "Żydowskie Stronnictwa," pp. 269–73, 280–84. See also Kantorowicz, *Arbeter Bavegung*. At the beginning of the 1930s the Poalei-Tsiyon Left party was beset with an active opposition displaying tendencies toward Communism and the Third International. In October 1931 a decision was taken to oust some opposition leaders from the party in order to strengthen the party's independent position. Hafftka, "Żydowskie Stronnictwa," pp. 283–84.

73. Altogether, ten Jews were elected to the Sejm in these elections, and one to the Senat. See Hafftka, "Życie parlamentarne," pp. 300–311. Gruenbaum was the driving force behind the establishment of the Minorities Bloc in 1922. The Bloc entered the lists again in the elections of 1928. On the establishment of the Bloc, see Netzer, *Ma'avak*, pp. 289–94. The difficulty in reestablishing the Bloc in the 1930 electoral campaign lay, among other factors, in the radicalization of the position of the Ukrainians, who now stressed that they were not a minority at all but a large majority in their areas of concentrated settlement, and as such should not participate in a minorities' list. Moreover, the influence of the White Russian minority declined sharply around this time. See Halpern, *Polityka*, p. 40.

74. In that year the Jewish caucus, under the leadership of the traditional advocate of cooperation with the government, Ozjasz Thon, voted against the government's proposed budget. Gruenbaum expressed his satisfaction with this development. Gruenbaum, *Milhamot*, p. 366. See also *Żydzi w Polsce Odrodzonej*, 2:352.

75. The Revisionist Party had been founded on a worldwide basis by Vladimir Jabotinsky in 1925 out of dissatisfaction with the unwillingness of the World Zionist Organization to declare publicly that it sought the establishment of a sovereign Jewish state (as opposed to an autonomous Jewish "national home") in Palestine.

76. Hafftka, "Żydowskie Stronnictwa," p. 274; see also pp. 283–84. On the growth of Po'alei Tsiyon C.S. during the early 1930s see Ritov, "Po'alei Tsiyon," pp. 136–37; *Finf Yor Po'alei Tsiyon Tetikayt*, p. 47.

77. See the secret report of the Security Division of the Government Commission in Warsaw about the 1930 elections to the Sejm and Senat, in *Warszawa II Rzeczypospolitej* 4:279–80 (1972).

78. See *Żydzi w Polsce Odrodzonej*, 2:255–58; Mendelsohn, "Politics," pp. 48, 54–57. In December 1931 the Hasidic Rebbe of Belz founded a party known as Mahzikei haDas, which hoped to compete with Augdas Yisroel. Within a short time this party had enrolled ten thousand members, mostly in Galicia. See *Żydzi w Polsce Odrodzonej*, 2:258.

79. The Bund enjoyed a certain success in the 1929 municipal elections. See Hafftka, "Żydowskie stronnictwa," p. 279. The party decided not to take part in the Jewish community elections of 1931 because of the contraction of the communities' secular functions. See Johnpoll, *Politics*, pp. 180–81.

80. A minority faction, led by Yosef Chmurner-Leszczyński and Meir Wasser, continued to insist that changes were in store within the Communist International and that the Bund would eventually become integrated into this body. This faction continued to exert influence upon the party's ideas.

81. The Communist Party of Poland also enjoyed considerable influence within the Jewish trade union movement. See Hafftka, "Żydowskie stronnictwa," pp. 276–78. On attempts at cooperation between the Bund and the Communist Party of Poland during 1933–34 and on

their eventual failure see Dziewanowski, *Communist Party*, p. 141; Kowalski, *Trudne Lata*, pp. 602–14; Auerbach, "Zagadnienia," p. 41. The government, especially the Minorities Department of the Interior Ministry, followed the divisions within the Bund and its negotiations with the Communists. See Ministerstwo Spraw Wewnętrznych, *Sprawozdanie*; also Nowogrodzki, "HaBund," pp. 77–79.

82. Ministerstwo Spraw Wewnętrznych, *Sprawozdanie*.

83. See the comments by Sokolow, *Ha-Tsofeh le-Veit Yisrael*, p. 243.

Chapter 2: Political Changes After Piłsudski

1. Pobóg-Malinowski, *Najnowsza historia*, 2:758.

2. See Stawecki, *Następcy Komendanta*, p. 10.

3. Constitution of the Republic of Poland, April 23, 1935. Warsaw, 1935.

4. *Nasz Przegląd*, March 24, 1935. Thon was not present for the Sejm vote on the new constitution. For evaluations of differing positions within the Jewish caucus and among the Jewish public, see Ministerstwo, *Sprawozdanie*.

5. *Folkstsaytung*, May 25, 1935.

6. *Warszawski Dziennik Narodowy*, June 13, 1935.

7. See, for example, *Nasz Przegląd*, September 15, 1935 (M. Bałaban, "U trumny budowniczego").

8. *Folkstsaytung*, June 18, 1935.

9. Only military officers, holders of state decorations, officials in local government or economic and social agencies, and those possessing a higher education were entitled to vote for electors, to the Senat in the regional assemblies. *Dziennik Ustaw* 46 (1935).

10. On the negative attitude of PPS, the Peasant Party, and the Communist Party to the electoral ordinance, see Żarnowski, *Polska*, pp. 31–32, 36, 59.

11. Polonsky, *Politics*, p. 399.

12. Przybylski, "Centrum," p. 582.

13. The conservatives dissented from Piłsudski's economic etatism and from what they believed had been the authoritarian, police-state character of his rule.

14. BBWR had attempted to organize several youth groups, the most important of which was known as Legion Młodych (Youth Legion). See Pilch, *Studencki Ruch*, pp. 36–48; Krzywicki, *Wspomnienia*, pp. 285–91. On the failure of BBWR among the youth see the evaluation of the British ambassador in Warsaw, Howard Kennard, in a memorandum to the British foreign minister of May 29, 1935, PRO — FO 371/18887; also Polonsky, *Politics*, pp. 356–59.

15. On the circumstances of the dissolution of BBWR, see Chojnowski, *Piłsudczycy*, pp. 236–42.

16. *Folkstsaytung*, June 24, 1935.

17. See Po'alei Tsiyon C. S., *Finf Yor*, p. 27.

18. *AJYB*, 1936/37, p. 338.

19. In late January 1935, the Jewish Sejm deputies from East Galicia, Emil Sommerstein and Henryk Rosmarin, had discussed this subject with the then minister of the interior, Marian Zyndram-Kościałkowski, who had promised them to take their desires into account. See the minutes of the meeting of the Executive Committee Presidium of the Zionist Federation of East Galicia, January 25, 1935, CZA — F3/4.

20. See Hartglas, "Mandaten un Glaykhberekhtigung," *Haynt*, April 26, 1935; speech by F. Rottenstreich, *Sprawozdanie Sejmu*, no. 145, June 25, 1935.

21. In making his case he referred to the decision of the Ukrainian National Democratic Organization(UNDO)to take part in the elections. Minutes of the Council of the Zionist Federation of East Galicia, July 16, 1935, CZA — F3/5. On the decision of UNDO regarding the elections, see *Chwila*, July 9, 1935. One month later this decision was reversed; ibid., August 19, 1935.

22. *Nasz Przeglad*, July 30, 1935.

23. *Haynt*, July 18, 1935 (M. Kleinbaum, "Vahl Ideologie un Vahl-Rekhiles"); ibid., August 13, 1935 (M. Kleinbaum, "A Bashlus fun frayen Vilen").

24. In Warsaw, Wiślicki received only one vote more than the General Zionist candidate from the Et Livnot faction, Yehoshua Gottlieb (12,199 votes to 12,198). When Wiślicki died shortly following the elections, Gottlieb took over his seat. *Nasz Przegląd*, September 10 and September 13, 1935.

25. The Ukrainians were the only ethnic minority to win Senat representation at the polls. *Chwila*, September 16 and September 24, 1935.

26. A debate over whether Polish Jewish leaders should migrate to Palestine was conducted in the pages of the Yiddish daily *Haynt*. One of the editors of the newspaper, Moshe Indelman, demanded that Zionist leaders remain in Poland and devote themselves to the struggle to secure the Jewish position in that country. Opposing this view, a prominent Zionist, Apolinary Hartglas, argued that migration to Palestine was the essence of Zionism and that no Zionist leader should be prevented from seeking personal fulfillment in this fashion. He believed that new leaders would be found to replace those who left. *Haynt*, April 21, 1935 ("Fihrer Veln Zikh Gefinen").

27. Thon did not believe that the new Sejm would be representative of the population of Poland. Even the previous Sejm had fallen, in his opinion, to the level of an "advisory bureau for the government." An assimilationist Jew was nominated for his seat in Kraków with the help of local Sanacja forces. The Zionists in Kraków urged the Jews, if they did not refrain from voting altogether, to vote for Polish candidates, and in the end the assimilationist was not elected. See Schwarzbart, "HaHistadrut haTsiyonit," p. 235.

28. At the seventh congress of the Communist International, which met in Moscow in July-August 1935, a resolution was adopted to take the initiative in forming "popular fronts" in various countries, uniting all forces opposed to fascism. On the basis of this resolution the Communist Party of Poland decided in November 1935 to establish a popular front of all of the democratic forces in Poland. See Dziewanowski, *Communist Party*, p. 140; Zachariasz, *Di Komunistishe Bavegung*, p. 81. The Bund opposed the popular front idea in general, particularly insofar as it involved the inclusion of the Peasant Party, supporting instead the idea of a "labor front," which would include PPS, the Bund, the Communists, and the socialist parties of the German and Ukrainian minorities. The Bund also criticized PPS's positive attitude toward the Kościałkowski government in its early stages. See *Myśl Socjalistyczna*, September 12, 1935 (W. Alter, "O jedną partię proletariacką").

29. See the report on the sixth general assembly of the Bund, in *Folkstsaytung*, February 19, 1935.

30. *Folkstsaytung*, August 7, 1935; also October 20, 1935 (H. Erlich, "Der Bund").

31. Bund, *Di Lage fun di Yidishe Masn*, pp. 6–9.

32. Żarnowski, *Polska*, pp. 61–62. This supportive attitude changed to one of non-support following the meeting of the supreme party council of PPS in November 1935; ibid., p. 63.

33. Pobóg-Malinowski, *Najnowsza historia*, 2:780–81; Polonsky, *Politics*, p. 402. See also Chajn, *Materiały*, 1:19.

34. Yaffe, *BeShelihut Am*, p. 175.

35. On the significance for the Jews of this policy of encouraging the formation of cooperatives, see the remarks by Emil Sommerstein on the floor of the Sejm on February 25, 1936, *Sprawozdanie Sejmu*, no. 17.

36. Although he did not say so in public, Rydz-Śmigły appears at this time to have held the opinion that Jews held decisive influence over the Polish economy. This influence worried him because of its security implications; the patriotism of Polish Jews was not to be trusted. See Szembek's account of his discussion with Rydz-Śmigły, September 30, 1936, Szembek, *Diariusz*, 2:291.

37. In Polish: "Walka ekonomiczna – owszem, ale krzywdy żadnej." *Sprawozdanie Sejmu*, no 26.

38. The distance between Składkowski's *owszem* declaration and the statement made by Premier Kazimierz Bartel on July 7, 1926 (in the immediate aftermath of the Piłsudski coup) concerning the policy of equality and objectivity with regard to the Jews and the struggle against economic antisemitism that the government would pursue is remarkable. See Mark, "Der Virtshaftlikher Krig," pp. 140–41; Landau, "Hafichat Mai," pp. 257–58. Following the *owszem* declaration Polish censors adopted a less severe attitude toward calls for an anti-Jewish economic boycott. Until that time the Polish courts had frequently declared the more extreme of such calls published in newspapers illegal. See Pietrzak, *Reglamentacja*, p. 440. See also the opinion of Jacob Marcus on the *owszem* statement and on the reactions to it among the Jewish public. Marcus, *Social and Political History*, p. 366.

39. Brandes, "Der Rekhtlikher Motsov," pp. 178–79.

40. Several months following the speech Składkowski explained to Yitshak Gruenbaum that his remarks should be interpreted simply as expressing opposition to all illegal manifestations of violence. See the typescript of Gruenbaum's travel diary, November 3, 1936, CZA – S46/285. In 1964 Składkowski indicated that his statement had been taken as encouraging a boycott and even pogroms against the Jews, although this had been neither the original meaning of his words nor his intention. On this occasion he presented himself as neither a fanatical nationalist nor a "servant of the Jews" but as one who sought a compromise for the good of Poland. Składkowski, *Nieostatnie slowo*, p. 226.

41. Segal, *The New Poland*, p. 142.

42. Mark, "Der Virtshaftlikher Krig," p. 143. On the *bojówki*, see above, chap. 1.

43. Sanacja Senator Konstanty Terlikowski remarked to the Senat on March 9, 1936 that Endecja and its allies were exploiting the Jewish question as a political playing card. Were there no Jewish question in Poland, he observed, it would be necessary for Endecja to invent one, for the only way that it could hope to gain public acceptance was to play upon anti-Jewish feeling. Moreover, he stressed, because the Jewish question was of only tactical interest to Endecja, that party proposed no constructive solutions to it in the economic and cultural realms but only anti-Jewish violence. *Sprawozdanie Senatu*, no 8.

44. *Chwila*, June 27, 1936 (H. Hescheles, "Morał Myślenic"). See details in chap. 4 below.

45. Hlond also castigated Jews as being extensively engaged in bribery and forgery and as exercising destructive influence on the Polish educational system. Terej, *Rzeczywistość*, p. 60; see also Heller, *On the Edge*, pp. 112–14.

46. *Nasz Przegląd*, April 4, 1936.

47. Terej, *Rzeczywistość*, p. 62. On the close collaboration between the lower clergy and Endecja in spreading anti-Jewish propaganda, see Jędrzejewicz, *Fragmenty*, p. 134. On the

Catholic establishment's hostile attitude toward Jews, see Biddle to Secretary of State, October 1, 1937, NA — 860C.4016/509.

48. "Folkshilf," September 9, 1936, AL — 243. See also *Haynt*, January 5, 1937.

49. Terej, *Rzeczywistość*, pp, 58–59.

50. See, for example, the statement made by Archbishop Sapieha following an illegal demonstration in Kraków on March 23, 1936, in which six demonstrators had been killed. *Tygodnik Polski*, April 5, 1936.

51. *Haynt*, January 19, 1936.

52. *Warszawski Dziennik Narodowy*, April 30, 1936.

53. Ibid., May 15, 1936.

54. *Nasz Przegląd*, May 12, 1936.

55. Ibid., January 11, 1936. The League for the Protection of the Rights of Man and the Citizen had been founded in 1921; among its purposes had been the protection of the rights of Poland's ethnic and religious minorities. Its most visible activity took place during the 1930s, when it was heavily influenced by Communist elements (although its president, the writer Andrzej Strug, was a member of PPS). In late 1937 it was disbanded by the Polish government. See Barcikowski, *Liga*, pp. 16–18.

56. *Haynt*, August 26, 1936. Among the contributers to the newsletter was the eminent Polish man of science Tadeusz Zaderecki.

57. On the PPS attitude toward the Jewish question, see also Cang, "Opposition Parties," pp. 251–53; Brumberg, "The Bund," pp. 83–92.

58. Quoted in *Nasz Przegląd*, May 6, 1936. On anti-Jewish tendencies within PPS, see Żarnowski, "PPS," pp. 120–21. Reports from provincial governors to the Polish Ministry of the Interior in late 1936 indicated that in many places branches of the Peasant Party were trying to dissociate themselves from PPS in response to Endek propaganda branding PPS a pro-Jewish party. Żarnowski, *Polska*, p. 141.

59. From an article in *Robotnik*, quoted in *Haynt* and *Nasz Przegląd*, July 2, 1936.

60. KPP, *Uchwały i Rezolucje*, pp. 533, 539.

61. KPP Central Committee to Bund, PPS, Ukrainian Social Democratic Party in Poland, German Social Democratic Party in Poland, Left Po'alei-Tsiyon, and Central Committee of Trade Unions, July 1936, *Dokumenty KPP*, doc. 23, pp. 138–39.

62. See, for example, Bund leader Wiktor Alter's comments in *Folkstsaytung*, February 3, 1936. See also Polonsky, *Politics*, pp. 415–16.

63. Resolutions of the Peasant Party Congress, December 8, 1935, *Materiały źródłowe*, doc. 92, pp. 252–53. In contrast, the platform held that the Slavic minorities must be guaranteed the opportunity to develop their own culture and be granted wide-ranging territorial and economic autonomy. See also Wynot, "The Polish Peasant Movement," pp. 49–50.

64. *Folkstsaytung*, February 3, 1936. See also the evaluation in Polonsky, *Politics*, pp. 415–16.

65. From an interview published in *Dziennik Popularny*, quoted in *Nasz Przegląd*, November 6, 1936.

66. Rudnicki, *Obóz Narodowo-Radykalny*, p. 313; Pobóg-Malinowski, *Najnowsza Historia*, 2:797–801.

67. Pobóg-Malinowski, *Najnowsza Historia*, 2:797–801. On Koc's approaches to ONR, see Rudnicki, *Obóz Narodowo-Radykalny*, pp. 315–16; Windyga, "Obóz," p. 183; Siemiaszko, "Grupa," pp. 2–4.

68. Micewski, *W cieniu*, pp. 397–440. Laeuen, "Polens," p. 445, views the founding of OZON

as a further stage, following the April constitution, on the road to turning Poland into a totalitarian state.

69. Pobóg-Malinowski, *Najnowsza Historia*, 2:802–5.

70. Evidently some circles within Sanacja also found the OZON platform as proclaimed by Koc unacceptable. Among government members who opposed the platform were Deputy Prime Minister and Treasury Minister Eugeniusz Kwiatkowski and Agriculture Minister Juliusz Poniatowski, who expressed reservations about the growing movement toward Endek positions. Some former members of the Piłsudskist youth organization *Legion Młodych* also withdrew from OZON following the influx of Falanga youth into ZMP. For further details see Polonsky, *Politics*, pp. 422–26; Stawecki, *Następcy Komendanta*, p. 149; Wynot, *Polish Politics*, p. 68.

71. Recognizing this new development, Endecja sought to clarify its differences with OZON, attacking the new camp's platform with the argument that its founders did not understand that the Jewish problem was essentially political and not limited to the areas of culture and the economy. *Warszawski Dziennik Narodowy*, February 23, 1937.

72. *Gazeta Polska*, April 21, 1937. He did state that he saw no reason why certain individual Poles "of the Muslim or Jewish faith" should not be admitted. The next day, however, following a request from the OZON newspaper, Gazeta Polska, for clarification of the membership issue, Kowalewski retreated, stating that Christianity was a requirement for membership and that even Jews who had fought for Poland's liberation would not be eligible to join OZON. On this clarification, see AAN — MSZ 9904/8–10. See also following note.

73. *Gazeta Polska*, April 22, 1937. See also the report by British Ambassador Kennard, April 27, 1937, PRO — FO 371/20759.

74. See the report by Emil Sommerstein to the Zionist Council of Eastern Galicia, November 14, 1937, CZA — F3/5. The derogatory term *Żydokomuna* was widely used in Poland at the time to indicate the allegedly close connection between the Jews and Communist subversion.

75. *Sprawozdanie Sejmu*, no. 60, December 2, 1937. The information was provided by Emil Sommerstein, who based his statement upon the Belorussian newspaper *Christiańska Dumka*. The Belorussian youth reportedly rebuffed the overture from OZON.

76. Cable, Kennard to Eden, September 22, 1937, PRO — FO 371/20765.

77. Polonsky, *Politics*, p. 431.

78. The seeming rapprochement between OZON and the Endecja youth was increasingly criticized during 1937 by various Sanacja circles, including the group of "colonels" coalesced around Walery Sławek. See, among others, *Nation und Staat*, 11:186 (1937–38). Biddle reported that Mościcki did not look with favor upon Rydz-Śmigły's policy of seeking a rapprochement between OZON and Endecja. Biddle to Secretary of State, October 22, 1937, NA — 860C.00/703.

79. The name was, of course, a play on "Night of the Long Knives" (in Polish, *noc długich nożów*). Rydz-Śmigły later denied ever having planned such a move, and some historians have cast doubt upon the purported plan's existence. Among those who believe that a coup was planned and who have adduced documentary support for their belief, see Chajn, *Materiały*, 1:37; Jędruszczak, *Ostatnie Lata*, p. 242. On the other hand, Stawecki, *Następcy*, p. 153, discounts the existence of a detailed plan for a coup, pointing out that the documents that speak of it all emanate from opponents of the regime. There does not, however, appear to be much doubt that the idea of a coup in general terms was seriously discussed. See Żarnowski, *Polska Partia*, pp. 272–74; Polonsky, *Politics*, pp. 430–32.

80. See *Gazeta Polska*, April 21, 1938. See also Pobóg-Malinowski, *Najnowsza historia*,

2:802–5; Terej, *Idee*, p. 166; Windyga, "Obóz," p. 184.

81. AJCB, *The Jewish Situation in Poland*, January-February 1938, pp. 2, 4.

82. *JTA Bulletin*, May 9, 1938; *Nowy Dziennik*, May 9, 1938.

83. *JTA Bulletin*, April 26, 1938.

84. Cables, Kennard to Halifax, PRO — FO 371/21804–805.

85. Full text in *Sprawy Narodowościowe*, 1938/3:278–79.

86. Polonsky, *Politics*, p. 440.

87. *JTA Bulletin*, December 4, 1938. He also stressed the importance of Jewish emigration from Poland.

88. *Der Tog*, December 22, 1938. *Der Tog* was a name taken temporarily by *Haynt* because of the newspaper's difficulties with the censor. See also Raczyński's favorable response to Skwarczyński's initiative, December 30, 1938, AIP — A.12/52/4.

89. *Słowo*, quoted in *Der Tog*, January 6, 1939. *Dziennik Ludowy*, January 5, 1939 also published an item about OZON's plans for introducing antisemitic legislation. See Korzec, "Antisemitism," pp. 97–98. However, the news agency Iskra denied this report; see *Nowy Dziennik*, January 16, 1939.

90. *Osteuropa* 14 (1938–39):362–63; *Der Tog*, January 20, 1939.

91. Hans von Moltke, Germany's ambassador to Warsaw, observed in a note to his Foreign Ministry as early as November 1938 that no anti-Jewish legislation was likely to be enacted because Polish-Ukrainian relations had deteriorated, and the Poles could not act against both the Ukrainians and the Jews at the same time. *DGFP*, Ser. D, 5:132, doc. 103. Moltke noted that OZON had prepared proposals for anti-Jewish laws. In another message Moltke expressed his belief that the Polish government lacked the courage to alter the legal status of the Jews. Moltke to German Foreign Ministry, January 3, 1939, YVA — JM 2220.

92. At this time the participants in the meeting already knew of the advances that had been made by OZON to a portion of the still illegal ONR.

93. They believed that this opposition group was oriented toward a pro-French foreign policy, whereas Koc's camp identified with Beck's more pro-German line.

94. In this connection the possibility was raised of sending a delegation consisting of Anshel Reiss, Moshe Kleinbaum, and Henryk Rosmarin to the United States for 6–8 weeks. Their plan was to establish a newspaper with pro-French tendencies in which Polish opponents of antisemitism, who did not wish to publish their views in Jewish or socialist publications, could express themselves. This idea was also discussed in the Jewish press; see, for example, the position of Juliusz Kalisz of Lwów, *Nasz Przegląd*, July 16, 1937.

95. Reiss to Secretariat, Israel Workers' Party (Mapai), March 17, 1937, LPA — 37/101b. With regard to the Congress of National Minorities, it is not clear exactly what was intended. The Jewish delegation had withdrawn from the yearly meetings in 1933 after the Congress that year had refused to condemn Nazi Germany's Jewish policy. The final such Congress was held in Stockholm in 1938. See *Sprawy Narodowościowe*, 1937, no. 6, pp. 658–59.

96. *Sprawozdanie Senatu*, no. 22, March 5, 1937.

97. Report on the third convention of the Polish Jewish Veterans Organization, 1937 (typescript in Jewish National Library, Jerusalem).

98. On this law, see below, chap. 5.

99. *Dos Yudishe Togblat*, May 24, 1938.

100. Ibid., May 23, 1938. See also *Sprawy Narodowościowe*, 1938/3, pp. 308–9.

101. *Folkstsaytung*, May 23, 1938 and May 26, 1938.

102. *Haynt*, March 2, 1937.

103. *Haynt*, April 21, 1938.

104. Ibid., February 10, 1939. Kleinbaum stood against the argument put forth by some other Jewish leaders that Jews ought to cooperate with the regime in an effort to exert a moderating influence upon its anti-Jewish policy.

105. See Kleinbaum's article in *Der Tog*, December 30, 1938.

106. *Chwila*, February 3, 1937; *Haynt*, February 3, 1937. The congress also declined to entertain a motion urged upon it by Bund members to include in the platform a plank encouraging the struggle against Zionism.

107. See Biddle to Secretary of State, October 1, 1937, NA — 860C.4016/509.

108. Żarnowski, "PPS w przededniu II wojny," p. 499. On police prohibition of joint Jewish-Christian demonstrations, see Tomicki, "Warszawska organizacja," p. 280.

109. Żarnowski, "PPS w przededniu II wojny," pp. 508–9. In this connection an article by W. Kosowski in the newspaper *Naye Folkstsaytung*, March 5, 1939, complained bitterly about the failure of a recent decision of the PPS supreme council to include clearly and specifically the struggle against antisemitism as part of the fight against "national chauvinism and racism." On the other hand, a memoir by a Łódź Bundist claims that in that city PPS leaders supported a joint demonstration with Jews wholeheartedly but were prevented from carrying out such a demonstration by the opposition of the local authorities. Hertz, *Geshikhte fun Bund*, p. 415. For details on the nature of the relationship between the Bund and PPS, see Brumberg, "The Bund," pp. 75–94.

110. On the pogroms and ghetto benches, see below, chaps. 4 and 5.

111. A joint PPS-trade union delegation submitted to Mościcki a memorandum on November 13, 1937 calling, among other things, for the government to change its policy on the Jewish question. See Żarnowski, "PPS w przededniu II wojny," pp. 507–10; *Nasz Przegląd*, November 14, 1937.

112. Berenstein, "KPP," p. 53.

113. Zachariasz, *Di Komunistishe Bavegung*," pp. 98–101. A similar proclamation was issued by the Warsaw committee of KPP in June 1937. See Bernstein, "KPP," p. 36.

114. At the end of 1937, the Warsaw branch of KPP numbered 1215 members organized in 182 party cells. Over 65 percent of the members were Jews. Drozdowski, *Klasa Robotnicza*.

115. See Zachariasz, *Di Komunistishe Bavegung*, p. 103; Jędruszczak, "O działalności KPP," p. 141. During the latter half of 1938 the Communist International disbanded KPP, charging that it had been infiltrated by "provocatory elements." See also Dziewanowski, *The Communist Party*, pp. 150–54.

116. The Jewish press viewed this silence as a positive development, indicating that the party no longer insisted upon including in its official pronouncements a paragraph calling for the displacement of the Jews from their positions in the economy. See, among others, *Chwila*, February 3, 1937 (J. Wurzel, "Rekordziści Górą"). In August 1937 the demand was embodied in the famous ten-day peasant strike, during which 42 protesters were killed and over 1200 people arrested. See also Wynot, "The Polish Peasant Movement," pp. 52–53.

117. *Zielony Sztandar*, as quoted in *Nasz Przegląd*, October 5, 1937.

118. *Materiały źródłowe*, doc. 150, p. 371.

119. *Dos Yudishe Togblat*, January 15, 1937 (H. Zeidmann, "Stam Politik un Real-Politik"). See also the article by A. B. Ekarman, "Orientatsie," in the same issue.

120. See *Unzer Velt*, March 26, 1937 (Y. Leyzerovitsh, "Vegn Orientatsie").

121. Among the mainstream Zionists, including the General Zionists and Mizrahi, there were no differences in principle over the diagnosis of the Jewish situation in Poland at that time. In practice, on the other hand, the General Zionists of Galicia, Et Livnot (representing the opposition to the dominant trend among the General Zionists of Congress Poland), and Mizrahi tended to differ with the Zionist Federation of Congress Poland over tactical issues. The former groups believed that Jewish interests required that Jews be represented among the parliamentary opposition, whereas the latter organization believed that such representation would merely strengthen the Sanacja regime, which was hostile to Jews.

122. Kleinbaum to Gruenbaum, January 17, 1937, CZA — A127/492/1. See also *Nasz Przegląd*, January 9, 1937.

123. See, for example, the editorial in *Folkstsaytung*, February 12, 1937 and the article by Henryk Erlich, "Tsiyonizm un Antisemitizm," in the same newspaper's issue of October 23, 1938. See also Alter, *Tsu der Yidn-Frage*, p. 108–11.

Chapter 3: The Economic Campaign Against the Jews

1. On the moratorium and its effects upon Polish Jewry, see above, pp. 3–4.

2. Opposition to the proposal to extend the scope of the debt moratorium was voiced in particular by two members of parliament from Agudas Yisroel, Sejm Deputy Leyb Mincberg and Senator Jakub Trockenheim. See *Sprawozdanie Sejmu*, no. 3, October 29, 1935; *Sprawozdanie Senatu*, no 3, November 5, 1935.

3. *Sprawozdanie Sejmu*, no. 10, February 17, 1936.

4. Ibid., no. 16, February 24, 1936.

5. On this policy, see above, p. 21.

6. *Sprawozdanie Sejmu*, no. 27, June 17, 1936. Sommerstein had spoken about the factors driving Jews toward Communism in an earlier speech as well; ibid., no. 16, February 24, 1936. On this subject see also Otiker, "Tenu'at HeHaluts," p. 67.

7. *Sprawozdanie Sejmu*, no. 3, October 29, 1935. Later that year Sejm deputy Izaak Rubinstein also spoke on the same theme. Ibid., no. 4, December 6, 1935. It should be pointed out that during this period general economic trends were also highly unfavorable to Jewish interests. Employment opportunities were expanding in the mineral, electrotechnical, chemical, metal, paper, and leather industries, in which the percentage of Jewish workers had been minimal, whereas employment opportunities were decreasing in the haberdashery, lumber, food, and building industries, in which Jewish workers had been much more strongly represented. See Tomaszewski, "Robotnicy," pp. 79–80.

8. *Sprawozdanie Senatu*, no. 17, June 24, 1936.

9. *American Jewish Year Book*, 1936/37, p. 342.

10. *Sprawozdanie Sejmu*, no. 18, February 26, 1936.

11. *Nasz Przegląd*, August 5, 1936.

12. Ibid., June 24, 1936. The Jewish Economic Committee was made up of representatives of the Jewish Merchants Association, the League of Jewish Small Businessmen, the Association of Jewish Artisans, and several associations of Jews in the free professions.

13. See above, chapter 1, n. 16.

14. *Folkshilf*, May 1935, November–December 1936.

15. Ibid., May 1935.

16. Ibid., November–December 1935. About 50 percent of the capital for the free loan funds came from the American Jewish Joint Distribution Committee.

17. *Nasz Przegląd*, December 19, 1936.

18. See the survey of the activity of the credit unions in *Ruch Spółdzielozy*, May 5, 1935.

19. Joint, *Aid to Jews Overseas*, 1936, p. 29.

20. J. C. Hyman, General Secretary, Joint Distribution Committee, to M. D. Bressler, October 30, 1935, CZA — S52/233.

21. See Szajkowski, "Reconstruction," p. 134. See also *Nasz Przegląd*, November 16, 1935; Bauer, *My Brother's Keeper*, p. 199.

22. *Di Kooperative Bavegung*, no. 9, September 1935.

23. Spokesmen for the Polish cooperative movement accused the cooperatives of the national minorities of possessing a political character and the Jewish cooperatives in particular of being tied to international Jewish finance. See Z. Łagiewski, "O spółdzielniach mniejszości narodowych w Polsce," *Spółdzielczy Przegląd Naukowy*, August-September 1935, quoted in *Ruch Spółdzielczy*, no. 12, 1935. See also Bernard Kahn, director, European Office, JDC, to A. G. Brotman, Board of Deputies of British Jews, January 5, 1936, BDBJ — Poland, 535; Tartakower, "Ma'avakam haKalkali," p. 167; Bauer, *My Brother's Keeper*, pp. 196–97.

24. *Nasz Przegląd*, June 26, 1936.

25. See Tartakower, "Pauperyzacja," p. 121. On the failure of efforts to maintain producers' and marketing cooperatives see Prowalski, "Społdzielczość," pp. 614–15.

26. *Folkstsaytung*, May 5, 1936 ("Rekht oif Arbet").

27. *Sprawozdanie Sejmu*, no. 3, October 29, 1935.

28. Haynt, July 7, 1936. See also Tartakower, "Pauperyzacja," p. 121; Tomaszewski, "Robotnicy," pp. 79–80.

29. Beck to Raczyński, June 10, 1936, AIP — A12/53/4.

30. Locker to Weizmann, October 22, 1936, Weizmann to Marks, October 28, 1936, WA — 1936.

31. *Chwila*, August 13, 1936.

32. Quoted in *Gazeta Polska*, January 26, 1938. On the policy of the government to remove Jews from various branches of commerce and to encourage peasants to move to cities and towns in order to assume Jewish positions, see Biddle to Secretary of State, October 1, 1937, NA — 860C.4016/509.

33. See Sommerstein's remarks at a meeting of the council of the East Galician Zionist Federation, September 12, 1937, CZA — F3/5.

34. "Joint-Barikht," January-July 1938, pp. 18–19, AL — 255. See also the editorial in *Folkstsaytung*, June 16, 1938.

35. *Nasz Przegląd*, December 31, 1937, represented Stanisław Cat-Mackiewicz, editor of the conservative Wilno newspaper *Słowo*, as holding this view.

36. *Tygodnik Polityczny*, April 10, 1938.

37. "Baricht Joint," January-July 1938, AL — 255. On the origins of Związek Polski, see above, p. 21.

38. Report dated September 21, 1937, Archives of the German Foreign Ministry, POL/V 5915 (microfilm in YVA).

39. *Nasz Przegląd*, November 16, 1937; Kennard to Eden, November 17, 1937, PRO — FO 371/20765; Landau and Tomaszewski, *Gospodarka Polski*, 4:453–54.

40. *Dos Yudishe Togblat*, November 15, 1937; Landau and Tomaszewski, *Gospodarka Polski*, 4:456–57.

41. *JTA Bulletin*, January 30, 1938.

42. *Sprawozdanie Sejmu*, no. 71, February 17, 1938.

43. *AJYB*, 1938/39, p. 243. On the change in government policy and on the open support given by government spokesmen to the Polonization of the country's economic life, see Landau and Tomaszewski, *Gospodarka Polski*, 4:457. Beck, in a conversation with Biddle, also presented the removal of Jews from economic life in Poland as a natural and necessary process. See Beck's report, August 25, 1938, HIA — Poland, Ambasada U. S., 64–4.

44. "Baricht-Joint," January-July 1938, pp. 23–25.

45. *Haynt*, February 10, 1938.

46. *Haynt*, April 1, 1938.

47. Ibid., September 22, 1938.

48. Ibid.

49. Ibid., April 12, 1938. See also Krzywicki, *Wspomnienia*, p. 373.

50. *JTA Bulletin*, April 21, 1938.

51. See Leyb Mincberg's remarks, *Sprawozdanie Sejmu*, no 67, February 11, 1938.

52. *Haynt*, January 18, 1938, published the text of two letters sent within a two-week interval by Falanga to the (Christian) owners of a canned goods business. The first warned against continued commercial contacts with a certain Jewish-owned factory, lest the adressees be identified as enemies of Polish commerce. When this letter did not achieve its goal, it was followed by a second one, signed by the Fighting Division (*Wydział Bojowy*) of ONR, threatening the business with destruction.

53. *Sprawozdanie Senatu*, no. 22 (March 5, 1937). According to *Rolnik Żydowski*, February-March 1937, the total estate holdings of Jews in these districts represented no more than 7 percent of the available land. On the forced redistribution of Jewish-owned lands in Galicia, see Levavi, "Ma'amadah shel haHakla'ut," pp. 186–87.

54. *Sprawozdanie Sejmu*, no. 37, February 11, 1937.

55. A copy of the report is in AL — 246.

56. *Folkshilf*, no. 7–8, July-August 1937.

57. Ibid., no. 11, November 1937.

58. *Chwila*, November 24, 1937. Almost a year later, in October 1938, this committee held two conferences about organizing Jewish-made products for export and prepared an exhibition of such products. See *Sprawy Narodowościowe*, 1938, no. 4–5, p. 480.

59. *Nowy Dziennik*, February 21, 1939. The committee's chairman, H. Ruttenberg, believed that conditions were especially ripe in the United States for acquiring merchandise produced by Polish Jews, because of the boycott of German, Italian, and Japanese produces and because of the desire of American Jewry to assist the Jews of Poland.

60. "United British Appeal for Polish Jewry," February 1937, BDBJ — Poland, 249. See also Schwarzbart, *Tsvishn beyde Velt-Milkhomes*, p. 44. The Jewish population of Katowice increased from 4.5 percent of the total population in 1931 to 6.7 percent in 1938. Goldin, "Yidn in Katovits," p. 248.

61. *Nasz Przegląd*, December 26, 1937. See also *Folkshilf*, no. 12, December 1937. There are no precise figures on the number of Jews. The funds devoted to their relief, however, were sizeable, suggesting that their number was considerable. See below.

62. Joint, *Aid*, 1937, pp. 27–28. For figures on the amount of aid distributed by the Joint in Poland between 1935–38, see Bauer, *My Brother's Keeper*, p. 190; Marcus, *Social and Political History*, p. 141.

63. See Yehoshua Gottlieb's comments on this matter in *Sprawozdanie Sejmu*, no. 71, February 17, 1938.

64. Coded telegram no. 44, April 16, 1937, AIP — A12/53/17.

65. See Szembek, *Diariusz*, 3:66, 184, 187–89.

66. Joint, *Aid*, Poland 1938, pp. 38, 41.

67. *Barikht-Joint*, January-July 1938, p. 16; *Haynt*, March 7, 1938. See also Brandes, "Der rekhtlikher motsev," p. 182; Trunk, "Der ekonomisher antisemitizm," p. 30.

68. *Nasz Przegląd*, August 7, 1937.

69. *Haynt*, May 4, 1938 (B. Yaushzahn, "Bravo,"). On the demands of the Gdańsk merchants, see also Mincberg's remarks in the Sejm, *Sprawozdanie Sejmu*, no. 67 (February 11, 1938). The author of the *Haynt* article contrasted the Łódź merchants favorably with several Jewish wholesalers from Warsaw, who in the winter of 1937–38 stopped extending credit to Jewish shopkeepers in provincial towns out of fear that the boycott would impair their ability to repay their debts. At the same time, they continued to extend broad credit to Christian merchants.

70. See, for example, *Haynt*, June 30, 1938 (A. Silberschein, "Der Veg fun Virtshaftlikher Zelbstshuts").

71. Minutes of meeting between representatives of the Joint in Poland and the Joint Executive for Europe, Warsaw, November 20, 1938, CAHJP — PL 224. See also the memorandum by D. Schweitzer, January 7, 1939, ibid. This idea was first discussed in July 1938 at a meeting between Bernard Kahn, director of the Joint's European office, and the heads of the Joint office in Warsaw. Kahn asked to set up a local body consisting of important Jewish figures in commerce, banking, industry, and manufacturing. Morris Troper, who replaced Kahn in October 1938, continued to pursue the same idea. See Bauer, *My Brother's Keeper*, pp. 294–95.

72. Minutes of meeting between Joint and Cekabe, Warsaw, February 23, 1939, CAHJP — PL 224.

73. *Der Tog*, December 4, 1938. See also Micewski, *Z geografii*, p. 223.

74. Quoted in *Dos Yudishe Togblat*, January 29, 1939.

75. See Potocki to Beck, June 21, 1937, AAN — MSZ 2299/3–5. The report mentioned a meeting held in New York by Potocki and Deputy Minister of Industry and Trade Mieczysław Sokołowski with the heads of the JDC and several Jewish bankers.

76. See Biddle to Secretary of State, October 20, 1937, NA — 860C.4016/516.

Chapter 4: Anti-Jewish Violence

1. See Drozdowski, *Polityka gospodarcza*, pp. 44–46.

2. Berenstein, "KPP," pp. 5–6, identifies three separate anti-Jewish pogrom waves in interwar Poland: 1918–20, during the first years of Polish independence; 1929–31, during the economic crisis and the intensification of the class struggle; and 1935–37, during a period of depression and mounting fascism in the country.

3. In analyzing these pogroms, it is not appropriate to rely exclusively upon the contemporary Jewish press. Often the Jewish newspapers had to ignore certain important details because of censorship restrictions, to delay publication of reports about the pogroms until an official statement about them had been issued, and to adjust their reports to the official statement. After a while the Jewish press developed a special style for describing anti-Jewish violence. It did not use the term "pogrom" and even refrained from speaking of "antisemitic excesses." It also generally spoke about "energetic intervention by the police." See Singer, *Od Witosa*, pp. 19, 34; also the remarks by Rubinstein in *Sprawozdanie Sejmu*, no. 4, December 6, 1935. For examples of the manner in which censorship restrictions affected reporting about

pogroms in Jewish newspapers, see Gothelf, "Itonut," pp. 156, 279.

4. For details about the Grodno pogrom and the trial that followed it, see *Nasz Przegląd*, June 13, September 22, and November 5 and 16, 1935.

5. *Nasz Przegląd*, June 13, 1935; Berenstein, "KPP," p. 19.

6. *Nasz Przegląd*, November 30, 1935; Berenstein, "KPP," p. 19. On June 6, 1936 twenty rioters from Odrzywół were put on trial. See *Haynt*, June 7, 1936.

7. See, for example, *Sprawozdanie Sejmu*, no 4, December 6, 1935.

8. See the report of a special correspondent in Przytyk, *Nasz Przegląd*, February 3, 1936.

9. *Sefer Przytyk*, p. 163.

10. *American Jewish Year Book*, 1936/37, p. 333.

11. *Nasz Przegląd*, June 17, 1936; *Folkstsaytung*, June 17, 1936.

12. *Warszawski Dziennik Narodowy*, June 10, 1936.

13. See *Haynt*, June 30, 1936.

14. *Chwila*, June 18, 1936.

15. *American Jewish Year Book*, 1936/37, p. 333.

16. Ibid.

17. *Sprawozdanie Senatu*, no. 11, March 12, 1936.

18. *Haynt*, June 19, 1936 (Y. Thon, "Przytyk als a Moshel").

19. Ibid., July 3, 1936 (Y. Thon, "Gor a groysen Toes gehat").

20. Rottenstreich to Jewish Agency Executive, March 27, 1936, CZA — S25/10004.

21. To be sure, a Communist Party activist wrote in his memoirs that in 1936 Jewish and Polish workers in Otwock organized to prevent a planned pogrom there by members of ONR. Rybak, "Wspomnienia," pp. 270–71. See also Berenstein, "KPP," p. 38. On the trial of three Jewish young people in Otwock on charges of attacking members of ONR, see *Nasz Przegląd*, May 16, 1936.

22. Dobkin Diary, September 28, 1936; report to the secretariat of the Central Committee of the Workers' Party of Palestine (Mapai), LPA — 36/101b.

23. This plan violated the Polish government's condition that those Jews who received military training leave Poland immediately. See *BeRu'ah Se'arah*, pp. 18, 33–34. See also Arazi testimony, AH; *Sefer Toledot HaHaganah*, 2:999–1000.

24. Enciphered cable, Beck to Raczyński, August 16, 1936 (no. 26), AIP — A12/53/15.

25. *Warszawski Dziennik Narodowy*, March 18, 1936.

26. Ibid., June 4, 1936. A Polish historian has attributed the Przytyk pogrom, as well as other pogroms occurring during the same period, to Jewish provocation. See Borkowski, 'O społeczeństwie,' pp. 132–33.

27. *Nasz Przegląd*, March 16, 1936.

28. *Dos Yudishe Togblat*, March 16, 1936 (A. M. Rogovi, "Nisht Davke Przytyk").

29. *Nasz Przegląd*, March 17, 1936.

30. Ibid., May 21, 1936.

31. *American Jewish Year Book*, 1937/37, p. 334.

32. *Der Yidisher Arbeter Klas*, pp. 14–15; see also Hertz, *Geshikhte*, pp. 388–89.

33. The circular is reproduced in *Der Yidisher Arbeter Klas*, p. 17.

34. See Berenstein. "KPP," p. 46. PPS did not take part in the strike of March 17, but its journal, *Robotnik*, did express solidarity with the Jewish strikers in its issues of March 17–18. Żarnowski, *Polska*, p. 58.

35. *Der Yidisher Arbeter Klas*, p. 29; Berenstein, "KPP," pp. 47, 50.

36. *Der Yidisher Arbeter Klas*, pp. 58, 63.

37. *Yudishe Togblat*, March 17, 1936. This stance also undoubtedly reflected the party's anger over the introduction of a bill in the Sejm to outlaw the slaughtering of kosher meat. On this bill, see below, chapter 5. See also Mendelsohn, "Politics," p. 57.

38. *Unzer Velt*, March 20, 1936.

39. *Nasz Przegląd*, March 18, 1936. For more on the actual course of the strike in Warsaw, see Goldstein, *Tsvantsik Yor*, pp. 43–45, 289–92; *Henryk Erlich un Wiktor Alter*, pp. 41–43.

40. *Yudishe Togblat*, March 18, 1936.

41. This effort was undoubtedly prompted by the simultaneous efforts of Jewish organizations to unite all Jews within a single World Jewish Congress.

42. *Der Yidisher Arbeter Klas*, pp. 164–65.

43. Ibid., p. 169. See also Mirkin, *Eyn Kongres*, pp. 12–13.

44. *Nasz Przegląd*, May 22, 1936; see also *Der Yidisher Arbeter Klas*, pp. 177–78.

45. *Der Yidisher Arbeter Klas*, pp. 216–17. The Bund called the Communists' approach "neoreformist," in contrast to its own "revolutionary socialist" orientation.

46. *Unter der Fon*, pp. 289–90. See also *Der Yidisher Arbeter Klas*, p. 166.

47. *Folkstsaytung*, 11, June 23, 1936.

48. In the indictment handed down against Chaskielewicz a year later, the possibility was raised that the accused had acted on behalf of an underground organization. Chaskielewicz maintained that he had killed Bujak, who had been his commander during the period of his military service eight years earlier, because the sergeant had singled him out for harsh treatment at the time. *Gazeta Polska*, June 3, 1937.

49. The Communist Rybak, "Wspomnienia," pp. 268–69, writes that local military authorities gave special leave to officers and NCOs so that they could take revenge upon the Jews for the death of their comrade.

50. In the Sejm, Sommerstein spoke out against holding all 6,000 Jews of Mińsk-Mazowiecki responsible for Bujak's death, arguing that those who did so effectively removed Jews from the circle of those protected by the law. *Sprawozdanie Sejmu*, no. 27, June 17, 1936. On the application of the principle of Jewish collective responsibility, see Rudnicki, *Obóz Narodowo-Radykalny*, p. 292.

51. *Nasz Przegląd*, June 3, 1936. An Endek newspaper wrote that several Jews had shot and killed Bujak without any provocation. In response, according to this account, Polish youth had begun to smash the windows of Jewish homes and businesses. *Warszawski Dziennik Narodowy*, June 3, 1936.

52. Leszczyński, "HaPera'ot beFolin," p. 46.

53. *Nasz Przegląd*, June 3 and 4, 1936.

54. Ibid., June 17, 1936.

55. Ibid., June 5, 1936. A normal daily routine began to be restored only on June 6, although reinforced police detachments continued to patrol the streets. Ibid., June 7, 1936.

56. Ibid., June 4, 1936.

57. *Haynt*, June 8, 1936. On the panic in Mińsk-Mazowiecki, see also Goldstein, *Tsvantsik Yor*, pp. 293–96. Goldstein, leader of the Bund's militia in Warsaw, had been sent by his party to Mińsk to organize self-defense units there, in case the riots were renewed.

58. *Nasz Przegląd*, June 25, 1936. See also Pobóg-Malinowski, *Najnowsza Historia*, 2:834.

59. *Chwila*, June 27, 1936. See also *Folkstsaytung*, June 24, 1936 ("Myślenice").

60. See, for example, *Warszawski Dziennik Narodowy*, June 3, 1936.

61. *Haynt*, June 7, 1936; *Folkstsaytung*, June 8, 1936.

62. See, for example, the speech of the attorney for defendant Yehiel Lesko, as reported in *Haynt*, June 24, 1936.

63. *Nasz Przegląd*, June 27 and August 11, 1936. In November 1936 a court of appeals in Lublin actually imposed even stiffer sentences upon several Jewish defendants. However, it also sentenced some of the Poles who had previously been acquitted to terms of up to 1.5 years in prison. On the whole, the appellate court upheld the reasons that the lower court had given for its verdict. See *Nasz Przegląd*, November 25, 1936, February 5–6, 1937.

64. *Nasz Przegląd*, June 28, 1936.

65. See *Folkstsaytung*, June 20, 1936. *Haynt*, October 26, 1936, lashed out bitterly against this wave of trials, arguing that one could not bring charges against every Jew who spoke sharply about Poles during a personal altercation while at the same time ignoring the daily crude insults to which Jews were subjected.

66. *Nasz Przegląd*, June 30, 1936.

67. This lack of response was noted in ibid., July 1, 1936.

68. See *Haynt*, July 5, 1936.

69. *Folkstsaytung*, June 29, 1936.

70. *Nasz Przegląd*, July 1, 1936; *Haynt*, July 1, 1936.

71. See, for example, *Nasz Przegląd*, July 2, 1936; *Folkstsaytung*, July 11, 1936.

72. See *Nasz Przegląd*, September 23, 1936.

73. *American Jewish Year Book*, 1937/38, p. 410.

74. As quoted in *Sprawozdanie Sejmu*, no. 30, December 2, 1936. At the same meeting Sommerstein railed against the Przytyk trial having turned the courts into fora for antisemitic agitation.

75. *American Jewish Year Book*, 1937/38, p. 413.

76. The details about the Brześć pogrom were revealed publicly only two weeks after the event, as the result of a parliamentary interpellation directed by Sommerstein to Składkowski. Although Jewish newspapers had possessed accounts of the course of events as early as the day following the pogrom, out of fear of the censors they delayed publishing any reports until a Polish government spokesman had made an official statement. See Singer, *Od Witosa*, p. 334. The details of the pogrom presented here are based on accounts in *Nasz Przegląd*, June 5, 1937, and in Goldstein, *Tsvantsik Yor*, p. 308.

77. In contrast, in two earlier smaller riots – one that took place in Czyżew on January 5, 1937 (in which two Jews were killed), and another in Sokołow Podlaski on April 1 – the police responded energetically. See *Nasz Przegląd*, January 7, 12 and April 2, 1937.

78. Goldstein, *Tsvantsik Yor*, pp. 304–10.

79. *Chwila*, May 21, 1937 (E. Sommerstein, "Brześć"). For the newspaper's late edition the censorship eliminated a portion of this article.

80. The newspaper stated, "We wish to warn the Jews that they are responsible for the results of the method of provocation thoughtlessly employed by them." Quoted in *Haynt*, May 18, 1937.

81. *Warszawski Dziennik Narodowy*, May 28, 1937 ("Na szlaku Prytyk-Brześć nad Bugiem").

82. *Haynt*, June 14, 1937, published a report about "Polish merchants from Poznań and Pomorze arriving in Brześć and expressing interest – for the time being without success – in acquiring Jewish shops."

83. *Robotnik*, as quoted in *Haynt*, May 18, 1937. The editor of the PPS organ inquired rhetorically, "If a Polish criminal murders a policeman somewhere, am I, the editor of *Robotnik*, responsible?" He argued further that it had become necessary to defend Poland against the penetration of the psychology and dubious morality of the Third Reich.

84. *Chwila*, May 24, 1937.

85. *Folkstsaytung*, May 27, 1937.

86. Ibid., May 23, 1937.

87. The Jewish press placed special emphasis upon this aspect of the response to the pogrom, arguing that the fundraising effort should not be regarded merely as a philanthropic undertaking but as an essential element in the struggle against anti-Jewish violence in general. Newspapers themselves took party in the fundraising campaign and criticized wealthy Jews who did not contribute in what they regarded as sufficient measure. See, for example, the editorial in *Haynt*, June 20, 1937.

88. *Haynt*, May 23, 1937.

89. *Nasz Przegląd*, June 11, 1937. The fundraising efforts extended even to small villages where Jews were in serious economic straits. Also, the Association of Jewish Merchants decided at its annual meeting on May 31 to exert every effort to assist the Jews of Brześć. Even earlier, on May 19, the Association had sent a special delegation to the site of the pogrom. See *Nasz Przegląd*, May 20 and June 3 and 18, 1937.

90. *Haynt*, July 12, 1938.

91. Report of U.S. Ambassador Biddle to Secretary of State, June 18, 1937, NA — 860C.4016/476.

92. This feeling was frequently reported by representatives of the Jewish community in Palestine who had been sent to Poland to assist Jews who wished to settle in the Jewish homeland. See, for example, the various letters in LPA — 37/101b.

93. *Nasz Przegląd*, June 9, 1937. In the Szczerbowski trial, too, the attorney for the family of the murdered policeman publicly praised the way in which the Polish community in Brześć had demonstrated national unity against the desire of the Jews to take over their country. Ibid., June 16, 1937.

94. Ibid., June 9, 10, and 12, 1937.

95. Ibid., October 13, December 2, 1937.

96. *Nasz Przegląd*, July 20, 1937, according to a report in *Warszawski Dziennik Narodowy*. During the first days following the pogrom the Jewish press was forbidden to publish information about it, although Endek newspapers described the frenzy in the streets in detail. The authorities even went so far as temporarily to block publication of the contents of a parliamentary interpellation by Yehoshua Gottlieb on June 23, 1937, which contained an explication of the course of the riots. See *Nasz Przegląd*, June 24, 1936.

97. "Igeret Michtavim Penimit," no. 1, July 4, 1937, AH — Mordechai Hadash, 221–32.

98. Ibid.; also *American Jewish Year Book*, 1937/38, p. 415. For additional details about the pogroms in Brześć and Częstochowa and their reflection in the Polish press, see the reports of the U.S. Embassy in Warsaw to the Secretary of State, May 19, 1937, NA — 860C.4016/469; June 18, 1937, NA — 860C.4016/476; June 25, 1937, NA — 860C.4016/480. During this entire time the Endek press thundered against the efforts of the Jews to rehabilitate the pogrom victims, including the fact that Jewish shopkeepers and owners of market stalls in the various towns that had been hit by violence were at times assisted by Jewish manufacturers, who gave them jobs in their factories. Not a few Jews from the Radom district (which included Przytyk

and Odrzywół) who had been hurt by pogroms were taken in by Jewish factories in Łódź and Tomaszów Mazowiecki. The organ of Endecja expressed concern over "the apparent possibility that the bankrupt Jewish element in Brześć will be revived in Warsaw." *Warszawski Dziennik Narodowy*, August 24, 1937. In contrast, the PPS newspaper published a proclamation signed by 29 Polish academics, writers, and public figures vigorously protesting the riots in Brześć and Częstochowa, which, it claimed, had broken out as a result of racist antisemitic agitation in the country. Among the signers of this proclamation were Professors Tadeusz Kotarbiński, Tadeusz Manteuffel, and Stefan Czarnowski. *Robotnik*, July 8, 1937.

99. *American Jewish Year Book*, 1938/39, p. 263; Berenstein, "KPP," p. 26. The town of Briańsk was especially hard hit by violence in which some 50 Jews were wounded. A large number of Jewish casualties was also reported in Bielsko and Bydgoszcz. Attacks were also reported against Jewish passersby in Warsaw; in some Jewish neighborhoods the attackers were chased away. See Biddle to Secretary of State, September 28, 1937, NA — 860C.4016/510.

100. *Folkstsaytung*, September 17, 1937.

101. Testimony of Menashe Amali, head of the delegation of instructors, AH — 2407; Amali Diary, October 31, November 20, 1937, AH — 2607. The instructors complained that in some places they were not allowed to operate legally and were not provided with the financial resources that they expected.

102. See the comments about the censorship in *Folkstsaytung*, December 24, 1937: "It is more and more difficult to write, and we must camouflage what we want to say. . . . We do everything we can to keep from having what we write rubbed out. We never know what will get by and what will not; there are no fixed rules." See also *Fun Noentn Over*, pp. 191, 384; Singer, *Od Witosa*, pp. 19–20.

103. See, for example, cables, Kennard to Eden, June 25, 1937, PRO — FO 371.4674/3950/55; September 22, 1937, PRO — FO 371/20765. The British government's evaluation of the extent of the violence was apparently related to pressures being applied against it to open the gates of immigration to Palestine in light of the deteriorating situation of Polish Jewry.

104. Joint, *Aid*, Poland 1937, p. 26.

105. *Unity in Dispersion*, p. 96. This decision was universally condemned in the Polish press. See, for example, *Robotnik*, July 17, 1937; *Gazeta Polska*, July 19, 1937.

106. See the memorandum by William Strang on his conversation with Maurice Perlzweig, October 27, 1937, PRO — FO 371/20765.

107. Szajkowski, "Western Jewish Aid," pp. 175–76.

108. Ibid., p. 202.

109. Ibid.

110. Ibid., p. 161. The American Jewish Committee took a similar attitude.

111. On the origins and aims of Szoszkies's mission, see the correspondence between the Polish Foreign Ministry and the Polish diplomatic offices in Washington and New York, AAN — MSZ 2298/221–22, 227–28.

112. On the time spent by Szoszkies in the United States in the service of Poland, as well as on the results of his activities, see the report of the Polish consul-general in New York, July 15, 1937, AAN — MSZ 2299/85–87; also Szoszkies's report to the Polish Foreign Ministry, entitled "Nastroje amerykańskie w kwestji polskiej w maju–czerwcu 1937 roku," 91–107. AAN — MSZ 2299/91–107. Szoszkies had made a similar trip to the United States on behalf of the Polish government in 1934. See Szembek to Polish ambassador, Washington, July 5, 1934, HIA-Poland, Ambasada US, 66–3.

113. Bauer, *My Brother's Keeper*, pp. 194–95.

114. Potocki to Polish Foreign Ministry, May 24, 1937, AAN — MSZ 2298/114–19; May 26, 1937, AAN — MSZ 2298/129–31; June 23, 1937, AAN — MSZ 2299/32–33.

115. This motif emerged during Perlzweig's conversation with Strang; see above, n. 106.

116. See Biddle's reports to the secretary of state, August 6, 1937, NA — 860C.4016/500; October 20, 1937, NA — 860C.4016/513.

117. Cable, Biddle to Hull, October 20, 1937, in *FRUS*, 1937/2:559.

118. *Sefer Toledot HaHaganah*, 2/2:1000–1001. This principle had been stated as early as July 15, 1937 in a circular distributed to *HeHaluts* leaders; AH — M. Hadash, no. 221–32. See also Amali Diary, December 31, 1937, AH — 2607. The decision had also contained a secret protocol stating that *HeHaluts* would need in the future to find a way to organize self-defense in the Jewish communities.

119. See Laeuen, "Das polnische Ultimatum."

120. For details see Krzywicki, *Wspomnienia*, pp. 374–79.

121. *JTA Bulletin*, March 20, 1938.

122. *Haynt*, March 20, 24, 1938.

123. Cable, Beck to Raczyński, March 21, 1938 (no. 17), AIP — A12/53/19.

124. See the memoirs of the director-general of the Polish state bank PKO, Gruber, *Wspomnienia*, pp. 376–77.

125. See, for example, the editorials in *Folkstsaytung*, March 21, 1938, and *Haynt*, March 22, 1938.

126. Gruber, *Wspomnienia*, p. 377. See also the report by British Ambassador Kennard to Foreign Secretary Lord Halifax on the anti-Jewish disturbances associated with the Lithuanian crisis, PRO — FO 371/21806.

127. *Haynt*, April 6, 1938.

128. Ibid., March 1, 1939.

129. See the report on the situation of the Jews in Poland, August 25, 1938, CZA — A173/250.

130. See, for example, *JTA Bulletin*, September 16 and October 9, 1938. On the other hand, Sommerstein complained from the floor of the Sejm in January 1939 that the courts were still imposing light sentences upon attackers of Jews. See *Nasz Przegląd*, January 13, 1939.

Chapter 5: "Ghetto Benches," Agitation, and Violence in the Universities

1. Generally officials spoke of the need to limit the proportion of Jewish students in universities to the proportion of Jews in the general population of Poland, including the rural as well as the urban sectors.

2. See Pilch, *Studencki*, p. 150. On the deterioration in the status of Jewish students in Polish universities during the 1920s, see Rudnicki, "Numerus Clausus," pp. 247–53.

3. Ibid., p. 151. See also Gruenbaum, *Milhamot*, p. 327.

4. Wapiński, "Endecja," p. 840. This situation brought about the temporary closing of the Universities of Kraków and Warsaw as well as the Warsaw Polytechnikum. The University of Warsaw was closed again in November 1932, and in March 1933 Endek students proclaimed a strike protesting a government decree curtailing university autonomy. See Polonsky, *Politics*, p. 361.

5. Mahler, *Yehudei Polin*, pp. 172–75; Bronsztejn, p. 193.

6. *Wiadomości Statystyczne*, 1938/5.

7. Pilch, *Studencki*, p. 157. In 1936 Ukrainian and Lithuanian students were also removed

from a number of Polish student societies; ibid., p. 159.

8. Typescript entitled "Tsu der Lage," AL — 244.

9. See Sommerstein's remarks on this matter before the Education Committee of the Sejm, as recorded in *Nasz Przegląd*, March 14, 1935.

10. *Nasz Przegląd*, November 10, 1935.

11. For details, see Krzywicki, *Wspomnienia*, pp. 291–92.

12. A previous attempt to institute separate seating had been made in 1933–34. Pilch, *Studencki*, p. 152.

13. See Krzywicki, *Wspomnienia*, pp. 291–92; see also *Nasz Przegląd*, November 8, 1935.

14. *Nasz Przegląd*, November 20, 1935.

15. *Warszawski Dziennik Narodowy*, January 17, 18, and 22, 1936.

16. *Nasz Przegląd*, November 26, 1935.

17. At a meeting of Lwów Jewish political leaders Sommerstein declared that the imposition of ghetto benches represented a political confrontation that demanded swift and sharp reaction from a united Jewish community. See *Chwila*, December 16, 1935.

18. *Robotnik*, as quoted in *Chwila*, December 16, 1935.

19. *Nasz Przegląd*, January 26, 1936.

20. *Chwila*, December 22, 1935.

21. See *Nasz Przegląd*, January 11, 1936.

22. *American Jewish Year Book*, 1936/37, p. 330. On January 2, 1936 Neville Laski, president of the Board of Deputies of British Jews, met with Raczyński and complained about the violence against Jewish university students. Raczyński told him not to exaggerate the importance of these incidents, as they were directed against the government no less than against the Jews. See the record of the conversation in BDBJ — Poland, 249.

23. *American Jewish Year Book*, 1936/37, p. 331.

24. *Sprawozdanie Sejmu*, February 17, 1936 (no. 10).

25. Ibid., February 21, 1936 (no. 14).

26. *Haynt*, January 31, 1936 (O. Thon, "Gheto Abvehr un nokh azelkhe zakhen").

27. Thon's attitude seems strange in light of his call for greater activism in the struggle against antisemitism contained in the same article. Perhaps he had not yet sufficiently understood the intention of the initiators of the ghetto benches as they became clear later — to use separate seating in the universities as a springboard for the isolation of the Jewish population in other areas of life as well, through the enactment of antisemitic legislation. On attempts to realize this goal, see below, chap. 6.

28. See, for example, *Nasz Przegląd*, October 21, 1936; *Dos Yudishe Togblat*, October 25, 1936.

29. *Nasz Przegląd*, October 21, 30, 1936.

30. Pilch, *Studencki*, pp. 159–60.

31. *Nasz Przegląd*, October 30, November 13, 1936; *Chwila*, November 4, 1936.

32. See the remarks by Izaak Rubinsztein on the Wilno riots, *Sprawozdanie Sejmu*, December 2, 1936 (no. 30). The disturbances at the University of Wilno on November 10, 1936 (the anniversary of the death of the student Wacławski), which spread into the city, were described in detail in a report from the U. S. Embassy in Warsaw to the Secretary of State, December 17, 1936, NA — 860C.4016/454.

33. The position of the newspaper was discussed in *Haynt*, December 11, 1936.

34. *Walka Młodych*, as quoted in Pilch, *Studencki*, p. 162.

35. Żarnowski, *Polska Partia Socjalistyczna*, p. 15.

36. *Folkstsaytung,* December 11, 1936.

37. Indeed, at around the same time Endek members of the Łódź city council had introduced a bill "to allocate separate seats to Jewish members of the council, behind [those of] Christian council members." See *Chwila,* December 18, 1936. They had also introduced a proposal to establish separate railroad cars for Jews. *ABC,* as quoted in *Dos Yudishe Togblat,* October 29, 1936.

38. *Folkstsaytung,* November 27, 1936; *Nasz Przegląd,* November 27, 1936. The small circle of Bundist students at the University of Warsaw occasionally called upon the local Bund militia to help defend them against the attacks of campus antisemites. For details, see Goldstein, *Tsvantsik Yor,* pp. 237–39.

39. *Chwila,* December 10, 1936.

40. *American Jewish Year Book,* 1937/38. pp. 418–19.

41. *ABC,* as quoted in *Haynt,* January 19, 1937.

42. See, for example, *Nasz Przegląd,* January 30, 1937.

43. *American Jewish Year Book,* 1937/38, p. 420.

44. As quoted in *Chwila,* January 29, 1937.

45. Pilch, *Studencki,* p. 160.

46. *Nasz Przegląd,* February 10, 11, 1937. On February 28, 1937, 760 Jewish students from the University of Lwów took part in a sitdown strike protesting antisemitic violence and the institution of ghetto benches on campus. See *Chwila,* March 2, 1937.

47. *American Jewish Year Book,* 1937/38, pp. 422–23; *Folkstsaytung,* March 18, 1937.

48. *American Jewish Year Book,* 1937/38, p. 423. Interestingly, the Ukrainian newspaper *Dilo* expressed difficulty understanding why Jews were so vigorously opposed to the ghetto benches; Ukrainians, the newspaper claimed, would be happy to be offered separate seating. It opined that the Jewish reaction reflected the Jews' eternal desire to push their way into strange surroundings and to assimilate completely. As quoted in *Chwila,* February 15, 1937.

49. Pilch, *Studencki,* p. 154.

50. The order contained the following provisions:

a. Students belonging to the Polish student organization *Bratnia Pomoc* will take up seats on the right side of the lecture halls, in areas marked with the letter B.

b. Jewish students belonging to the organization *Wzajemna Pomoc* will take up seats on the left side of the lecture halls, in areas marked with the letter W.

c. Students not belonging to either organization will take up seats in areas marked with the letter N. See *American Jewish Committee Bulletin,* February 1, 1938 (Special Bulletin on "The Ghetto Question in the Universities in Poland"). Details on the order are also given in a report by Biddle to the U. S. Secretary of State, October 7, 1937, NA — 860C.4016/513.

51. *American Jewish Year Book,* 1938/39, pp. 264–65. One of the Warsaw institutions to issue such an order was the Wawelberg Government School. This school had been founded as the result of a donation by a Jewish philanthropist, who had included in the terms of his donation a stipulation that Jewish students would not be subject to any discrimination. The order thus violated the terms under which the institution had been established. See *Nasz Przegląd,* December 4, 1937. Cf. Sommerstein's Sejm speech on the ghetto benches, *Sprawozdanie Sejmu,* December 2, 1937 (no. 60).

52. *American Jewish Year Book,* 1938/39, pp. 264–65. This arrangement was to be submitted to a plebiscite of non-Jewish students. Ukrainian students at the University of Lwów refused

to take part in such a plebiscite, fearing that eventually a "Ukrainian-free day," like a "Jewish-free day," would be declared. They demanded that a separate Ukrainian university be established in Lwów. See *Chwila*, October 25, November 12, 1937.

53. For the text of Kulczyński's letter, see Chajn, *Materiały*, 1:238–40. For details about the incident, see *American Jewish Year Book*, 1938/39, pp. 265–66; Pilch, *Studencki*, p.165. Two deans, Prof. Ostrowski of the Faculty of Medicine and Prof. Samsonowicz of the Faculty of Natural Sciences, also resigned their posts in solidarity with Prof. Kulczyński. See *Nowy Dziennik*, January 13, 1938.

54. *Nasz Przegląd*, October 8, 1937.

55. *Nowy Dziennik*, March 13, 1938.

56. *Folkstsaytung*, October 15, 1937.

57. See, for example, the remarks by Izaak Rubinsztein in the Sejm, *Sprawozdanie Sejmu*, February 20, 1937 (no. 43). Jews were not the only ones to sense such a trend; in a diplomatic cable U.S. Ambassador Biddle spoke of the danger of ghettoization in the areas of public transportation, culture, and art. Biddle to Secretary of State, October 7, 1937, in *FRUS*, 1937, 2:558. And actually such suspicions were not without basis; attempts had already been made to set aside separate areas for Jewish stalls in marketplaces and separate cars for Jews on certain tramway lines (ostensibly in order to protect Jews from Endek attacks). See *Tygodnik Polski* August 1, 1937; *Nasz Przegląd*, July 14, August 10, 1937; *Folkstsaytung*, December 8, 1937. See also Rudnicki, "Numerus Clausus," p.261. Moreover, an Endek newspaper wrote explicitly that the ghetto benches were meant to be the first stage toward the goal of establishing separate Jewish neighborhoods in Poland's cities. *Warszawski Dziennik Narodowy*, October 9, 1937.

58. *Folkstsaytung*, October 15, 1937. The phrase "Polish Streichers" referred to Julius Streicher, the Nazi Gauleiter of Franconia, known as one of the Hitler regime's crudest and most vociferous Jew-baiters.

59. *Chwila*, October 16, 19, 1937.

60. *Nasz Przegląd*, October 15, 1937.

61. See above, n. 59.

62. *Dos Yudishe Togblat*, October 20, 1937, published the names of many Jewish businessmen in Warsaw who did not participate in the strike. See also *Haynt*, October 20, 1937. British Ambassador Howard Kennard, evidently unimpressed by the Jewish response, reported that the strike did not lead to further action during the next month. He observed that "the Jews are beginning to understand that protests such as this will not prevent further restrictions upon their rights." Cable, Kennard to Eden, November 17, 1937, PRO – FO 371/20765.

63. *Chwila*, December 12, 1937.

64. *Haynt*, December 19, 1937.

65. *Nasz Przegląd*, December 10, 1937; Krzywicki, *Wspomnienia*, pp. 357–71.

66. See *Nasz Przegląd*, December 23, 1937; *Haynt*, February 2, 1938.

67. Rudnicki, "Numerus Clausus," p. 261.

68. *JTA Bulletin*, March 28, 1938.

69. *Haynt*, May 19, 1938.

70. On this resolution, see *JTA Bulletin*, October 14, 1938.

71. Ibid., November 29, 1938.

72. Ibid., November 25, December 5, 12, 1938.

73. Ibid.

74. *Nowy Dziennik*, November 28, 1938.

75. *Haynt*, February 10, 1939.

76. *JTA Bulletin*, December 8, 1938. Jewish students walked out of the academy in protest.

77. *Folkstsaytung*, January 14, 1939. The Bar Association explained that the reason for segregation was to protect the Jewish students. Jews, however, refused to participate in this scheme. See also *Nowy Dziennik*, January 10, 1939, March 5, 1939.

78. *Haynt*, February 9, 1939; *JTA Bulletin*, February 19, 1939. The family of Michael Wawelberg, who had founded the school, sued the institution's trustees, claiming that the institution of ghetto benches violated the agreement that the school's benefactors had signed with the Ministry of Education. See *Nowy Dziennik*, January 16, 1939.

79. See *Nowy Dziennik*, November 30, 1938; *Der Tog*, November 30, 1938.

80. *Haynt*, February 10, 1939.

81. *Folkstsaytung*, March 12, 1939.

82. Ibid., January 21, 1939.

83. *Haynt*, February 12, 1939; *JTA Bulletin*, February 15, 1939.

84. *Haynt*, February 5, 1939. There were some Jewish students who lost a full academic year for refusing to comply with ghetto bench orders. See *Folkstsaytung*, May 12, June 17, 1939.

85. Quoted in *Haynt*, March 14, 1939. Bartel singled out the rector of the Polytechnikum for criticism for not acting aggressively against those who committed violent acts within the walls of the institution.

86. *JTA Bulletin*, May 31, 1939.

87. *Haynt*, June 15, 1939.

88. *JTA Bulletin*, June 16, 1939.

89. *Gazeta Polska*, the semi-official government organ, published two editorials, on July 3 and 11, 1939, against university autonomy, arguing that Endek circles were using this autonomy to impose a reign of anarchy and terror as a means of advancing their own political purposes.

90. In 1937–38 there were 4,790 Jewish students in Poland, representing about 10 percent of the total number of university students in the country. In 1938–39 their number fell to 4,113, or 8.2 percent of the total student body. See Mahler, *Yehudei Polin*, p. 172. Also, it should be noted that during the same period the number of students from other minorities remained fairly level. See the table in Pilch, *Studencki*, pp. 169–70.

91. For a discussion of the reactions of Polish students to anti-Jewish violence, see Pilch, *Studencki*, p. 167.

Chapter Six: The Kosher Slaughtering Ban and Other Anti-Jewish Legislation

1. Revenues from kosher slaughtering constituted the largest source of income for Jewish communities. See Lestschinski, "Economic Aspects," p. 327.

2. See, for example, the polemics by Cynamon, "Momenty," and Wojtyna, *Handel mięsny*.

3. See Lewin, Munk, and Berman, *Religious Freedom*.

4. Rozenmann, *Zagadnienie*, p. 9.

5. Trzeciak, *Ubój Rytualny*. See also *Nasz Przegląd*, May 3, 1935.

6. They did draw a devastating refutation from the noted Orientalist Prof. Tadeusz Zaderecki of Lwów, who exposed Trzeciak's ignorance of Judaism. Zaderecki, *Z Biblią*, p. 12.

7. See, for example, Awigdor, *Ubój Rytualny*, esp. p. 10 (stressing the Jewish religion's traditional emphasis upon the prevention of suffering by animals), and Seidman, *Prawda*, esp. pp. 17–18, 70–72.

8. Asz, *W obronie*, pp. 16, 25, 34–35. The author mentioned sections 112 and 113 of the April constitution, which guarantee freedom of religion.

9. *Nasz Przegląd*, July 17, 1935.

10. *Nasz Przegląd*, September 20, 1935. See also "Barikht Joint," January-July 1938, AL – 255; Brandes, "Der Rekhtlikher Motsev," pp. 180–81. The Hebrew/Yiddish word translated in the text as "decree" is *gezerah*, which conveys the sense of a punishment inflicted from above.

11. See *Nasz Przegląd*, May 7, 1936.

12. *Sprawozdanie Sejmu*, no. 9 (February 7, 1936).

13. Among them were Poznań, Wilno, Częstochowa, Grudziądz, and Gniezno.

14. "Sprawy Uboju Rytualnego," *Sprawy Narodowosciowe*, 1936, pp. 108–11.

15. *Nasz Przeglad*, February 28, 1936.

16. Szembek, *Diariusz*, 2:129–30.

17. Even before his discussion with Kościalkowski, Szembek had instructed Ambassador Raczyński in London to explain to the press that Prystor's motion did not stem from antisemitic motives, although certain circles in Poland were interested in attributing such motives to it. Cable, Szembek to Raczyński, February 13, 1936, AIP – A.12/53/14. This explanation, of course, conflicted with Kościalkowski's later explanation.

18. *Nasz Przegląd*, February 17, 1936; *Chwila*, February 18, 1936.

19. See Gitman, *Jews*, pp. 141–43. The Polish government was well aware of the interest shown by the Joint Foreign Committee in the situation of Polish Jewry. See Ministerstwo, *Sprawozdanie*. Jewish organizations also exerted some pressure upon the British government regarding the proposal to ban kosher slaughtering. A staff member of the British Embassy in Warsaw, who investigated the matter on his government's instructions follwing the dispatch of a letter from the chief rabbi of Great Britain to the Polish ambassador in London, concluded that such intervention was not warranted, because economic and humanitarian motives rather than antisemitic ones stood behind the proposal. His assessment was that the Polish government did not support the proposal because of the heavy opposition in Jewish circles; he believed that the government would try to have the proposal amended in order to permit kosher slaughtering in quantities limited but sufficient for Jewish needs. Cable, Evling, British Embassy, Warsaw, to Eden, February 28, 1936, PRO – FO 371/19963.

20. Gruenbaum to Goldmann, March 10, 1936, CZA – L22/201.

21. Gruenbaum did not believe that kosher slaughtering would be outlawed altogether but merely strictly limited.

22. The journalist Bernard Singer also wrote that the initiators of the anti-*sheḥita* legislation were really interested in getting at Kościałkowski, knowing that he would not dare to oppose an antisemitic bill. *Haynt*, January 1, 1937 (B. Singer, "Di For-Geshikhte un Nokh-Geshikhte fun Shite-Gezets").

23. It is interesting to note that Gruenbaum did not mention the pogrom in Przytyk, which had taken place the previous day. Probably he was not yet aware of what had happened there. It is interesting also to compare Gruenbaum's evaluation with that of Chaim Weizmann, president of the World Zionist Organization. Some two weeks earlier he had written to Stephen Wise, "I think that the situation in Poland is worse even than in Germany. There [in Poland] we are dealing with a population that is used to making pogroms, one that is entirely uncontrollable, as well as with a larger Jewish community than in Germany possessing much less ability to resist and already half-starved." Weizmann to Wise, February 27, 1936, WA – 1936.

24. Actually, Wise did visit Poland in July 1936 to investigate the situation, but he spoke merely about organizing relief for Jews who had been injured by adverse legislation or by pogroms. See *Chwila*, July 20, 1936.

25. Goldmann to Gruenbaum, March 19, 1936, CZA — L22/201.

26. Grudzanski, *Avi'ezer*, pp. 359–60.

27. Ibid.

28. *Sprawozdanie Sejmu*, no. 21, March 17, 1936.

29. *Nasz Przegląd*, March 21, 1936.

30. *Sprawozdanie Sejmu*, no 22, March 20, 1936.

31. *Sprawozdanie Senatu*, no. 15, March 27, 1936.

32. They did not, however, take part in any of the debates over the bill.

33. From an article in the UNDO organ, *Dilo*, as quoted in *Chwila*, March 9, 1936. See also the report from Lwów in *Haynt*, March 11, 1936 (B. Cegrowski, "Di Shtelung fun di Ukrainer in der Shite-Frage").

34. Interview with Baran in *Haynt*, March 30, 1936.

35. In the 1935 elections Agudas Yisroel candidates had even run on the Sanacja list.

36. *Sprawozdanie Sejmu*, no. 22, March 20, 1936. Mincberg evidently meant to point out that part of Prystor's original proposal had been modeled after a Bavarian law that had been enacted at the instigation of the Nazis. See Lewin, Munk, Berman, *Religious Freedom*, p. 85.

37. See, among others, Grudzanski, *Aviezer*, pp. 360–61; *Dos Yudishe Togblat*, March 17, 1936 (Lamed Vav, "Shite un Przytyk").

38. "Sprawy Uboju Rytualnego," *Sprawy Narodowościowe*, 1936, pp. 101–108.

39. Ibid.

40. *Folkstsaytung*, March 21, 1936. The Bund had condemned the outlawing of kosher slaughtering even before the law had been enacted, stating that the initiators of the idea were antisemites no less than those who advocated physical violence against Jews. They had proposed such legislation in order to protect the interests of Polish butchers and slaughterhouses, but they sought to disguise their motive in a cloak of "humanitarianism." See *Folkstsaytung*, February 14, 1936.

41. There were some ten thousand kosher butchers in Poland in 1936, and another five thousand Jews were involved in other aspects of the meat industry. Assuming that these people headed families of four, it can be estimated that some sixty thousand Jews were dependent on the meat industry for their livelihoods. See the memorandum presented to the World Jewish Congress by the Central Professional Council of Jewish Trade Unions in Poland, August 5, 1936, CZA — S25/10004.

42. As Moshe Kleinbaum explained following the renewal of debate in the Sejm over the *shehita* issue in February-March 1938, the Jews had previously suffered discrimination only in administrative practice, not in law. In his view, the ban on kosher slaughtering set an ominous precedent, for "if one brick is removed from the foundation of legal equality, the entire structure of public order is shaken." *Haynt*, March 25, 1938 (M. Kleinbaum, "Di Shtim fun Idisher Varnung").

43. *Nasz Przegląd*, October 28, 1937.

44. Representatives of the larger Jewish communities met in Warsaw on November 28, 1937 to discuss ways of making up the lost income that had resulted from the limitation of *shehita*. They estimated that their incomes had been reduced by as much as fifty percent, and they proposed that each Jew now be required to pay community dues amounting to ten percent of

his income tax obligation. See *Sprawy Narodowościowe*, 1937, no. 6, p. 678.

45. Actually, between February and November 1937 quotas for kosher meat were reduced significantly in Warsaw, Łódź, Lwów, and Kraków. See *Haynt*, January 7, 1938.

46. See the diary of Yitshak Gruenbaum, February 19, 1937, CZA — A127/37.

47. *Sprawozdanie Sejmu*, no. 65, February 1, 1938. Dudzinski was among twelve Sejm deputies and senators representing OZON who resigned from the camp in April 1938, citing, among other things, what they believed to be the camp's moderation with regard to the Jewish question. In August 1938, Dudziński was invited to take part in a Congress of Experts on the Jews (*Kongres Żydoznawczy*), set to take place in Erfurt under German government sponsorship. The Polish Foreign Ministry expressed objection to participation by members of the Polish parliament in this event. See the opinion of the Emigration Department, August 16, 1938, AAN — MSZ 9906/148–49.

48. *Haynt*, March 20 and 22, 1938.

49. *JTA Bulletin*, March 24, 1938.

50. *Haynt*, March 27, 1938.

51. The bill was initially scheduled to be considered by the Senat on March 29, but it appears that the government acted to delay the deliberation. See *Nowy Dziennik*, March 29, 1938.

52. The ferment on the Jewish street was noted in the reports of British and American diplomats in Poland. See cable, Kennard to Halifax, April 1, 1938, PRO — FO 371/21806; cable, Biddle to Secretary of State, March 29, 1938, NA — 860.6/4016/545. Biddle believed that the Senat would not pass the bill that it had received from the Sejm, for the Senat was generally more liberal than the Sejm with regard to the Jewish question.

53. *Folkstsaytung*, March 27, 1938.

54. *Dos Yudishe Togblat*, March 20, 1938 (M. Rogovy, "An Ezsamen fun Natsionaler Distsiplin").

55. *Haynt*, March 28, 1938.

56. Ibid., March 29, 1938.

57. Ibid., April 1, 1938. See also *Sprawy Narodowościowe*, 1938, nos. 1–2, pp. 121, 138.

58. Cable, Szembek to Raczyński, March 29, 1938 (no. 22), AIP — A12/53/19. Szembek sought to prove that the amendment's motives were economic rather than religious by pointing out that the Bund (which might be assumed to have shown no interest in the matter were it entirely of a religious nature) was active in protests against it.

59. *American Jewish Year Book*, 1938–39, pp. 256–57.

60. See above, n. 47.

61. *JTA Bulletin*, December 9, 1938. The Senat did not have time to consider the bill during its 1938 session. In November 1938 new elections to the Polish parliament were held and, according to the legislature's by-laws, it was necessary for the Sejm to pass the law again.

62. Ibid., February 28, 1939. Agriculture Minister Poniatowski told the committee that the government was disappointed that the existing law had not managed to prevent the sale of kosher-slaughtered meat to non-Jews.

63. Ibid.; also *Haynt*, March 1, 1939.

64. *JTA Bulletin*, March 8, 1939.

65. *Haynt*, March 10, 1939.

66. *Dos Yudishe Togblat*, March 12, 1939.

67. *JTA Bulletin*, March 12, 1939; *Haynt*, March 16, 1939. Jewish newspapers managed to work around this restriction by publishing recipes for meatless meals.

68. *Haynt*, March 23, 1939.

69. *JTA Bulletin*, May 12, 1939. In his memoirs Składkowski wrote that he was opposed to a total ban, mainly because he feared that such a ban would injure Polish cattle raisers. Thus, he claims, he sought to draw out debate on the bill so that it would eventually fall. Składkowski, *Nieostatnie*, p. 226.

70. The Germans forbade kosher slaughtering altogether in occupied Poland on Octover 26, 1939. See Trunk, "Der Ekonomisher Antisemitizm," p. 31.

71. See the appendix to the report by A.Drexel-Biddle to the U.S. Secretary of State, October 1, 1937, NA — 860C.4016/509. See also Gitman, *The Jews,* p. 166; Majchrowski, "Obóz," p. 147.

72. *Chwila*, May 10, 1937. Forty Jewish doctors who had been present at the convention walked out following the vote. It should also be pointed out that the Warsaw, Kraków, and Lwów branches of the medical association declared their opposition to the Aryan paragraph at special meetings. See *Chwila*, May 28 and June 21, 1937.

73. The lawyers' assembly spoke with alarm of the "Judaization" of the legal profession in Poland, noting that of the country's 7,189 attorneys, 3,806 (53 percent) were Jews. See *Gazeta Polska*, May 10, 1937.

74. *Gazeta Polska*, January 7, 1938.

75. Giertych, *O wyjściu*, p. 262.

76. *Nowy Dziennik*, January 10, 1938.

77. *Haynt*, April 14, 1938.

78. Mahler, "Jews," p. 339. A German publication devoted to the study of Eastern Europe noted with praise that the Thirteen Theses on the Jewish Question of OZON and the desire of Endecja to imitate the anti-Jewish legislation in Hungary had encouraged "Aryanization" procedures in various organizations, such as the Young Lawyers Organization, the Journalists Association of Pomorze, and the Architects and Geographers Association. *Osteuropa*, 13 (1937/38), p. 766.

79. *American Jewish Year Book*, 1938/39, p. 253.

80. *JTA Bulletin*, June 13, 1938. For further details on legislation aimed at closing the legal profession to Jews, see Mahler, "Jews," pp. 319–21.

81. In his report to the British Foreign Office, British Ambassador Kennard in Warsaw spoke of the law as a means of fighting against Jewish "monopolisation" of various professions, adding that further laws would permit the limitation of Jewish entry into the medical profession as well. The ambassador expressed understanding for this aim; however, he noted with concern that such anti-Jewish measures were not likely to remain confined to the economic field and that they possessed political significance. Cable, Kennard to Halifax, June 24, 1938, PRO — FO 371/21806. Moreover, during the second half of 1938, the Polish Bar Association petitioned the minister of justice for exceptions to be made in the case of 100 potential attorneys, all non-Jews. According to *Haynt*, February 7, 1939, the association had requested that Christian lawyers be granted special consideration for their talents "in view of the situation in the [legal] profession from an ethnic point of view." Similarly, in early 1939 the governing body of the Bar Association considered 99 applications for admission; it forwarded the applications of all 36 non-Jews to the justice minister with favorable recommendations, whereas it did so for none of the 63 applications from Jews. See *JTA Bulletin*, January 23, 1939; *Haynt*, January 27, 1939.

82. *Nowy Dziennik*, March 19 and March 30, 1938. For more on this law and its application, see below, chap. 8.

83. *Barikht Joint*, AL — 255, p. 22.

84. On the import of this law, see Brandes, "Der Rekhtlikher Motsev," p. 181.

85. *Haynt*, February 4, 1938.

86. See above, chap. 4.

87. *Sprawozdanie Sejmu*, no. 40, February 16, 1937. Sommerstein continued to speak out on this theme throughout the next two years. Eventually Justice Minister Grabowski upbraided him for using the Sejm to criticize the Polish judiciary. See *JTA Bulletin*, January 23, 1938; *Der Tog*, January 13, 1939.

88. Gitman, *The Jews*, pp. 168–69.

89. See *Haynt*, January 25 and 26, 1938; *JTA Bulletin*, January 26, 1938. Emil Sommerstein argued that the Jews in question were not "foreigners" at all but had merely fled from Polish territories during the war and returned to them following the conclusion of hostilities.

90. As reported in *Der Tog*, October 30, 1938.

91. On OZON and the Thirteen Theses, see above, chap. 2.

92. See *Gazeta Polska*, January 24, 1939.

93. "Notatka w sprawie knoferencji Pana DDK u Pana Ministra Becka (ściśle tajne)," February 15, 1939, AAN-MSZ 9908/53–54. Drymmer, who also served as head of the Personnel Department of the Foreign Ministry, prepared a list of the names of forty permanent employees of the Ministry who were allegedly "of non-Aryan (Semitic) descent." The list included some senior Ministry officials. "Wykaz urzędników statowych MSZ pochodzenia niearyjskiego (semickiego) — stan wiosna 1939r," AAN — MSZ 9981/56–57.

94. See *Fun Noenten Over*, p. 191.

95. See, for example, *Nasz Przegląd*, June 3, 1937.

96. See, for example, the editorials in *Nowy Dziennik*, March 24, 1938, and in *Folkstsaytung*, March 28, 1938. Actually, the Citizenship Law facilitated the expulsion of Polish Jews from Germany in October 1938. On this see below, chap. 8.

97. *Haynt*, February 3, 1939 (M. Kleinbaum, "Es fehlt Mut oyf der Poylisher Zayt"). Kleinbaum portrayed the government as being torn between its responsibility to all Polish citizens and its inability, because of domestic and foreign political pressures and a basic lack of courage on its part, to state decisively that Jews were equal citizens under the 1935 constitution.

98. *JTA Bulletin*, June 23, 1938. The Polish censorship authorities forbade publication of any news about the hunger strike. It became known only as the result of an interpellation in the Sejm by Emil Sommerstein. "Barikht Joint," AL — 255, p. 15.

99. See, for example, the remarks of the two parliamentarians as quoted in *Der Tog*, January 12 and 13, 1939.

Chapter 7: The Failure of Jewish Leadership in Poland

1. The modern Hebrew pronunciation is represented here. Most Polish Jews would have pronounced the word *kehiles*, with a Yiddish inflection.

2. Tomaszewski, "Walka polityczna," p. 85; Brandes, "Der Rekhtlikher Motsev," pp. 154–55, 157.

3. Sakowska, "Z dziejów," p. 164.

4. Grynsztejn, *Regulamin*. For details about this ordinance, see Krasowski, *Związki wyznaniowe*, p. 188. The ordinance did not include the communities of Upper Silesia.

5. *Nasz Przegląd*, January 24, June 18, 1935. The appointed Lwów board also failed to satisfy the authorities, and it was replaced again on February 13, 1936. See *Chwila*, February 14, 1936.

6. See the evaluation in *Nasz Przegląd*, August 7, 1936.

7. See above, chap. 4.

8. This rising prestige was noted by Zionist activists. See, for example, the letter from the Central Council of Jewish Trade Unions (an organization of Po'alei-Tsiyon C.S.) to the Executive Committee of the General Federation of Jewish Workers in Palestine (*Histadrut*), February 21, 1936, HA — HL/4/24. See also the entry in the diary of Eliyahu Dobkin from Poland, August 29, 1936, LPA — 36/101b.

9. *Folkstsaytung*, July 5, 1936. See also ibid., July 10, 1936 (H. Erlich, "Moychel di Privilegie"). The Bund had refrained from taking part in the communal elections in Warsaw in 1931 because of the community's thoroughly religious character. See Johnpoll, *Politics of Futility*, pp. 180–81.

10. *Folkstsaytung*, July 30, 1936.

11. 94,300 Jews in Warsaw had the right to vote in these elections; voter turnout was thus approximately 45 percent.

12. See the table in *Yidisher Arbeter*, pp. 224–25.

13. *Haynt*, September 8, 1936.

14. *Yudishe Togblat*, September 8 and 10, 1936.

15. *Folkstsaytung*, September 13, 1936.

16. See Sakowska, "Z dziejów," p. 180.

17. *Chwila*, September 8, 1936.

18. *Yidisher Arbeter*, pp. 222–24. The Zionist bloc won three seats in this election.

19. Agudas Yisroel received 21 percent of votes cast, the General Zionists 17 percent, the so-called nonparty Orthodox 15.5 percent, other independents 9.5 percent, representatives of artisan associations 9.4 percent, the Bund 8.8 percent, Mizrahi 6.2 percent, Po'alei-Tsiyon C. S. 5.5 percent, the Revisionists 2.7 percent, Left Po'alei-Tsiyon 1.8 percent, representatives of merchant associations 1 percent, and the Folkspartay 1 percent. See *Sprawy Narodowościowe*, 1937:123–24.

20. All segments of the population took an active role in the Łódź elections; this had not been the case in the parliamentary elections of September 1935.

21. Kowalski, *Trudne Lata*, p. 548; Strauch, "Mo'etset haIr," p. 295. The Zionists received four seats in this election, a German national list one, and Left Po'alei-Tsiyon one.

22. See *Nasz Przegląd*, July 5, 1935.

23. *Yidisher Arbeter*, p. 236. 24. See Gruenbaum, *Milhamot*, p. 415; *Yudishe Togblat*, September 29, 1936.

25. See Rowe, "Jewish Self-Defense," p. 125.

26. *Yidisher Arbeter*, pp. 237–38; *Nasz Przegląd*, August 10, 1936. Four Jewish communists were included in the PPS list. PPS argued that only its list contained candidates from all national groups and that only Polish socialists could protect Jews from the Endeks. See Hertz, "Geshikhte," p. 399. On the other hand, the party worked to convince Polish voters that it was not, as the Endeks charged, essentially a "Jewish list." See Żarnowski, *Polska Partia Socjalistyczna*, p. 149.

27. *Yidisher Arbeter*, pp. 239–40; *Haynt*, September 29, 1936; Polonsky, *Politics*, p. 415.

28. *Nasz Przegląd*, October 1, 1936.

29. *Yidisher Arbeter*, pp. 243–44, 248–49.

30. *Warszawski Dziennik Narodowy*, September 29, 1936. The British ambassador in Warsaw, who prepared a detailed report on the elections for his government, did not accept the argument that masses of Jews had voted for PPS. This report, which emphasized the

importance of the elections as the first opportunity since the death of Piłsudski for the Polish public to vote democratically, concerned itself mainly with the absolute defeat of Sanacja just when it was reorganizing itself into a new camp under the leadership of Colonel Koc and when Endek strength was declining compared to the elections of 1934. Kennard to Eden, October 2, 1936, PRO − FO 371/19957.

31. Cf. the analysis of the elections by Berl Locker of the Jewish Agency Executive, who had visited Poland during the campaign. He noted that many Zionists had voted for the PPS list in Łódź and for the Bund in the Warsaw community elections. The reason for this behavior, he suggested, was that during a time when possibilities for immigration to Palestine were small, the Polish Zionist movement, which was in any case suffering from a leadership crisis, was bound to become weaker, whereas the Bund possessed "a leadership that naturally tended to stay in Poland and was directed [in its thinking] toward Poland." Circular dated December 9, 1936, LPA − 36/101g.

32. *Folkstsaytung*, December 17, 1936. See also Hertz, *Geshikhte*, pp. 403–404.

33. Central Committee of the Zionist Federation of [Congress] Poland to Gruenbaum, May 7, 1936, CZA − A127/459. See also Circular No. 32 of the Zionist Federation of [Congress] Poland, February 28, 1936, in which the first organizational steps toward establishing a Polish Jewish Congress were discussed.

34. See *Haynt*, May 3, 1937 (M. Kleinbaum, "Bay der Geendeter Lage in Poyln").

35. See below, n. 45.

36. *Chwila*, June 18, 1937. See also *Sprawy Narodowościowe*, 1937, no. 6:658–59.

37. *Chwila*, June 13, 1937.

38. See *Haynt*, June 30, 1937; *Sprawy Narodowościowe*, 1937, no. 3:304–305.

39. See *Sprawy Narodowościowe*, 1937, no. 4–5:47.

40. A copy is located in LPA − 37/101.

41. See Cukierman to the Organizing Committee, January 19, 1938, CZA − F3/21. A copy of the electoral ordinance is located in CZA − F3/20. The ordinance provided that any Jew over age 18 who purchased a voter's card was eligible to vote in the elections, which were to be equal, secret, general, direct, and proportional. Any Jew over age 24 who purchased a voter's card was elegible for election to the Congress.

42. See, for example, Schwarzbart to Nahum Goldmann, World Jewish Congress, October 22, 1937, and Chaim Hilfsztein to Goldmann, October 24, 1937, CZA − L22/219/2.

43. See the minutes of the meetings of the Zionist Federation of East Galicia, September 12 and November 14, 1937, CZA − F3/5.

44. For example, the organizing committee discussed the possibility of explicitly eliminating religious and cultural issues from the Congress's purview, so as to avoid the appearance that the Congress claimed authority over the internal spiritual content of Jewish life. See the reports on the conferences of Zionist representatives in Warsaw, October 15, 1937 and January 21, 1938, CZA − F3/21. Emil Schmorak, a Zionist leader from Lwów, proposed that delegates from Agudas Yisroel be returned to the Congress without elections. Minutes of the Directorate of the Council of the Zionist Federation of East Galicia, October 18, 1937, CZA − F3/5.

45. Agudas Yisroel demanded that delegates to the Congress be chosen not through elections but by a standing committee of representatives of the Jewish communities. The party argued that, instead of promoting Jewish unity, the Congress would injure that unity; unity without a Congress was to be preferred to a Congress without unity. See *Dos Yudishe Togblat*, November 22 and December 27, 28, and 31, 1937.

46. See, for example, the editorials in *Folkstsaytung*, October 30 and December 28, 1937. Interestingly, the Communist Party of Poland at first supported the idea of a Congress, even with Zionist leadership, as a potentially effective, broadly-based weapon in the battle against fascism. Later, however, it claimed that the Zionists were using the Congress merely to advance their own ideological position. The Communists believed that any all-Jewish Congress should concern itself only with the struggle of the Jews inside Poland and should not deal with issues dividing the Jewish public. *Unter der Fon*, pp. 293–95.

47. See *Sprawy Narodowościowe*, 1938, no. 1–2:121, 129. On the debate within Polish Jewry over emigration, see below, chap. 9.

48. *Nasz Przegląd*, November 1, 1937.

49. In January 1938 they even prepared a detailed agenda for the Congress. See *Sprawy Narodowościowe*, 1938 (no. 1–2):120.

50. *Nowy Dziennik*, February 27, 1938.

51. The Bund had already raised this idea once before, in 1936. See above, chap. 5.

52. See *Folkstsaytung*, January 1, 1938.

53. *Haynt*, February 8 and 24, 1938.

54. See *Nowy Dziennik*, April 9, 1938; Haynt, April 10, 1938.

55. Kleinbaum to Goldmann, April 26, 1938, CZA — L22/219/2. Several days earlier Emil Schmorak had come to a similar conclusion. See the minutes of his meeting with Anshel Reiss, April 21, 1938, CZA — F3/21.

56. See above, chap. 6.

57. See below, chap. 8.

58. See above, chap. 6.

59. *JTA Bulletin*, April 3, 1938.

60. Reiss to Goldmann, March 27, 1938, CZA — A180.

61. *Haynt*, July 1, 1938 (Moshe Kleinbaum, "Etapn").

62. See ibid., September 25, 1938; *Der Tog*, October 28, 1938 (A. M. Hartglas, "Di Idishe Achdes un di Shtodtrat-Vahlen"). See also Sommerstein's remarks to the Zionist Federation of East Galicia, October 2, 1938, CZA — F3/5.

63. The official name of the body proposed by the Bund was Congress of the Jewish Working Masses (*"Kongres fun di Yidishe Arbetende Masen"*).

64. See *Sprawy Narodowościowe*, 1938, nos. 4–5, p. 477.

65. See *Haynt*, September 11, 1938.

66. See *Folkstsaytung*, August 12, 1938 (Sh. Lerer, "Tsu der Platform fun Kongres fun di Yidishe Arbetende Masen"). Left Po'alei-Tsiyon did not participate in the efforts to organize such a Congress, thus reversing the stance that it had taken in 1936. See Trunk, "Der ekonomisher Antisemitizm," p. 94.

67. *Folkstsaytung*, July 29, 1938 (Shimon Dubnow, "Vegn der Izolatsie fun Bund").

68. Ibid., July 29, 1938, continued July 31, 1938 (H. Erlich, "Tsi iz der Tsiyonizm a Bafrayendik Demokratishe Bavegung?").

69. Ibid., October 30, 1938. See also Hertz, *Geshikhte*, p. 414.

70. Turlejska, *Rok*, pp. 9–14; Welkisch, "Die Wahlen," pp. 162–64.

71. See *Nowy Dziennik*, September 20, 1938 (B. Singer, "Na Froncie Wyborczym"); *Robotnik*, as reprinted in *Nowy Dziennik*, October 8, 1938; Welkisch, "Die Wahlen," p. 166.

72. Turlejska, *Rok*, p. 141; Składkowski, *Nieostatnie słowo*, p. 155; Jędruszczak, *Ostatnie Lata*, pp. 309–10.

73. *JTA Bulletin*, September 13, 1938. See also *Haynt*, September 15, 1938 (M. Kleinbaum, "Dos Ayz hot gerihrt").

74. *Haynt*, September 30, 1938 (M. Kleinbaum, "Gehn oder nisht gehn").

75. Minutes of the meeting of the Zionist Federation of East Galicia, October 2, 1938, and its Political Committee, CZA — F3/5. See also *JTA Bulletin*, October 3, 1938.

76. See *Sprawy Narodowościowe*, 1938, no. 6, p. 651; *JTA Bulletin*, September 16 and 29, 1938.

77. See Turlejska, *Rok*, pp. 145–47. Składkowski, *Nieostatnie słowo*, p. 221, testified that he instructed his administration not to interfere in any way with the electoral process. His instruction, though, was not always carried out; see Żarnowski, *Polska Partia*, p. 331.

78. Szczypiórski, "Samorząd Warszawy," pp. 97–98. Elections for the Warsaw city council had not been held since 1927; since 1934 an appointed provisional council had governed the city.

79. *Der Tog*, January 1, 1939. Actually, the *Al HaMishmar*-Right Po'alei-Tsiyon alliance polled more votes than the opposing alliance led by *Et Livnot*, but because of the geographical division of electoral districts it received one less mandate. Similarly, although the Bund received less than 62 percent of the total Jewish vote, it received 85 percent of the seats on the council held by representatives of Jewish parties (17 of 20). The Left Po'alei-Tsiyon polled 2.6 percent of the votes cast for Jewish parties, but did not win a seat on the council.

80. Polonsky, *Politics*, p. 442; Żarnowski, *Polska Partia*, pp. 330–31. See also Schwarzbart, *Tsvishn*, pp. 67–68; *Folkstsaytung*, December 21, 1938. As in 1936, the Bund in Łódź had sought to present a united socialist list together with PPS, but PPS had refused, allegedly prefering practical electoral considerations to considerations of principle. See Hertz, *Di Geshikhte*, p. 427.

81. *Kurier Poranny*, as quoted in *Der Tog*, December 21, 1938.

82. *Robotnik*, as quoted in *Der Tog*, December 21, 1938.

83. Moltke to German Foreign Ministry, December 22, 1938, YVA — JM 2342.

84. Gruenbaum, *Milhamot*, pp. 427–29.

85. *Der Tog*, December 20, 1938 (M. Kleinbaum, "Der Vahl Rezultat"); December 30, 1938 (M. Kleinbaum, "Elementn un Sinteze").

86. *Folkstsaytung*, December 20, 1938. In early December 1938 over 100 Bund and trade union activists had been arrested, and five halls of unions close to the Bund had been closed by the authorities. See *Sprawy Narodowościowe*, 1938, no. 6, p. 660.

87. *Folkstsaytung*, January 6, 1939.

88. The Bund received 31,000 votes in Łódź (as compared with 24,000 in 1936), representing 57.4 percent of the total number of votes cast for Jewish lists. The so-called Zionist-Democratic Bloc polled 12,000 votes (up from 11,000 in 1936), for 22.2 percent, while Agudas Yisroel received 11,000 votes (down from 15,000 in 1936) for 20.4 percent. See *Der Tog*, January 1, 1939; *Folkstsaytung*, January 8, 1939.

89. See Żarnowski, "PPS w przededniu," p. 516.

90. *Haynt*, May 17, 1939; *Folkstsaytung*, May 23, 1939.

91. On anti-Jewish agitation prior to municipal elections, see *Haynt*, February 9 and 15, 1939.

92. *Haynt*, May 28, 1939.

93. See the Reports of the Nineteenth, Twentieth, and Twenty-First Zionist Congresses. In East Galicia no elections to the Congress were held in 1937 (the list of delegates had been agreed upon before the vote); in West Galicia and in Silesia the same situation prevailed both in 1937 and in 1939.

94. Zerubavel, Warsaw, to Histadrut Executive, Tel Aviv, February 3, 1939, HA — Poland, 1939/40, HL/4/12; Steinwachs, Warsaw, to Mereminski, Histadrut Executive, February 10, 1939, ibid., HL/4/24.

95. *Folkstsaytung*, June 2, 1939. The Zionist leader from Kraków, Yitshak Schwarzbart, believed that the Bund victory stemmed from negative factors. In his view the "Zionist orientation" had been dominant among the Jewish public in Poland, and its primary competition had come from an "orthodox-assimilationist orientation." Lately, however, the Jews, mainly in Congress Poland, had turned toward a third orientation — the Bundist. He believed that many Zionists and orthodox Jews in Congress Poland had voted for the Bund list as a protest against "the emigrationist illusion." Schwarzbart, *Tsvishn beyde Velt-Milkhomes*, pp. 66–76. Cf. Tartakower, *Yidn*, p. 208.

96. On this idea and its use as a political slogan, see below, chap. 10.

97. The electoral results in Tarnów, the second-largest Jewish community in Western Galicia, represent an exception to this generalization. In the elections held in this city on March 5, 1939 the Bund received 8 mandates and a Zionist-Agudas Yisroel bloc 5. PPS received 15 mandates, OZON 10, and Endecja 2. See *Folkstsaytung*, March 7, 1939.

Chapter 8: Ukrainians and Germans in Poland

1. For details on the major Ukrainian population centers in Poland, see Horak, *Poland*, pp. 83–84.

2. See *Nasz Przegląd*, April 28, 1933. On the connection between OUN and German espionage during the 1930s, see Torzecki, *Kwestia Ukraińska*, pp. 63, 80; Gondek, *Działalność*, pp. 237–43.

3. See Torzecki, *Kwestia Ukraińska*, p. 66.

4. *Gazeta Warszawska*, as quoted in *Nasz Przegląd*, May 3, 1933. The Endeks viewed much of the Ukrainian population in Poland as Poles of Ruthenian origin (*"gente Ruthenus — natione Polonus"*). See Terej, *Rzeczywistość*, p. 65.

5. Torzecki, *Kwestia Ukraińska*, p. 115.

6. Ibid., p. 129.

7. Ibid., pp. 119–20, 128.

8. See above, pp. 85–86.

9. *Haynt*, March 30, 1936.

10. Cable, Kennard to British Foreign Office, March 11, 1936, PRO — FO 371/C1787/445/55.

11. See Torzecki, *Kwestia Ukraińska*, pp. 152–53. On factors causing antisemitism among the Ukrainians in Poland, see Seraphim, "Der Antisemitismus," p. 341.

12. *Dos Yudische Togblat*, September 30, 1936 ("Ukrainer un Yuden").

13. *Ster*, 25 July 1937 (M. Kleinbaum, "Trójkąt polsko-ukraińsko-żydowski"). See also *Haynt*, January 14, 1938 (M. Kleinbaum, "Di Ukrainishe Politik — un di Idishe").

14. Gruenberg, *Niemcy*, pp. 15–26; Kuhn, "Das Deutschtum." Breyer, *Das Deutsche Reich*, pp. 61–62.

15. See Gruenberg, *Niemcy*, pp. 53–65; on the process of Nazification within the German organizations in Poland, see Melzer, "Relations," pp. 194–96.

16. *Nation und Staat*, 10 (1936–37): 39–40; *Osteuropa*, 13 (1937–38): 123. The Germans complained especially about the provincial governor of Silesia, Michał Grażyński. The Polish ambassador in Berlin, Józef Lipski, also complained to Polish Foreign Minister Beck that Grażyński's anti-German attitudes were hurting German-Polish relations. See Gruenberg, *Niemcy*,

pp. 119–20; Chojnowski, *Koncepcje*, pp. 106–15; Rechowicz, *Wojewoda Śląski*, pp. 145–46.

17. For details, see *The German Fifth Column*, pp. 36, 41–46; Cygański, *Hitlerowskie organizacje*, p. 182; Polonsky, *Politics*, pp. 463–64.

18. *Folkstsaytung*, July 12, 1935. For all its efforts to maintain a moderate appearance, the German-language press in Poland was rife with articles reprinted from the Erfurt-based *Weltdienst*, an international antisemitic news service that sent provocative material about Jews to Poland. See *Chwila*, November 14, 1935. Polish Senator Michał Róg claimed during a plenary session of the Senat that 25–27 German periodicals were being published in Poland and that these publications received financial assistance and instructions from the German Propaganda Ministry in Berlin. *Sprawozdanie Senatu*, No. 8 (March 9, 1936).

19. See Micewski, *Z geografii*, pp. 363–64.

20. Studnicki, *Sprawa*, pp. 88–90.

21. See *Chwila*, August 3, 1937.

22. *Słowo*, as quoted in *Warszawski Dziennik Narodowy*, April 24, 1937. See also Rudnicki, *Obóz Narodowo-Radykalny*, p. 308.

23. For more on this ambivalence, see above, chap. 1.

24. *Warszawski Dziennik Narodowy*, August 14, 1936.

25. Ibid., August 30, 1936, citing an article published in the organ of the German SA, *Der SA Mann*.

26. *Chwila*, October 28, 1935. See also Niemunis, "Stronnictwo," pp. 119–20; Wapiński, "Endecja," p. 841.

27. Such an accusation was made, for example, by the Sejm deputy Kopeć from Silesia at a meeting of the Sejm Budget Committee on January 21, 1936. See *Nasz Przegląd*, January 22, 1936.

28. *Nasz Przegląd*, September 28, 1936.

29. *Haynt*, May 13, 1938 (M. Kleinbaum, "Ven iz Kwiatkowski gerekht"). The PPS organ *Robotnik* discussed the extent to which Nazi doctrine allegedly influenced Sanacja and Endecja circles alike: "Under the guise of strengthening cultural relations between Poland and Germany, German Hitlerist proaganda is being injected [into Poland].... Not only a Polish-German treaty assists Nazi propaganda; the fascist sympathies that are widespread today in Poland assist it as well. The influential group in Sanacja — the fascist 'colonels' — is more or less sympathetic to Hitler. Endecja, as is well known, is influenced by Nazism, as proven by the numerous incidents of attacks upon Jews, of bomb plantings in Śląsk, etc. When the Endeks riot against the Jews they are collaborating with the Nazis." Quoted in *Nasz Przegląd*, February 19, 1936.

30. *American Jewish Year Book*, 1936/37, p. 339; *Nasz Przegląd*, June 27, 1935.

31. *Sprawozdanie Sejmu*, no. 4 (December 6, 1935).

32. See Polonsky, *Politics*, pp. 472–74; Cygański, *Hitlerowskie organizacje*, p. 177. On the joint declaration regarding the German and Polish minorities in the two countries, see Gruenberg, *Niemcy*, pp. 75–77; Mroczko, *Polska myśl*, pp. 252–54. On Polish-French relations during this period, see Ciałowicz, *Sojusz*, pp. 212–41.

33. See, for example, the remarks of Leyb Mincberg, *Sprawozdanie Sejmu*, no. 30 (December 2, 1936).

34. See *The German Fifth Column*, pp. 42–46; Gruenberg, *Niemcy*, p. 96; *Haynt*, June 17, 1938 (M. Kleinbaum, "Der Shotten fun Prag tsvishen Varshe un Berlin").

35. On these developments, see Polonsky, *Politics*, pp. 474–76. Beck assumed that following the Munich pact Hitler would turn against the West, and France would require assistance

from Poland. Ciałowicz, *Sojusz*, pp. 255–56.

36. See Kowalak, *Prasa*, p. 338.

37. During the interval in which it was officially closed, *Haynt* continued to appear under the name *Der Tog*. See *Fun Nontn Over*, p. 194; Finkelstein, *Haynt*, p. 130.

38. Ber, "Sochnut," p. 333.

39. See *Haynt*, February 3, 1937.

40. See the report by Joseph Cohen on the situation of the Jews in Poland, August 25, 1938, CZA – A173/250.

41. See, for example, Esch, *Polen 1939*, p. 138.

42. Nevertheless, in early 1937 the German Press Service from Poland announced in its inaugural publication that its purpose was to cultivate a satisfactory set of relationships between Poland and Germany and to serve the struggle against Jewry. Kowalak, *Prasa*, p. 237.

43. There were three ethnic German socialist organizations that did not fall to Nazi influence. One worked together with PPS, and all three condemned the annexation of Austria and the occupation of Czechoslovakia. Nevertheless, their strength diminished markedly among the German minority in Poland following Hitler's accession to power. Most of the German press in Poland began to refer to ethnic Germans as members of the German *Volksgruppe*, implying that they did not look upon themselves as Polish citizens of German national origin but demanded recognition as an integral part of the German nation, whose leader was Adolf Hitler and whose ideological orientation was expressed in the ideas of National Socialism. See Gruenberg, *Niemcy*, pp. 96, 104–106.

44. Ibid., p. 99.

45. Ibid., pp. 86–87.

46. See, for example, *Chwila*, December 1, 8, and 11, 1937; *Nowy Dziennik*, May 25, 1939. For its part, the Polish Foreign Ministry viewed the participation of Sejm deputies Wacław Budzyński and Juliusz Dudziński in the Congress of Jewish Experts scheduled for Erfurt in 1938 as undesirable on the grounds that the Polish government, seeking to solve the Jewish problem through emigration, needed the political good will of the West. The Foregn Ministry also stressed that Poland did not share the racist attitudes that were widespread in German propaganda. "Opinia E. I. w sprawie udziału posłów polskich w Kongresie Żydoznawczym w Erfurcie," August 16, 1938, AAN-MSZ 9906/148–49.

47. *Haynt*, February 10, 1939 (M. Kleinbaum, "Di Iden-Frage in Poylen – Es fehlt mut oyf der Idisher zayt").

48. Lipski, *Diplomat in Berlin*, pp. 411, 453. For further details, see Melzer, "HaDiplomatiyah haPolanit," pp. 228–29.

49. This deportation actually began on October 28. It was justified on the premise that Poland intended to revoke the citizenship of these Jews in accordance with the new Polish citizenship law of March 31, 1938. That law gave the Polish interior minister the power to revoke the citizenship of any Polish citizen who had lived abroad for five years and had given up all connection with the Polish state. For more on the adoption of this law, see above, p. 91. For its full text, see Szembek, *Diariusz*, 4:432. On German reactions to the law, see Melzer, "HaDiplomatiyah haPolanit," p. 225; Ben-Elissar, *La diplomatie*, pp. 301–21.

50. See Melzer, "HaDiplomatiyah haPolanit," p. 229.

51. Szembek, *Diariusz*, 4:207–208.

52. Report of the director of the Political Section, German Foreign Ministry, October 20, 1938, *DGFP*, D, doc. 92. See also Ben-Elissar, *La diplomatie*, p. 304. The Germans adopted this

position despite their fear that the Polish government would retaliate by expelling thousands of German citizens from Poland; as for the new Polish citizenship law, see above, n. 49.

53. Szembek, *Diariusz*, 4:217. These discussions were conducted with the utmost secrecy, so that they were not reported in the contemporary press.

54. Ibid., 4:447. See also Lipski, *Diplomat in Berlin*, pp. 461–62; Turlejska, *Rok*, p. 161.

55. Telephone message from the German Foreign Ministry to the Polish Embassy in Berlin, in *DGFP*, D, doc. 84. See also Szembek, *Diariusz*, 4:329; instruction of the Reich chief of police in Berlin to local authorities, October 26, 1938, YVA – JM 3163. Most likely this step by the Germans was a tactic in its strategy of seeking an "all-encompassing solution" to the outstanding issues of Polish-German relations.

56. Szembek, *Diariusz*, 4:332.

57. Ibid., 4:334. On October 29, to be sure, the Polish authorities arrested 50 German citizens, including 19 Jews. However, the non-Jews were released the next day, while the Jews were sent to the Polish-German frontier. Kaul, *Der Fall*, pp. 33–34.

58. Cable, Biddle, U.S. ambassador, Warsaw, to Secretary of State, October 29, 1938, in *FRUS*, 1938, 2:654. See also Adler, *Der verwaltete Mensch*, pp. 93–97; Tomaszewski, *Rzeczpospolita wielu narodów*, p. 206.

59. Ben-Elissar, *La diplomatie*, p. 309.

60. Cable, Kennard, British ambassador, Warsaw, to British Foreign Minister Halifax, November 1, 1938, in *DBFP*, DIII: 250–51. See also the report of the Joint Distribution Committee office in Warsaw from late 1938, AL – 247.

61. Heydrich to Lammers, December 2, 1938, in *DGFP*, D, doc. 107.

62. For details, see Ben-Elissar, *La diplomatie*, pp. 311–13. See also Lipski's memorandum to Beck about his conversation with Ribbentrop on November 19, 1938, AIP – A.11/49/N/7.

63. For the text of the agreement, see Adler, *Der verwaltete Mensch*, pp. 98–100. See also Ben-Elissar, *La diplomatie*, pp. 316–19.

64. Ben-Elissar, *La diplomatie*, p. 320.

65. See Sommerstein's remarks at the meeting of the Sejm Budget Committee, as quoted in *Dos Yudishe Togblat*, January 22, 1939.

66. Moltke to German Foreign Ministry, November 22, 1938, in *DGFP*, 5, doc. 103.

67. Składkowski, *Nieostatnie słowo*, p. 227.

68. Ibid., p. 226. See also *Nowy Dziennik*, January 14, 1939.

69. In fact, twenty-seven Jewish citizens of Germany were incarcerated in the camp by the Polish government. See the following note.

70. Annual report of the Joint Distribution Committee office in Warsaw, 1938, AL – 247; *JTA Bulletin*, November 2, 1938; *Der Tog*, January 13, 1939. On conditions in the camp, see Emanuel Ringelblum to Rafael Mahler, November 14, 1938, in Mahler, "Michtavim," pp. 22–25.

71. *Sprawy Narodowościowe*, 1938, 6:658–59.

72. *Unity in Dispersion*, p. 97.

73. Ringelblum to A. Fishman-Tamir, May 25, 1939, in Mahler, "Michtavim," pp. 28–29; *American Jewish Year Book*, 1939/40, p. 303.

74. Bauer, *My Brother's Keeper*, p. 293.

75. See *Nowy Dziennik*, May 1 and June 7, 1939; *Haynt*, June 7, 1939; *JTA Bulletin*, June 6 and 21, 1939.

76. Cable, German Foreign Ministry, Berlin, to German Embassy, Warsaw, May 23, 1939, YVA – JM 3163.

77. *JTA Bulletin,* June 8, 1939.

78. See, for example, *Haynt,* June 12, 1939.

79. *Haynt,* June 28, 1939. On the eve of the meeting there were 16,000 Polish Jews from Germany who had entered Poland, of whom 12,000 were dependent upon relief. *JTA Bulletin,* June 15, 1939.

80. Joint, *Aid to Jews,* 1939, pp. 25–26.

81. See Polonsky, *Politics,* p. 459.

82. See the speech by the Ukrainian deputy Mudryj, *Sprawozdanie Sejmu,* no. 60 (December 2, 1937). On Nazi propaganda among Ukrainians in Galicia, see Biddle to Secretary of State, October 10, 1937, NA – 860C.4016/509.

83. Horak, *Poland,* p. 169.

84. *Sprawy Narodowościowe,* 1938/3:285–86. See also *Haynt,* May 12, 1938. The Endek press attributed the UNDO proclamation to German influence, which aimed at weakening Poland. *Warszawski Dziennik Narodowy,* May 21, 1938. At the same time, the radical Ukrainian organization OUN continued to cooperate closely with the German espionage services – a situation reflected in the close relation between Konovalets and the head of German intelligence, Canaris. Konovalets was shot to death on May 23, 1938 in Rotterdam, evidently by a Soviet agent; nevertheless the organization's relations with the Germans continued. In the summer of 1939 a select group of 200 members was prepared in Austria to provide assistance to the German army in the event that the Germans occupied Poland. It was also to serve as the nucleus for a military uprising throughout the Ukraine. For details see Gondek, *Działalność,* pp. 236–39; Torzecki, *Kwestia,* p. 156; Armstrong, *Ukrainian Nationalism,* pp. 23, 42–43.

85. For details, see Hrushevsky, *Ukraine,* pp. 571–72; Torzecki, *Kwestia Ukraińska,* pp. 74, 160–61. See also *Nowy Dziennik,* January 8, 1939.

86. Torzecki, *Kwestia Ukraińska,* pp. 160, 175.

87. Moltke, Warsaw, to German Foreign Ministry, November 15, 1938, YVA – JM 3234.

88. See Wojciechowski, *Stosunki,* p. 523.

89. For details, see Torzecki, *Kwestia Ukraińska,* pp. 167–68. An additional factor in the German decision was the desire to see Ukrainian nationalist propaganda moderated, so as not to entice the Soviet Union out of its position of neutrality.

90. German diplomats in Poland followed this development with alarm and urged their government to issue a pro-Ukrainian declaration in order to encumber the Polish-Ukrainian rapprochement. See the letters from the German Consulate in Lwów to the German Foreign Ministry, March 21, May 12, 1939, YVA – JM 3234.

91. See above, pp. 85–86.

92. As quoted in *Chwila,* May 31, 1937.

93. *Chwila,* October 25, 1937; also *Nowyj Czas,* as quoted in *Chwila,* November 12, 1937.

94. *Dilo,* as quoted in *Chwila,* February 15, 1937.

95. *Dilo,* June 24, 1937, as quoted in *Folkstsaytung,* June 26, 1937.

96. Quoted in *Sprawy Narodowościowe,* 1937, 3:292–93.

97. See *Chwila,* July 27, 1937, in which the former Ukrainian deputy Mychajlo Strutyński recounted offers of such cooperation from ONR.

98. See the remarks of Stefan Baran in *Dilo,* November 3, 1937, as quoted in Chwila, November 4, 1937.

99. *Ster,* July 25, 1937 (M. Kleinbaum, "Trójkąt polsko-ukraińsko-żydowski").

100. Moltke to German Foreign Office, November 22, 1938, in *DGFP,* D, 5:132.

101. *Haynt*, February 10, 1939 (M. Kleinbaum, "Es fehlt mut oyf der Idisher zayt").

102. "Situation of Jews in Poland," November 29, 1938, BDBJ — Poland, 1939.

Chapter 9 : Jewish Emigration

1. For further details, see Melzer, "HaDiplomatiyah haPolanit," passim. Beginning in 1935, all of the Foreign Ministry's dealings with Jewish matters were concentrated in the Consular Division, which dealt also with emigration policy. This organizational step undoubtedly reflected a policy of dealing with Jewish matters from the perspective of emigration. The Emigration Department of the Consular Division was charged with investigating the problem of Jewish emigration and with developing proposals toward the formation of policy in this regard.

2. See ibid., p. 218; Garlicki, "Problemy kolonialne," pp. 109–110.

3. Quoted in *American Jewish Year Book*, 1937/38, p. 385.

4. French plenipotentiary in Berlin to French foreign minister, September 24, 1936, *Documents Diplomatiques Francais, 1932–1939*, Series 2, 3:414–15; cables, French ambassador, Warsaw, to French foreign minister, September 22 and 30, 1936, ibid., 3:395, 449–50.

5. See above, pp. 9–10.

6. See "Rozmowa Pana Ministra Becka z Ministrem Edenem w Londynie," November 1936, AAN — MSZ 2293/119; also Pobóg-Malinowski, *Historia*, 2:816.

7. See Biddle's summaries of his conversations with Beck about the Jewish question in Poland, Biddle to Secretary of State, October 1, 1937, NA — 860C.4016/509.

8. Goldmann to Political Department, Jewish Agency, 2 October 1936, CZA — S25/10004; Tytus Komarnicki, Polish representative to the League of Nations, to Beck, September 19, 1936, AAN — MSZ 2293/83–84.

9. Beck, *Final Report*, p. 136. For further details, see Melzer, "HaDiplomatiyah haPolanit," p. 214.

10. Lepecki, *Madagaskar*, p. 20.

11. *Sprawy Narodowościowe*, 1937, 6:672–73. For further details see Biddle to Secretary of State, January 14, 1938, NA — 860C.4016/528.

12. "Rozmowa Pana Min. Becka z Min. Edenem w Londynie," November 1936, AAN — MSZ 2293/119. See also Melzer, "HaDiplomatiyah," p. 217.

13. Beck to Raczyński, April 21, 1936, AIP — A.12/53/14.

14. See Vansittart's report on his meetings with Raczyński, May 22, 1936, PRO — FO 371/E4529/94/31; September 14, 1936, PRO — FO 371/E5814/94/31; November 2, 1936, PRO — FO 371/E6909/94/31. See also Melzer, "HaDiplomatiyah," p. 216.

15. Kennard to Eden, September 4, 1936, PRO — FO 371/E5654/94/31.

16. *Warszawski Dziennik Narodowy*, August 7, 1936.

17. Ibid., November 17, 1936.

18. Quoted in *Chwila*, November 9, 1936.

19. *Materiały*, pp. 252–53.

20. The destinations of the 30,703 Jews who left Poland in 1935 were distributed as follows: Palestine — 80.6 percent, Argentina — 6.6 percent, Brazil — 3.5 percent, United States — 2.4 percent, Canada — 1.8 percent, Uruguay — 0.9 percent, other countries — 4.2 percent. The following year, the destinations of the 16,942 Jewish emigrants were as follows: Palestine — 61.1 percent, Argentina — 15.8 percent, Brazil — 5.3 percent, United States — 3.4 percent, Canada — 1.8 percent, Uruguay — 2.1 percent, other countries — 10.5 percent. See Tartakower, "The Mi-

gration." The decline in the number of emigrants and the percentage of them going to Palestine was undoubtedly related to the tightening of immigration restrictions into that country that were imposed in 1936.

21. See JEAS, *Sprawozdanie*, pp. 3–7.

22. See Tartakower, "The Migration," p. 26. On July 1, 1935, a Territorialist Conference was held in London, where it was decided to unite the three Jewish territorialist organizations into a single organization, to be known as Freiland, the League for Territorialist Settlement. The most active branches of this organization in Poland were in Łódź and Wilno. The Paris committee of Freiland submitted a memorandum to French Colonial Minister Marius Moutet regarding opening the French colonies of New Caledonia, Madagascar, and Guiana to Jewish settlement. See Astor, *Geshikhte*, pp. 121, 134–35, and 189–90. At the head of Freiland operations in Poland stood Josef Kruk. However, the organization did not arouse a strong response in Poland. See *Nasz Przegląd*, March 3, 1936. The Polish government was said to have encouraged the activities of another organization, the Jewish-Asian Society (*Towarzystwo Żydowsko-Azjatyckie*), which promoted Jewish settlement in Asian countries other than Palestine. See Jewish-Asian Society to S. S. Wise, July 28, 1936, CZA — A243/119.

23. Gruenbaum was, of course, originally from Poland, but he had left the country several years before. Jabotinsky was not a Polish Jew at all.

24. *Nasz Przegląd*, August 4, 1936; *Haynt*, August 6, 1936.

25. *Chwila*, August 6, 1936.

26. *Nasz Przegląd*, August 4, 1936.

27. *Folkstsaytung*, August 4 and 17, 1936.

28. As quoted in *Nasz Przegląd*, August 14, 1936. Like *Folkstsaytung*, the Folkist journal also condemned Gruenbaum's 1927 remarks about the "million superfluous Jews."

29. *Haynt*, August 14, 1936 (Y. Gruenbaum, "A getsvungener Entfer"); Gruenbaum, *Milhamot*, pp. 407–10.

30. See Schechtman, *Jabotinsky*, p. 96; Remba, *Jabotinsky's Teg*, pp. 158–74; Niv, *Ma'arachot HaIrgun*, pp. 120–29.

31. The article appears in Jabotinsky, *Ketavim: BaSa'ar*, pp. 223–27. The idea of a ten-year plan for mass Jewish migration to Palestine had been mentioned earlier, in a letter from Jabotinsky to Weizmann on May 29, 1936, CZA — Z4/17135. The presidium of the New Zionist Organization in London issued a publication about the ten-year plan in August 1936: Klinger, *10 Jahres Plan*.

32. *Nasz Przegląd*, September 11, 1936. See also Schechtman, *Jabotinsky*, p. 105.

33. Jabotinsky regarded this interval as one of the most exasperating of his life. Schechtman, *Jabotinsky*, p. 113.

34. *Nasz Przegląd*, September 19, 1936.

35. Report of the Warsaw Presidium of the New Zionist Organization, June 7 to November 7, 1936, JA — New Zionist Organization, Presidium, Warsaw. See also Schechtman, *Jabotinsky*, p. 116.

36. Schechtman, *Jabotinsky*, p. 117. Jabotinsky hoped that these meetings would bring the desired results within weeks. See Jabotinsky to Jacoby, September 25, 1936, JA — A/1/2/26/2, in which he wrote that he hoped soon to obtain "a declaration coupling in some form our conception of Zionism with 'Gleichberechtigung.'"

37. Goldmann to Jewish Agency Political Department, October 2, 1936, CZA — S25/10004.

38. See Melzer, "HaDiplomatiyah," pp. 213–14. The Presidium of the New Zionist Organiza-

tion took sharp exception to the Polish call for alternate territories. See Report of the Warsaw Presidium of the New Zionist Organization, June 7 to November 7, 1936, JA — New Zionist Organization, Presidium, Warsaw.

39. See *Nasz Przegląd*, September 14, 1936; *Dos Yudishe Togblat*, September 11, 1936. On Polish press responses, see cable, Kennard to Eden, September 16, 1936, PRO — FO 371/20025. See also Garlicki and Weinbaum, "The Zionist Revisionists," pp. 93–106.

40. Jabotinsky stopped contributing to Moment thereafter, telling the editors, "I am sorry that you do not see the black clouds gathering over the heads of the Jews of Europe." He also ceased publishing his articles in *Nasz Przegląd*, to which he had been a regular contributor since 1935. See Schechtman, *Jabotinsky*, pp. 97–98.

41. Jabotinsky to Jacoby, September 25, 1936, JA — A/1/2/26/2.

42. See *Unzer Velt*, November 6, 1936 (V. Jabotinsky, "A Vort tsum Poylishen Yid).

43. See the remarks by Karol Pacznik, in *Biuletyn Okręgu Krakowskiego*, November 11, 1936.

44. *Folkstsaytung*, September 16, 1936.

45. Ibid., September 18, 1936. See also the caricature of Gruenbaum and Jabotinsky that appeared in the edition of September 26, 1936, based upon a parody of the popular Yiddish film *Yidl mit'n Fidl*, in which the two were said to be "playing the tune of [Warszawski] Dziennik [Narodowy] and Czas."

46. *Haynt*, September 20, 1936 ("Di Naye Hamtsoe"). See also Marcus, *Social and Political History*, p. 408.

47. See, for example, Fischel Rottenstreich to Chaim Weizmann, February 23, 1936, WA — 1936. Rottenstreich indicated that the Zionist leadership in Poland found it difficult to insist upon migration to Palestine as the sole solution to the Jewish question when the gates of the country were practically closed altogether. Communists, he claimed, were using this situation to argue against the Zionists, and they were "making inroads among Jewish youth. The situation," he remarked, "is frightening."

48. See the exchange of letters between N. M. Gelber and Goldmann, January 26 and 30, 1937, CZA — L22/219/2. On Weizmann's negative attitude toward the Madagascar plan and his discussions with French Prime Minister Leon Blum about it, see his letters to Moshe Shertok, October 14 and 18, 1936, and to Leon Blum, October 15, 1936, WA — 1936.

49. Gruenbaum to Goldmann, October 29, 1936, CZA — L22/201.

50. Bund, *Di Lage*, p. 10.

51. See *Haynt*, October 23, 1936 (Y. M. Nayman, "Der Bund geht nokh yerushe"). Some of the Bund's critics even charged that the party was itself involved in organizing emigration from Poland and that it had urged some of its members to join Zionist training farms in preparation for immigration to Palestine. See the remarks by Yitshak Schipper to the Warsaw Jewish Community Council, as quoted in *Haynt*, September 23, 1936.

52. *Folkstsaytung*, January 5, 1937.

53. *Dokumenty Komunistycznej Partii Polskiej*, pp. 224–26.

54. Zachariasz, *Di komunistishe Bavegung*, p. 97.

55. See the correspondence in CZA — S46/289.

56. The British mandatory authorities in Palestine delegated the responsibility for approving applications for immigrant visas from Jews to the Jewish Agency, within a quota set by the British government. In other words, the Jewish Agency was able to distribute immigrant visas among Jews in any way it saw fit.

57. See Gruenbaum's diary entry for October 27, 1936, CZA — S46/285.

58. Gruenbaum to Jewish Agency Executive, November 1, 1936, ibid.

59. The Agreement was to be concluded between the Jewish Agency and the Polish Bureau for the Settlement of Accounts (Polska Izba Rozrachunkowa — PIR). According to its terms Polish Jews possessing capital who wished to migrate to Israel would deposit their funds with PIR in Warsaw and would be entitled to draw upon them in Palestine as long as the balance of trade and payments between the two countries was in Poland's favor. For details, see *Chwila*, November 10, 1936.

60. Gruenbaum to Goldmann, November 13, 1936, CZA — L22/201.

61. The final text of the agreement is located in CZA — S46/289. See also *Haynt*, March 5, 1937; *Sprawy Narodowościowe*, 1938, p. 156.

62. See *BeRu'ah Se'arah*, pp. 18, 24, 31.

63. Pobóg-Malinowski, *Historia*, 2:819–21. See also above, p. 57.

64. *Gazeta Polska*, January 28, 1937 ("Możliwości emigracji żydowskiej").

65. See Melzer, "HaDiplomatiyah haPolanit," pp. 214–15, 220–21; *Sprawy Narodowościowe*, 1937, 6:672–73.

66. *FRUS*, 1937/2:552. See also "Notatka z konferencji u P. Min. Becka," November 13, 1937, AAN — MSZ 10004/6.

67. Szembek, *Diariusz*, 3:188–89.

68. Szembek to Potocki, January 8, 1938, HIA — Amb. US, 65–4. See also Melzer, "HaDiplomatiyah haPolanit," p. 222.

69. Mention was also made in this discussion of the possibility that Baruch would assist in providing Poland with 50 million dollars in credits for strengthening the country's industrial base. See Melzer, "HaDiplomatiyah haPolanit," p. 222. See also the working paper (*notatka*) prepared by Drymmer for his discussions with Bullitt on Jewish emigration to Latin America, Novermber 15, 1937, AAN — MSZ 9905/2–5. On various programs to engage the Jews of the West in assisting Polish Jewry, see Szajkowski, "Western Jewish Aid," pp. 196–99.

70. The government demanded that the international conference not limit itself merely to consideration of refugees from Nazi Germany but take up the issue of emigration from Eastern Europe as well. See W. T. Drymmer, "Notatka dla Pana Ambasadora R. P. w Waszyngtonie," September 19, 1938, HIA — Amb. US, 65–4. See also "Problem emigracji żydowskiej w oświetleniu MSZ," January 4, 1939, AAN — MSZ 10004/126.

71. See the report of the head of the Central European department of the British Foreign Office, William Strang, on his conversation with Raczyński, December 9, 1938, PRO — FO 371/22540. See also Melzer, "HaDiplomatiyah haPolanit," pp. 225–27.

72. Lipski, *Diplomat*, p. 411.

73. See above, pp. 122–26.

74. Raczyński to Winterton, July 31, 1939, PRO — FO 371/24093.

75. See Melzer, "Poland, the United States," pp. 64–65.

76. Roosevelt also tried to interest the British government in this scheme, but to no avail. Ibid., p. 67–80.

77. *Der Tog*, December 22, 1938; *Dos Yudishe Togblat*, January 24, 1939. On Skwarczyński's interpellation, see also Biddle to Secretary of State, December 22, 1938, NA — 860C.4016/576.

78. "Sprawa żydowska w resorcie MSZ," February 16, 1939, AAN — MSZ 10004/131–35; "Notatka w sprawie Konferencji Pana DDK u Pana Ministra Becka," February 1939, AAN — MSZ 9908/53–54.

79. Mimeographed copy in BDBJ — Poland 1939.

80. *Gazeta Polska*, May 30, 1938.

81. Ibid., November 27, 1938.

82. See, for example, *Nasz Przegląd*, December 15, 1937; *Haynt*, January 19, 1937; *Folkstsaytung*, January 19, 1937.

83. *Nasz Przegląd*, March 6, 1937.

84. *Sprawozdanie Sejmu*, no. 39, February 14, 1937.

85. An exception to this generalization can be found in the attitude of the Folkspartay, which in its conventions of 1937 and 1938 reaffirmed its determination to work against the spread of propaganda calling upon Jews to leave the country. Party leader Noah Prylucki sought alliances with Polish political groups that did not regard the Jews as foreigners. See *Sprawy Narodowościowe*, 1937/1–2, p. 122; 1938/1–2, p. 129.

86. The Bund maintained a Workers Emigration Bureau in Warsaw, whose purpose was to assist candidates for emigration in making arrangements for their departure and in obtaining tickets for transportation. During 1937–38, 456 people left Poland with the help of this bureau, including 356 to destinations outside of Europe. *Folkstsaytung*, August 1, 1939.

87. *Folkstsaytung*, April 1, 1937 (H. Erlich, "Der Eyntsiker Veg").

88. Ibid., May 29, 1938 (W.A., "Dos iz Bundizm"). In May 1938 the Bund Central Committee adopted a resolution opposing "emigrationism" as a solution to the Jewish question and castigating the Zionists. Ibid., May 26, 1938.

89. Borski, *Sprawa*, pp. 15–19.

90. *Folkstsaytung*, April 21, 1937. Cf. *Haynt*, April 19, 1937. In fact the official institutions of PPS did not adopt a clear position on this matter. In any event, they did not dissociate the party from Borski's views.

91. Ster, April 18, 1937 (M. Kleinbaum, "Pomówmy o emigracji uczciwie i po męsku").

92. A. Tarshish to Histadrut Executive Committee, November 8, 1937, HA – CL/4/2.

93. Ibid. See also Moshe Kolodny to Histadrut Executive Committee, September 1937, HA – CL/4/4.

94. Cable, Raczyński to Beck, July 13, 1937; cables, Łubieński, Polish Foreign Ministry, to Raczyński, July 17, 1937, September 26, 1937, AIP – A.12/53/18.

95. Report by Goldmann, CZA – S25/1322.

96. Goldmann to Shertok, January 11, 1938, CZA – A172; Melzer, "HaDiplomatiyah ha-Polanit," pp. 220–21.

97. Goldmann to Gruenbaum, June 2, 1938, CZA – L22/219/2. Indeed, the Polish diplomatic offices in the Middle East began to examine the possibilities of directing Jewish emigrants from Poland to Middle Eastern destinations close to Palestine, such as Transjordan or the Sinai Peninsula, which, they hoped, would prove attractive to the Zionists. See Polish Foreign Ministry to Potocki, May 20, 1938, AAN – MSZ 9905/109–13.

98. *Sprawy Narodowościowe*, 1937/1–2, pp. 117–18.

99. Jabotinsky to Haskel and Judes, Johannesburg, JA – A1/2/27. Jabotinsky asked that the Polish government conduct its own investigation in order to determine how inadequate was the small territory allocated for a Jewish state under the partition plan.

100. Ibid. See also Schechtman, *Jabotinsky*, pp. 119–20.

101. Szembek to Raczyński, November 13, 1937, AIP – A.12/53/18.

102. Gruenbaum to Goldmann, August 11, 1938, CZA – L22/194/1.

103. See Goldmann's report, September 30, 1938, CZA – S25/10004.

104. This idea was a variation on a plan initially proposed by Zionist leader Max Nordau

in 1919. See Jabotinsky to Danziger, November 29, 1938, JA — A1/2/28/2.

105. Jabotinsky to Benjamin Akzin, January 2, 1939, JA — A1/2/29/1. Jabotinsky envisioned half of the proposed million immigrants coming from Poland.

106. A copy of the memorandum to the Polish government is located in JA, among Jabotinsky's letters for 1938. See also Schechtman, *Jabotinsky*, pp. 120–21.

107. Drymmer to Beck, June 1939 ("w sprawie sejmu syjońskiego"), AAN — MSZ 9918/115; Jabotinsky to Presidium, New Zionist Organization, London, June 22, 1939, JA — A1/2/29/1; Jabotinsky to A. Propes, July 2, 1939, JA — A1/2/29/2. See also Schechtman, *Jabotinsky*, pp. 122–23.

108. See the section of the report of the Consular Department of the Polish Foreign Ministry for January 1939 entitled "Sprawa emigracji żydowskiej," AAN — MSZ 10004/87–89. See also Astor, *Geshikhte*, 1:361.

109. Anshel Reiss, Warsaw, to Eliezer Kaplan, Jerusalem, December 14, 1938, LPA — 38/101b. In addition to Schorr, three Zionists participated in the committee: Henryk Rosmarin, Yehoshua Gottlieb, and Leon Lewite.

110. See *Der Tog*, January 5, 1939.

111. See Schwarzbart, *Tsvishn Beyde Velt-Milkhomes*, pp. 66–67.

112. *Dos Yudishe Togblat*, February 1, 1939. A year earlier Beck had spoken at an internal meeting of the Foreign Ministry of the need to draw Agudas Yisroel, "loyal to the state, into cooperation with us" on the emigration issue. "Notatka z konferencji u Pana Ministra Becka," November 13, 1937, AAN — MSZ 10004/6.

113. The memorandum is attached to a letter from Moshe Schorr to Lord Winterton, December 31, 1938, PRO — FO 371/24074. It fell in with the Polish government's efforts at the time to bring the question of Polish Jewish emigration to the agenda of the Intergovernmental Commission on Refugees in London. See above.

114. See the Polish Foreign Ministry document entitled "Wytyczne dla delegatów Żydowskiego Komitetu Kolonizacyjnego," January 1939, AAN — MSZ 9914/41–42.

115. See Raczyński's reports on the activities of the delegation in London, February 4 and 10, 1939, AAN — MSZ 9914/54, 60–62. See also *JTA Bulletin*, February 9, 1939; Korzec, *Juifs*, p. 264.

116. See the minutes of the meeting of the Executive Committee of the World Jewish Congress, January 14, 1939, CZA — A172.

117. There were also more specific, personal reasons for the JDC's opposition. Two members of the Colonization Committee, Moshe Schorr and Henryk Rosmarin, maintained close ties to the American Federation of Polish Jews, which the JDC regarded as a competitor in fundraising campaigns. See Bauer, *My Brother's Keeper*, pp. 249–49.

118. Ibid.

119. See B. Eiger to Sir Robert Waley Cohen, February 27, 1939, BDBJ — Poland 1939, 515; Eiger to Neville Laski, March 2, 1939, with attached copies of letters between Eiger and Wolf, ibid.

120. Special conditions existed for the entry of so-called capitalist immigrants, who, because of their wealth, would presumably not tax the economic absorptive capacity of Palestine. The Clearing Agreement essentially permitted Jews of means seeking to enter Palestine to retain much of the wealth they had assembled in Poland so that they could enter under this special category.

121. See Jewish Agency Executive to Polish Consulate, Tel Aviv, November 25, 1937, CZA — S46/289.

122. See Hindes to Gruenbaum, September 27, 1937, CZA — S46/289.

123. See Gruenbaum to Jewish Agency Executive, May 31 and June 8, 1938, CZA — L22/194/1.

124. See Schechtman's account of his discussions with the economic advisor to the Polish Foreign Ministry, Jan Wszelaki, in *Unzer Velt*, May 20 and July 1, 1938.

125. Government involvement in this area had been approved by Rydz-Śmigły after Beck had raised the matter with him. See Drozdowski, "Polityczna rola." On the Foreign Ministry's positive attitude toward government assistance in training Jewish military organizations in Palestine and toward financing partially illegal immigration to Palestine, see "Problem emigracji żydowskiej w oświetleniu MSZ," January 4, 1939, AAN — MSZ 10004/127.

126. *Sefer Toledot haHaganah*, 2/2:972–73; *BeRu'ah Se'arah*, p. 24.

127. *Sefer Toledot haHaganah*, 2/2:972–73. Wolf actually paid only ú20,000; the payment of the remaining four installments that he had promised could not be made because of the outbreak of war.

128. In 1938 Moshe Kleinbaum proposed, in the name of the Jewish Agency, that the blocked accounts of various Zionist funds in Poland be used to pay for arms purchases. "Notatka dla Pana D.D.K. w sprawie zakupu broni do Palestyny przez Agencję Żydowską," October 18, 1938, AAN — MSZ 9908/20.

129. *Sefer Toledot HaHaganah*, 2/2:1000–1002. Courses were inaugurated in twenty-eight training farms throughout the country in the weeks prior to the outbreak of war.

130. See Jabotinsky to Zarychta, May 12, 1939, in Drymmer, "Zagadnienia," p. 77. See also Pobóg-Malinowski, *Najnowsza Historia*, 2:819–21; Schechtman, *Jabotinsky*, pp. 233–34.

131. See Drymmer to Ministries of Industry and Commerce and Treasury, June 1939, AAN — MSZ 9918/119. In the meantime the representative of the New Zionist Organization in Warsaw, Josef Schechtman, had made arrangements with the Romanian ambassador in Poland to permit the transit of Jews from Poland through Romania for embarkation from the Black Sea port of Constanza without the need to present immigrant visas to another country. Schechtman, *Jabotinsky*, p. 202. In August 1939 the Polish authorities promised the British government to take steps against illegal Jewish emigration to Palestine from Poland. See Polish Foreign Ministry to British Embassy, Warsaw, August 16, 1939, PRO — FO 371/24094; Jan Wagner to Ministries of Interior and Social Welfare, August 21, 1939, AAN — MSZ 9935/9.

132. See Lenkin, *Sipuro shel Mefaked*, pp. 47–49. Interestingly, by this time Etsel had begun to conduct political and propaganda activities on its own in Poland, bypassing the Revisionist organizational structure and angering Jabotinsky. It published its own newspapers in Yiddish (*Die Tat*) and in Polish (*Jerozolima Wyzwolona*) independently of the official Revisionist publications. The assimilated Jewish attorney from Warsaw, Henryk Strassmann, was instrumental in serving as an intermediary between *Etsel* and the Polish officer corps. See *Sefer Toledot haHaganah*, 2/2:1066–69; Niv, *Ma'arachot*, pp. 163–65, 171–174.

Chapter 10: Toward War

1. The German ambassador in Warsaw, Moltke, reported to the German Foreign Ministry a month before the outbreak of war that "when it comes to the battle against Germany, the Jews of Poland are a natural and fanatical ally of Polish chauvinism." Moltke to German Foreign Ministry, August 1, 1939, in *Dokumente zur Vorgeschichte des Krieges*, p. 403. The Ukrainian parties in Poland, including the relatively moderate UNDO, based their policies after Munich on a pro-German orientation, for they viewed the autonomous Ruthenian regime that was established in Subcarpathian Ruthenia as a possible nucleus for a greater Ukraine, to be established under German sponsorship. They were deeply disappointed when, following the dismemberment of Czechoslovakia, those regions were transferred to Hungary, creating a

common Polish-Hungarian frontier. Despite this disappointment, however, UNDO never declared a negative attitude toward Germany's territorial demands upon Poland in 1939. Many Ukrainians evidently continued to hope that in the future Germany would have need of a greater Ukraine as an ally against its Polish and Russian enemies. Obviously, this attitude was not looked upon with favor by either the Polish or the Jewish communities. See *Gazeta Polska*, May 19, 1939; *Haynt*, August 1, 1939 (L. Halpern, "Gornisht Fargesen, Gornisht Gelernt").

2. See, for example, *Haynt*, March 22, 1939.

3. Lipski to Beck, March 21, 1939, AIP — A.12, "Stosunki Polsko-Niemieckie, 1939."

4. A. Reiche to German Foreign Ministry, May 4, 1939, YVA — JM 2220. The writer suggested that referring to the Polish government's policy as *"Judenpolitik"* would severely damage the morale of the Polish population, adding that "Zerstoerung der seelischen Geschlossenheit eines Volkes ist ja nicht zuletzt nach der Erfahrungen des Weltkrieges eine der erfolgreichsten Waffen vor und waehrend eines Krieges." See also Korzec, *Juifs*, p. 273.

5. *JTA Bulletin*, March 30, 1939.

6. Chajn, *Materiały*, 1:513–14, 519.

7. *Haynt*, April 18, 1939 (A. Einhorn, "Di naye Demokratishe Partay").

8. See *JTA Bulletin*, March 22, 1939. See also the summary of a meeting of the Joint Foreign Committee of the Board of Deputies of British Jews and the Anglo-Jewish Association, in which it was observed that "whatever part antisemitism had played in Poland of yesterday it was no longer today an atmospheric factor and as long as the present crisis persisted it was likely that such a situation would continue." BDBJ — Poland, 1939.

9. For example, it was on March 22, 1939 that the plenum of the Sejm passed the bill calling for a phased ban on kosher slaughtering. See above, p. 89.

10. See, for example, *Nowy Dziennik*, March 22, 1939 (I. Schwarzbart, "Błędy"). As early as January-February 1939 many Jews had been forced to leave several cities and towns along the border. See Bauer, *My Brother's Keeper*, p. 185.

11. Rudnicki, *Obóz Narodowo-Radykalny*, p. 328; Niemunis, "Stronnictwo Narodowe," p. 116.

12. *Warszawski Dziennik Narodowy*, April 6, 1939.

13. Ibid., July 9 and 11, 1939.

14. *Haynt*, July 12, 1939 (A.M. Hartglas, "Di Hitleristishe Agresie un dos Poylishe Identum").

15. See, for example, *Dos Yudishe Togblat*, April 16, 1939.

16. See *JTA Bulletin*, July 25, 1939.

17. *Gazeta Polska*, May 16, 1939 (W. Lenkiewicz, "Oczyścić Zakamarki").

18. Ibid., July 4, 1939.

19. Ibid., March 26, 1939; *Chwila*, March 24, 1939.

20. *JTA Bulletin*, July 9, 1939. The purpose of such differential labelling was to enable Polish retailers to boycott products produced by Jewish firms.

21. Ibid., June 29, 1939; *Warszawski Dziennik Narodowy*, June 25, 1939. The resolution was passed in the presence of government representatives.

22. *Warszawski Dziennik Narodowy*, April 6, 1939. See also *Nowy Dziennik*, April 6, 1939.

23. See *JTA Bulletin*, March 13 and 26, 1939.

24. See *Gazeta Polska*, May 19, 1939.

25. *JTA Bulletin*, July 16, 1939.

26. The press was forbidden to report on these events by the government censor in Warsaw. See Trepiński, Cenzura," pp. 142–43.

27. The majority was so large because the vote was taken on the eve of the Passover holiday,

when all Jewish council delegates save those from the Bund were not in attendance. See *Haynt*, April 6, 1939; *Folkstsaytung*, April 6, 1939. The PPS newspaper, *Robotnik*, argued with reference to this decision that it was dangerous to place the entire burden of the country's defense upon ethnic Poles alone, without involving the Jews. See *Nowy Dziennik*, May 16, 1939. Endek representatives attempted to introduce similar resolutions in other city councils, but where there was no Endek-OZON majority the resolutions were not adopted. See Hertz, *Geshikhte*, pp. 433–34.

28. See *Haynt*, May 16, 1939. In general, anti-German sentiment grew during this period, and pressure upon the German minority in Poland increased. For details see Esch, *Polen 1939*, pp. 92–93, 100–101; Polonsky, *Politics*, pp. 464–65.

29. Quoted in *JTA Bulletin*, May 31, 1939.

30. See above, n. 4.

31. *Gazeta Polska*, July 21 and 23, 1939. The newspaper also charged that the German radio programs called upon Poles to support Endecja. The German press argued that the Polish government had defined antisemitic propaganda as "a Nazi attempt at subversion." See *Osteuropa* 14 (1938/39):686.

32. *Dziennik Ludowy*, as quoted in *Nowy Dziennik*, July 19, 1939.

33. German consul-general, Katowice, to German Foreign Ministry, August 23, 1939, YVA – JM 3235.

34. See the analysis in *Nowy Dziennik*, April 18, 1939. Still, antisemitic circles continued to present emigration as the only solution to the Jewish problem. See Szembek to Raczyński, May 12, 1939, HIA – Poland. Ambasada US, 66–8.

35. Beck told British Ambassador Kennard that he wished to discuss the question of colonies for Poland in general and in this context to raise the Jewish question. Kennard objected, but the Polish side would not give in. In the end it was decided that the Jewish question would be discussed in the context of a general survey of Poland's situation. See cable, Kennard to Cadogan, March 7, 1939, in *DBFP* 4:203; cable, Kennard to Halifax, March 10, 1939; ibid., p. 217; cable, Halifax to Kennard, March 17, 1939; ibid., p. 290.

36. British Embassy, Warsaw, to British Foreign Office, March 18, 1939, PRO – FO 371/24084.

37. Foreign Office memorandum, April 11, 1939, ibid.

38. For the text of the communique, see *DBFP* 5:36.

39. Raczyński to Cadogan, June 10, 1939, PRO – FO 371/24084.

40. Undersecretary for colonial affairs to undersecretary for foreign affairs, June 22, 1939, ibid.

41. Roman Dmowski's death in January 1939 also made it a bit easier for OZON and Endecja spokesmen to speak with one another constructively.

42. See Polonsky, *Politics*, pp. 446–47.

43. See *American Jewish Year Book*, 1939/40, pp. 294–95.

44. *Gazeta Polska*, May 3, 1939. In response, the Jewish press asked about the contribution of Polish heavy industry and landed estates to the loan. See *Nasz Przegląd*, May 5, 1939.

45. *Warszawski Dziennik Narodowy*, May 4, 1939. See also *ABC*, as quoted in *Haynt*, May 9, 1939. For a reflection of the ferocity of accusations against Jews for shirking loan subscriptions, see also M. Grabowski, Warsaw, to the Secretariat of Mapai (Palestine Jewish Workers' Party), June 6, 1939, LPA – 39/101b.

46. *Folkstsaytung*, May 9, 1939. Unofficial sources reported that in Białystok, where Jews had been accused of undersubscribing to the loan, Jewish subscriptions amounted to 2.3 million

zł. out of a total of 3 million *zł.* total subscriptions collected in the city. *Haynt*, May 10, 1939.

47. *Haynt*, May 9, 1939.

48. Bauer, *My Brother's Keeper*, p. 188.

49. See *Haynt*, April 25 and 30, May 2, 1939; ibid., May 11, 1939 (M. Mark, "Der Emes vegen dem Idishen Ontayl in der Halvoeh").

50. Quoted in *Haynt*, May 10, 1939.

51. See the remarks of Deputy Stanisław Jóźwiak at the Sejm session of June 6, as quoted in *Haynt*, June 8, 1939.

52. *JTA Bulletin*, May 7, 1939.

53. Ibid., July 17, 1939; *Nowy Dziennik*, July 15, 1939. Actually, Friede's trip was sponsored by the Polish government, which was trying to obtain territory in British Guiana for Jewish resettlement. See cable, Drymmer to Raczyński, June 2, 1939, AIP – A.12/53/24.

54. Report by A. G. Brotman, secretary of the Board of Deputies of British Jews, July 5, 1939, BDBJ – 515. There is evidence that around this time the Board of Deputies was in contact with figures in the Polish opposition – mainly former Sanacja members then associated with the Democratic Party – who had expressed attitudes favorable to Jewish interests. The Board appears to have offered these Polish politicians financial assistance in their organizational efforts, through the mediation of the Polish Jewish industrialist B. Eiger. See Sir Robert Waley Cohen to Brotman, March 20, 1939, BDBJ – Poland, 1939; Brotman to Pierre Mantoux, Alliance Israelite Universelle, Paris, March 27, 1939, ibid.; report on meeting with a "Polish friend," March 31, 1939, ibid.

55. See the speech by Yitshak Schwarzbart at the convention of the Zionist Federation of West Galicia, March 25, 1939, as reported in *Nowy Dziennik*, March 28, 1939.

56. *Folkstsaytung*, August 3, 1939.

57. Bauer, *My Brother's Keeper*, pp. 297–98. At one point the Polish government tried to persuade the JDC to sever its connections with the Bund; it was interested in encouraging such a development because of the Bund's steadfast opposition to the emigration idea and because it hoped to see JDC funds used to support emigration projects rather than projects designed to improve the Jews' economic situation in Poland. See Drymmer to Polish Consulate-General, New York, March 31, 1939, HIA – Poland, Ambasada Great Britain, 07/08. JDC, however, did not bow to such pressure.

58. On the negotiations, see Bauer, *My Brother's Keeper*, pp. 299–300. JDC headquarters in New York was notified on September 2, 1939, the second day of the war, that the central organization had been established. Ibid., p. 301.

59. *Haynt*, August 8, 1939 (M. Kleinbaum, "'Tkhies Hameysim' fun a Vort").

60. *Gazeta Polska*, August 26 and 27, 1939.

61. *Warszawski Dziennik Narodowy*, August 23, 1939. During the final days of August, this newspaper published disproportionately large lists of names of Jews who had been accused of profiteering and accounts of their trials, including their pictures and pictures of their shops, which had been closed by the authorities. No mention was made of Poles who were accused of profiteering. See ibid., August 28–30, 1939.

62. Hertz, *Di Geshikhte*, pp. 436–37.

63. See, for example, *Haynt*, August 28, 1939 ("In shvere Minuten").

64. *Warszawski Dziennik Narodowy*, August 23, 1939; *ABC*, August 24, 1939, as quoted in *Folkstsaytung*, August 25, 1939.

65. See Trepiński, "Cenzura," p. 146.

66. See Drozdowski, *Alarm*, p. 66.

Bibliography

This list includes only those works actually cited in the text or notes.

Archives

1. Archive of the Board of Deputies of British Jews, London
   515, 535 Poland

2. Archive of the Israel Labour Party, Beit Berl, Tsofit, Israel
   101b Poland (including letters from party emissaries, 1936–38, and the diary of Eliahu Dobkin, 1936)

3. Archiwum Akt Nowych, Warsaw
   MSZ Ministerstwo Spraw Zagranicznych

4. Archiwum Instytutu Polskiego, London
   A.11 Polish Embassy, London
   A.12 Ministerstwo Spraw Zagranicznych

5. Central Archives for the History of the Jewish People, Jerusalem
   PL Poland

6. Central Zionist Archives, Jerusalem
   A127 Yitshak Gruenbaum
   F3 Zionist Federation of Eastern Galicia
   L22 World Zionist Organization and Jewish Agency for Palestine, Representation, Geneva
   S25 Jewish Agency for Palestine, Political Department
   S46 Jewish Agency for Palestine, Office of Yitshak Gruenbaum

7. Haganah Archive, Tel Aviv
   2607 Amali Diary
   —Testimonies of emissaries to Poland

8. Histadrut Archive, Tel Aviv
   HL Foreign Affairs (including letters of emissaries to Poland)

9. Hoover Institution Archives, Stanford, California
   Poland. Ambasada Great Britain
   Poland. Ambasada US

10. Jabotinsky Archive, Tel Aviv
    G4 New Zionist Organization, Presidium, London
    —Jabotinsky Letters

11. Jacob Lestschinski Archive, Hebrew University, Jerusalem
    236–295 [Various materials relating to Poland]

12. National Archives, Washington
    860C Department of State Decimal File, Poland
13. Weizmann Archives, Rehovot, Israel
    Letters, 1936–37
14. Yad Vashem Archives, Jerusalem
    JM Microfilms of German Foreign Ministry Documents

Newspapers and Periodicals

American Jewish Year Book	*Naye Folkstsaytung*
Chwila	*Nowy Dziennik*
Dos Yudishe Togblat	*Osteuropa*
Folkshilf	*Ruch Spółdzielczy*
Gazeta Polska	*Ster*
Haynt	*Tygodnik Polski*
JTA Bulletin	*Unzer Velt*
Miesięcznik Żydowski	*Warszawski Dziennik Narodowy*
Myśl Socjalistyczna	*Wiadomości Statystyczne*
Nasz Przegląd	*Yidishe Ekonomik*
Nation und Staat	

Additional Primary Sources

Alter, Wiktor. *Tsu der Yidn Frage in Poyln*. Warsaw, 1937

Asz, Nachum. *W obronie Uboju Rytualnego*. 1936

Awigdor, Jakób. *Ubój Rytualny*. Drohobycz, 1937

Barcikowski, Wacław. *Liga Obrony Praw Człowieka i Obywatela i Kongres Pokoju w Brukseli: Księga wspomnień (1919–1938)*. Warsaw, 1960.

Beck, Józef. *Final Report, 1926–1939*. New York, 1957

BeRu'ah Se'arah: Perakim miHayav umiMifalo shel Yehuda Arazi. Jerusalem, 1966

Borski, Jan Maurycy. *Sprawa żydowska a socjalizm*. Warsaw, 1937

[Bund]. *Di Lage fun di Yidishe Masn in Poyln*. Warsaw, 1935

Cang, Joel. "The Opposition Parties in Poland and their Attitude Towards the Jews and the Jewish Problem." *Jewish Social Studies* 1(1939):241–56

Chajn, Leon. *Materiały do Historii Klubów Demokratycznych i Stronnictwa Demokratycznego w latach 1937–39*. Vols. 1–2, Warsaw, 1964

Constitution of the Republic of Poland — April 23rd 1935. Warsaw, 1935

Cynamon, A. "Momenty gospodarcze Sprawy Uboju Rytualnego." *Zagadnienia Gospodarcze*, 1935, nos. 3–4:164–69

Der Yidisher Arbeter Klas in Yor 1936. Łódź, 1937

Dmowski, Roman. *Świat powojenny i Polska*. Warsaw, 1937

Documents Diplomatiques Français, 2nd series (1936–39). Vols. 1–2, Paris, 1964; Vol. 7, Paris, 1972

Documents on British Foreign Policy, 1919–1939, 3rd series. Vols. 3–4, London, 1950–51

Documents on German Foreign Policy, series C (1933–37), series D (1937–45). Washington, 1949–62

Dokumente zur Vorgeschichte des Krieges. Berlin, 1939

Dokumenty Komunistycznej Partii Polski 1935–1938. Warsaw, 1968

Drymmer, Wiktor Tomir. "Zagadnienie żydowskie w Polsce w latach 1935–1939." *Zeszyty Historyczne*, 13(1968):55–77

Esch, Peter. *Polen 1939*. Berlin, 1939

Haynt: A Tsaytung bay Yidn 1908–1939. Tel Aviv, 1978

Fun Noentn Over. New York, 1956

Foreign Relations of the United States: Diplomatic Papers, 1937–1938. Washington, 1954–55

German Fifth Column in Poland. London, 1940

Giertych, Jędrzej. *O wyjściu z kryzysu*. Warsaw, 1938

Gitterman, Isaac. "Perspektywy rzemiosła żydowskiego w Polsce." *Zagadnienia Gospodarcze, 1935*, nos. 1–2:7–20

Goldin, H. "Yidn in Katovits." *Yidishe Ekonomik*, 1939, nos. 4–6:248–50

Goldstein, Bernard. *Tsvantsik Yor in Varshever Bund (1919–1939)*. New York, 1960

Grodzanski, Hayim Ozer. *Aviezer*. Benei Berak, 1970

Gruber, Henryk. *Wspomnienia i Uwagi, 1892–1942*. London, n. d.

Gruenbaum, Yitshak. *Milhamot Yehudei Polin*. Jerusalem, 1941

Grynsztejn, Jakób. *Regulamin wyborczy do Gmin Żydowskich*. Warsaw, 1936

Hafftka, Aleksander. "Życie parlamentarne Żydów w Polsce Odrodzonej." In *Żydzi w Polsce Odrodzonej*, edited by Ignacy Schipper, Arieh Tartakower, and Aleksander Hafftka. Warsaw, n. d., 2:286–311

———. "Żydowskie stronnictwa polityczne w Polsce Odrodzonej." In *Żydzi w Polsce Odrodzonej*, edited by Ignacy Schipper, Arieh Tartakower, and Aleksander Hafftka. Warsaw, n. d., 2:249–85

Halpern, Leopold. *Polityka Żydowska w Sejmie i Senacie Rzeczypospolitej Polskiej, 1919–1933*. Warsaw, 1933

Hartglas, Apolinary. *Na pograniczu dwóch światów*. Typescript, n. d.

Henryk Erlich un Wiktor Alter: A Gedenk Bukh. New York, 1951

Hertz, Yakov Sholem. *Di Geshikhte fun Bund in Lodz*. New York, 1958

Jabotinsky, Ze'ev. *Ketavim: BaSa'ar*. Jerusalem, 1953

Jaffe, Leib. *BiShelihut Am*. Jerusalem, 1968

JEAS, Żydowskie Centralne Towarzystwo Emigracyjne. *Sprawozdanie.*
Warsaw, 1925–35

Jędrzejewicz, Janusz. *Fragmenty pamiętnika i pism*. London, 1972

Joint [Distribution Committee]. *Aid to Jews Overseas: Report on the Activities of the American Jewish Joint Distribution Committee for the Years 1935–1939* — Poland. N. p, n. d.

Klinger, S. *10 Jahres Plan für die Ansiedlung von Ca 1.5 Millionen Juden in Palästina*. london, 1936

KPP, Uchwały i Rezolucje. Warsaw, 1956

Krzywicki, Ludwik. *Wspomnienia*, vol 3. Warsaw, 1959

Laeuen, Harald. "Das Polnische Ultimatum." *Osteuropa*, 13 (1937-38):513–24

——. "Der Kampf um das polnische Bauertum." *Osteuropa*, 12
(1936–37):1–11

——. "Polens Lager der nationalen Einigung." *Osteuropa*, 12 (1936–37):
445–60

Lemański, Józef. "Generalizacja zobowiązań mniejszościowych a Polska."
Sprawy Narodowościowe, 8(1934):527–36

Lenkin, Eliyahu. *Sippuro shel Mefaked Altalena*. Tel Aviv, 1967

Lepecki, Mieczysław. *Madagaskar — Kraj, Ludzie, Kolonizacja*. Warsaw, 1938

Lestschinski, Jacob. "Di Ekonomishe Entviklung fun Poyln un der
Poylisher Antisemitizm." *Tsukunft*, December 1937

——. "Vegn a konstruktivn Plan fun Hilf far di Poylishe Yidn." *Yidishe
Ekonomik*, 1 (1937):129–48, 209–22

Lipski, Józef. *Diplomat in Berlin, 1933–1939*, edited by Wacław Jędrzejewicz.
Cambridge MA, 1963

Mahler, Rafael. "Michtavei E. Ringelblum miZbonshin veAl Zbonshin."
Yalkut Moreshet, 1964:17–31

Mały Rocznik Statystyczny 1939. Warsaw 1939

Maschke, Erich. "Roman Dmowski." *Osteuropa*, 10 (1934–35):391–410

Materiały źródłowe do historii polskiego Ruchu Ludowego. Vol. 3 (1931–1939).
Edited by Jan Borkowski and Józef Kowal. Warsaw, 1966

Ministerstwo Spraw Wewnętrznych. *Sprawozdanie z życia Mniejszości Narodowych za 1 kwartał 1935r*. Warsaw, 1935

Mirkin, N. *Ein Kongres oder Tsvey Kongresn*. Warsaw, 1936

Po'alei-Tsiyon C. S. *Finf Yor Po'alei-Tsiyon Tetikayt*. Warsaw, 1936

Prowalski, Abraham. "Spółdzielczość żydowska w Polsce Odrodzonej." In
Żydzi w Polsce Odrodzonej, edited by Ignacy Schipper, Arieh Tartakower,
and Aleksander Hafftka. Warsaw, n. d., 2:590–617

Remba, Isaac. *Jabotinsky's Teg un Nekht*. Paris, 1951

Report of the Nineteenth Zionist Congress. Jerusalem, 1935

Report of the Twentieth Zionist Congress. Jerusalem, 1937

Report of the Twenty-First Zionist Congress. Jerusalem, 1939

Rozenman, Gedalja. *Zagadnienie Uboju Rytualnego*. Warsaw, 1936

Rybak, P. "Wspomnienia o walce KPP z antysemityzmem i pogromami."
 Biuletyn Żydowskiego Instytutu Historycznego, 1955:268–73

Schechtman, Joseph. *Ze'ev Jabotinsky*. Tel Aviv, 1959

Schwarzbart, Yitshak. "HaHistadrut haTsiyonit haArtsit shel Ma'arav Galit-
 siyah veShleziyah." *Sefer Kroke*, Jerusalem, 1959, pp. 207–255

———. *Tsvishn Beyde Velt-Milkhomes*. New York, 1958

Sefer Betar: Korot uMekorot. Vol. 2. Jerusalem and Tel Aviv, 1953

Sefer Przytyk. Edited by David Sztokfisz. Tel Aviv, 1973

Sefer Toledot HaHaganah. Edited by Yehuda Slutsky. Vol. 2, Part 2; Vol. 3.
 Tel Aviv, 1963

Seidman, Hillel. *Prawda o Uboju Rytualnym*. Białystok, 1936

Seraphim, Peter Heinz. "Der Antisemitismus in Ost-Europa." *Osteuropa*,
 14 (1938–39):332–50

Singer, Bernard. *Od Witosa do Sławka*. Paris, 1962

Składkowski-Sławoj, Felicjan. *Nieostatnie słowo oskarżonego*. London, 1964

*Sprawozdanie Egzekutywy Organizacji Syjonistycznej dla Zachodniej Mał-
 opolski i Śląska, 1934–1935 i 1935–1936*. Kraków, 1935–36

Sprawozdanie Stenograficzne Sejmu Rzeczypospolitej, 1935–1938. Warsaw,
 1935–38

Sprawozdanie Stenograficzne Senatu Rzeczypospolitej, 1935–1938. Warsaw,
 1935–38

Studnicki, Władysław. *Sprawa Polsko-Żydowska*. Wilno, 1936

Szembek, Jan. *Diariusz i teki Jana Szembeka*. Vols. 1–3, edited by T. Komarnicki; vol. 4, edited by J. Zarański. London, 1964–72

Szlamowicz, L. "Oddłużenie rolnictwa a handel żydowski." *Zagadnienia
 Gospodarcze*, 1935:52–57

Sztrauch, Zerah. "Mo'etset ha'Ir Lodz uVe'ayat haYehudim lifnei Milhemet
 HaOlam HaSheniyah." *Sefer HaShanah/Yorbukh*, 3 (1970):294–99

Tartakower, Arieh. "Pauperyzacja Żydów polskich. *Miesięcznik Żydowski*,
 5 (1935):97–122

Trzeciak, Stanisław. *Ubój Rytualny w świetle Biblji i Talmudu*. Warsaw, 1935

Unter der Fon fun KPP: Zamlbukh. Warsaw, 1959

Wodzicki, Roman. *Wspomnienia: Gdańsk-Warszawa-Berlin*. Warsaw, 1972

Wojtyna, J. *Handel mięsny w świetle organizacji rynku warszawskiego*.
 Warsaw, 1935

Zachariasz, Szymon. *Di komunistishe Bavegung tsvishn der Yidisher Arbetndiker Bafelkerung in Poyln.* Warsaw, 1954

Zaderecki, Tadeusz, *Z Biblią i Talmudem w walce.* Warsaw and Lwów, 1936

Secondary Sources

Adler, Hans Günther. *Der verwaltete Mensch: Studien zur Deportation der Juden aus Deutschland.* Tübingen, 1974

Armstrong, John Aleksander. *Ukrainian Nationalism.* New York, 1963

Astor, Michael. *Geshikhte fun der Frayland-Lige.* Buenos Aires and New York, 1967

Bauer, Yehuda. *My Brother's Keeper: A History of the American Jewish Joint Distribution Committee, 1929–1939.* Philadelphia, 1974

Ben-Elissar, Eliyahu. *La diplomatie du IIIe Reich et les Juifs (1933–1939).* Paris, 1969

Ber, Arieh. "Sochnut haTelegrafit haYehudit (JTA)." In *Itonut Yehudit She-Haytah.* Tel Aviv, 1973, pp. 311–35

Berenstein, T. "KPP w walce z pogromami antyżydowskimi w latach 1935–1937," *Biuletyn Żydowskiego Instytutu Historycznego,* 1955:3–74

Brandes, Leo. "Der Rekhtlikher Motsev fun Yiden in Poyln tsvishen beyde Velt-Milkhomes." *YIVO Bleter,* 42 (1962):147–86

Breyer, Richard. *Das Deutsche Reich und Polen 1932–1937: Aussenpolitik und Volksgruppenfragen.* Würzburg, 1955

Bromke, Adam. *Poland's Politics.* Harvard, 1967

Bronsztejn, Szyja. *Ludność żydowska w okresie międzywojennym.* Wrocław, 1963

Brumberg, Abraham. "The Bund and the Polish Socialist Party in the late 1930s." In *The Jews of Poland Between Two World Wars.* Edited by Yisrael Gutman, Ezra Mendelsohn, Jehuda Reinharz, and Chone Shmeruk. Hanover NH and London, 1989, pp. 75–94

Budurowycz, Bohdan Basil. *Polish-Soviet Relations 1932–1939.* New York and London, 1963

Chojnowski, Andrzej. *Koncepcje polityki narodowościowej rządow polskich w latach 1921–1939.* Wrocław, 1979

——. *Piłsudczycy u władzy: Dzieje Bezpartyjnego Bloku Współpracy z Rządem.* Wrocław, 1986

Ciałowicz, Jan. *Polsko-Francuski sojusz wojskowy (1921–1939).* Warsaw, 1970

Cygański, Mirosław. *Hitlerowskie organizacje dywersyjne w województwie śląskim, 1931–1936.* Katowice, 1971

Drozdowski, Marian Marek. *Polityka gospodarcza rządu polskiego, 1936–1939.* Warsaw, 1963

———. *Alarm dla Warszawy*. Warsaw, 1964

———. *Klasa robotnicza Warszawy 1918–1939*. Warsaw, 1968

———. "Polityczna rola wojska w latach 1935–1939." *Nowe Książki*, 18 (30 September 1970)

Dziewanowski, Marian Kamil. *The Communist Party of Poland*. Cambridge MA, 1959

Garlicki, Andrzej. "Problemy kolonialne w opinii MSZ w 1936r." *Naród i Państwo*. Warsaw, 1969

———, and Weinbaum, Laurence. "The Zionist Revisionists, the Sanacja Regime, and the Polish Press, 1936–1939." *Gal-Ed*, 12 (1991):93–106

Garncarska-Kadary, Bina. "Shichvot haOvedim beFolin bein Shetei Milhamot haOlam." *Gal-Ed*, 3 (1976):141–89

Gitman, Joseph. "The Jews and the Jewish Problem in the Polish Parliament 1919–1939." Unpublished PhD dissertation, Yale University, 1962

Gondek, Leszek. *Działalność Abwehry na terenie polskim 1933–1939*. Warsaw, 1971

Groth, Alexander J. "Dmowski, Pilsudski and Ethnic Conflict in Pre-1939 Poland." *Canadian Slavic Studies*, 3 (1969):69–91

Grünberg, Karol. *Niemcy i ich organizacje polityczne w Polsce międzywojennej*. Warsaw, 1970

Heller, Celia Stopnicka. "Assimilation: A Deviant Pattern among the Jews of Inter-War Poland." *Jewish Journal of Sociology*, 15 (1973):231–37

———. *On the Edge of Destruction: Jews of Poland between the Two World Wars*. New York, 1977

Holzer, Jerzy. "Partie polityczne w międzywojennej Polsce." *Kwartalnik Historyczny*, 80 (1973):64–74

———. *Mozaika polityczna Drugiej Rzeczypospolitej*. Warsaw, 1974

Horak, Stephen. *Poland and her National Minorities, 1919–1939*. New York, 1961

Hrushevsky, Michael. *A History of Ukraine*. Hamden CT, 1970

Jędruszczak, Hanna. "O działalności KPP na terenie Warszawy, 1932–1937." In *Warszawa II Rzeczypospolitej*. Vol. 2, Warsaw, 1970

———, and Jędruszczak, Tadeusz. *Ostatnie lata 2-giej Rzeczypospolitej, 1935–1939*. Warsaw, 1970

Jędruszczak, Tadeusz. *Piłsudczycy bez Piłsudskiego*. Warsaw, 1963

Johnpoll, Bernard. *The Politics of Futility: General Jewish Workers' "Bund" of Poland, 1917–1943*. Ithaca NY, 1967

Kagan, G. "The Agrarian Regime of Pre-War Poland." *Central European Affairs*, 3 (1943):241–63

Kalicka, Felicja. *Z zagadnień Jednolitego Frontu KPP i PPS w latach 1933–1934.* Warsaw, 1967

Kantorowicz, Nahum. *Di Tsionistishe Arbeter Bavegung in Poyln (1918–1939).* New York, 1964

Kaul, Friedrich Karl. *Der Fall des Herschel Grynszpan.* Berlin, 1965

Korzec, Paweł. "Antisemitism in Poland as an Intellectual, Social and Political Movement." In *Studies on Polish Jewry, 1919–1939.* Edited by Joshua A. Fishman. New York, 1974, pp. 12–104

——. *Juifs en Pologne: La question juive pendant l'entre-deux-guerres.* Paris, 1980

Kowalak, Tadeusz. *Prasa niemiecka w Polsce 1918–1939.* Warsaw, 1971

Kowalec, Krzystof. *Narodowa Demokracja Wobec Faszyzmu, 1922–1939,* Warsaw, 1989

Kowalski, Józef. *Trudne lata: Problemy rozwoju polskiego Ruchu Robotniczego, 1925–1935.* Warsaw, 1966

Krasowski, Krzystof. *Związki wyznaniowe w II Rzeczypospolitej.* Warsaw and Poznań, 1988.

Kuhn, Walter. "Das Deutschtum in Polen und sein Schicksal in Kriegs- und Nachkriegszeit." In *Osteuropa Handbuch — Polen.* Edited by Markert Werner. Köln, 1959, pp. 138–64

Kulesza, Władysław. *Koncepcje ideowo-polityczne obozu rządzącego w Polsce w latach 1926–1935.* Wrocław, 1985

Landau, Moshe. "Hafichat Mai 1926: Tsipiyot beYahadut Polin liTemurah Medinit veTahalich Hitbadutan." *Gal-Ed,* 2 (1975):237–86

——. *Mi'ut Le'umi Lohem: Ma'avak Yehudei Polin 1918–1928.* Jerusalem, 1986

Landau, Zbigniew, and Tomaszewski, Jerzy. *Gospodarka Polski międzywojennej.* Vol. 4, 1936–1939. Warsaw, 1989

——. *Zarys Historii Gospodarczej Polski (1918–1939).* Warsaw, 1971

Lestschinski, Jacob. "Economic Aspects of Jewish Community Organization in Independent Poland." *Jewish Social Studies,* 9 (1947):319–38

——. "HaPera'ot beFolin 1935–1937." *Dappim leHeker haSho'ah vehaMered,* 2 (1952):37–72.

Levavi, Ya'akov. "Ma'amadah shel haHakla'ut haYehudit beFolin biShenot 1918–1939." *Gal-Ed,* 2 (1975):179–207

Lewin, Isaac, Munk, Michael L., and Berman, Jeremiah J., eds. *Religious Freedom: The Right to Practice Sheḥitah.* New York, 1946

Mahler, Raphael. "Jews in Public Service and the Liberal Professions in Poland (1918–39)." *Jewish Social Studies,* 6 (1944):291–350.

——. *Yehudei Polin bein Shetei Milhamot haOlam*. Tel Aviv, 1968

Majchrowski, Jacek. "Obóz Zjednoczenia Narodorego wobec kwestii żydowskiej." In: *Polska-Polacy — mniejszości narodowe* (ed. Wojciech Wrzesiński, Wrocław 1992, pp. 139–47

Marcus, Joseph. *Social and Political History of the Jews in Poland, 1919–1939*. Berlin, New York, Amsterdam, 1983

Mark, Moshe. "Der Virtshaftlikher Krig gegen Iden in Poylen." *Haynt Yoyvel-Bukh, 1908–1938*, pp. 140–46

Melzer, Emanuel. "HaDiplomatiyah haPolanit uVe'ayat haHagirah haYehudit baShanim 1935–1939." *Gal-Ed*, 1 (1973):211–49

——. "HaHerem haKalkali haAnti-Germani beFolin baShanim 1933–1934." *Gal-Ed*, 6 (1982):149–66

——. "Poland, the United States, and the Emigration of East European Jewry: The Plan for a 'Supplemental Jewish Homeland' in Angola, 1938–1939." *Gal-Ed*, 11 (1989):55–86

——. "Relations between Poland and Germany and their Impact on the Jewish Problem in Poland, 1935–1938." *Yad Vashem Studies*, 12 (1977):193–229

Mendelsohn, Ezra. "The Politics of Agudas Israel in Inter-War Poland." *Soviet Jewish Affairs*, 2 (1972):47–60

——. *Zionism in Poland: The Formative Years, 1915–1926*. New Haven and London, 1982

Micewski, Andrzej. *Z geografii politycżnej II Rzeczypospolitej*. Warsaw, 1964

Michowicz, Waldemar. *Walka dyplomacji polskiej przeciwko Traktatowi Mniejszościowemu w Lidze Narodów w 1934r.* Łódź, 1963

Mroczko, Marian. *Polska myśl zachodnia*. Poznań, 1986

Netzer, Shlomo. *Ma'avak Yehudei Polin al Zechuyoteihem haEzrahiyot ve-haLe'umiyot (1918–1922)*. Tel Aviv, 1980

Niemunis, Jolanta. "Stronnictwo Narodowe wobec hitleryzmu jako prądu ideowo-politycznego w latach 1933–1939." *Gdańskie Zeszyty Humanistyczne*, 10 (1967):99–122

Niv, David. *Ma'arachot haIrgun haTseva'i haLe'umi*. Vol. 2: *MeHaganah leHatkafah*. Tel Aviv, 1965

Ottiker, Yisrael. *Tenu'at heHaluts beFolin 1932–1935*. Lohamei haGeta'ot, 1972

Pietrzak, Michał. *Reglamentacja wolności prasy w Polsce (1918–1939)*. Warsaw, 1963

Pilch, Andrzej. *Studencki ruch polityczny w Polsce w latach 1932–1939*. Warsaw, 1972

Pobóg-Malinowski, Władysław. *Najnowsza historia polityczna Polski*

(1864–1945). Vol. 2. London, 1967

Polonsky, Antony. *Politics in Independent Poland, 1921–1939*. Oxford, 1972

Przybylski, Henryk. "Centrum polityczne wobec Konstytucji i Wyborów parlamentarnych w 1935r." *Kwartalnik Historyczny*, 77 (1971):576–89

Rechowicz, Henryk. *Wojewoda śląski — Dr. Michał Grażyński*. Warsaw, 1988

Ritov, Yisrael. "Po'alei-Tsiyon C. S., Tse'irei-Tsiyon, Hitahdut." In *Entsiklopediyah shel Galuyot: Varshah*. Vol. 2. Jerusalem, 1959, pp. 105–42

Rothschild, Joseph. *Pilsudski's Coup d'Etat*. New York, 1966

Rowe, Leonard. "Jewish Self-Defense: A Response to Violence." In *Studies on Polish Jewry 1919–1939*. Edited by Joshua A. Fishman. New York, 1974, pp. 105–49

Rudnicki, Szymon. "From 'Numerus Clausus' to 'Numerus Nullus.'" *Polin*, 2 (1987):246–68

———. "Narodowa Demokracja po przewrocie majowym." *Najnowsze Dzieje Polski*, 11 (1967):352–69

———. *Obóz Narodowo-Radykalny: Geneza i działalność*. Warsaw, 1985

———. "Obóz Wielkiej Polski w okresie Kryzysu gospodarczego." *Przegląd Historyczny*, 62 (1971):251–70

———. "Program społeczny Obozu Narodowo-Radykalnego (ONR)." *Z Pola Walki*, 8 (1965):25–46

Sakowska, Ruta. "Z dziejów gminy żydowskiej w Warszawie, 1918–1939." In *Warszawa II Rzeczypospolitej*. Vol. 4. Warsaw, 1972

Schipper, Ignacy. *Dzieje handlu żydowskiego na ziemiach polskich*. Warsaw, 1937

Segal, Simon. *The New Poland and the Jews*. New York, 1938

Siemiaszko, Zbigniew. "Grupa Szańca i narodowe siły zbrojne." *Zeszyty Historyczne*, 21 (1972):2–26

Stawecki, Piotr. *Następcy Komendanta*. Warsaw, 1969

Szajkowski, Zosa. "'Reconstruction' vs. 'Palliative Relief' in American Jewish Overseas Work, 1919–1939." *Jewish Social Studies*, 32 (1970):111–47

———. "Western Jewish Aid and Intercession for Polish Jewry, 1919–1939." In *Studies on Polish Jewry 1919–1939*. Edited by Joshua A. Fishman. New York, 1974, pp. 150–241

Szczypiórski, Adam. "Samorząd Warszawy (1916–1939)." In *Warszawa II Rzeczypospolitej*. Vol. 1. Warsaw, 1968, pp. 83–116

Tartakower, Arieh. "HaMahshavah haMedinit shel Yehudei Polin bein Milhamah leMilhamah." *Sefer HaShanah/Yorbukh*, 3 (1970):123–52

———. "Ma'avakam haKalkali shel Yehudei Polin miMilhamah leMilhamah." *Gal-Ed*. 2 (1975):145–77

——. "The Migration of Polish Jewry in Recent Times." *Sefer HaShanah/ Yorbukh*, 1 (1964)

——. "Yidishe Politik un Yidishe Kultur in Poyln tsvishn di tsvey Velt-Milkhomes." In *Algemayne Entsiklopedie: Yidn*. Vol. 6. New York, 1963, pp. 147–63

——. "Yidn in Poylishn Parlament." *Sefer HaShanah/ Yorbukh*, 3 (1970): 197–233

Terej, Jerzy. *Idee, mity, realia*. Warsaw, 1971

——. *Rzeczywistość i polityka*. Warsaw, 1971

Tomaszewski, Jerzy. "Robotnicy żydowscy w Warszawie międzywojennej." *Biuletyn Żydowskiego Instytutu Historycznego*, 1972:71–84

——. *Rzeczpospolita wielu narodów*. Warsaw, 1985

——. "Walka polityczna wewnatrz gmin żydowskich w latach 30-tych w świetle interpelacji posłów."*Biuletyn Żydowskiego Instytutu Historycznego*, 1973:85–110.

Tomicki, Jan. "Warszawska organizacja Polskiej Partii Socjalistycznej (1929–1939). In *Warszawa II Rzeczypospolitej*. Vol. 1. Warsaw, 1968, pp. 239–87

Torzecki, Ryszard. *Kwestia ukraińska w polityce III Rzeszy (1933–1945)*. Warsaw, 1972

Trepiński, A. "Cenzura w prasie warszawskiej przed Drugą Wojną Światową. *Rocznik Historii Czasopiśmiennictwa Polskiego*, 11 (1972):117–47

Trunk, Isaiah. "Der Ekonomisher Antisemitizm in Poyln tsvishn di tsvey Velt-Milkhomes." In *Shtudies vegn Yidn in Poyln 1919–1939*. Edited by Joshua A. Fishman. New York, 1974, pp. 3–98

Turlejska, Maria. *Rok przed klęską*. Warsaw, 1965

Unity in Dispersion: A History of the World Jewish Congress. New York, 1948

Wapiński, Roman. *Endecja na Pomorzu 1920–1939*. Gdańsk, 1966

——. "Endecja wobec kwestii narodowej." *Kwartalnik Historyczny*, 80 (1973):817–44

Windyga, M. "Obóz Narodowo-Radykalny w Warszawie międzywojennej." In *Warszawa II Rzeczypospolitej*. Vol. 2. Warsaw, 1970, pp. 173–86

Wojciechowski, Marian. *Stosunki Polsko-Niemieckie 1933–1938*. Poznań, 1965

Wynot, Edward D. *Polish Politics in Transition*. Athens GA, 1974

——. "The Polish Peasant Movement and the Jews 1918–1939." In *The Jews of Poland Between Two World Wars*. Edited by Yisrael Gutman, Ezra Mendelsohn, Jehuda Reinharz, and Chone Shmeruk. Hanover NH and London, 1989, pp. 36–55

Żarnowski, Janusz. "PPS w latach 1935–1936." *Najnowsze Dzieje Polski*,

3(1960):93–160

——. "PPS w przededniu II wojny światowej." *Przegląd Historyczny,*
    52(1961):495–520

——. *Polska Partia Socjalistyczna w latach 1935–1939.* Warsaw, 1965

Zieliński, Józef. "Reorganizacja Obozu Wielkiej Polski (r. 1931)." *Dzieje
    Najnowsze,* 2(1975):255–74

Zweig, Ferdynand. *Poland between Two Wars.* London, 1944

Index